Seventies British Cinema

Seventies British Cinema

Edited by Robert Shail

A BFI book published by Palgrave Macmillan

For J. A. and J. M. Shail

First published in 2008 by
PALGRAVE MACMILLAN

on behalf of the

BRITISH FILM INSTITUTE
21 Stephen Street, London W1T 1LN
www.bfi.org.uk

There's more to discover about film and television through the BFI.
Our world-renowned archive, cinemas, festivals, films, publications and learning resources are here to inspire you.

Palgrave Macmillan in the UK is an imprint of Macmillan Publishers Limited, registered in England, company number 785998, of Houndmills, Basingstoke, Hampshire RG21 6XS.

Palgrave Macmillan in the US is a division of St Martin's Press LLC, 175 Fifth Avenue, New York, NY 10010.

Palgrave Macmillan is the global academic imprint of the above companies and has companies and representatives throughout the world.

Palgrave® and Macmillan® are registered trademarks in the United States, the United Kingdom, Europe and other countries.

Cover design: Mark Swan
Cover image: *Jubilee* (Derek Jarman, 1978, Whaley-Malin Productions/Megalovision)
Text design: couch

Set by Cambrian Typesetters, Camberley, Surrey
Printed in China

This book is printed on paper suitable for recycling and made from fully managed and sustained forest sources. Logging, pulping and manufacturing processes are expected to conform to the environmental regulations of the country of origin.

British Library Cataloguing-in-Publication Data
A catalogue record for this book is available from the British Library

ISBN 978-1-84457-273-1 (pb)
ISBN 978-1-84457-274-8 (hb)

Contents

Acknowledgments

My warmest thanks go to all the contributors to this volume for their sterling efforts and their patience throughout the process of its completion. I would also like to extend my appreciation to those who do not appear in these pages but who gave generously of their advice and support, particularly Duncan Petrie and Andrew Spicer. As ever, I'm grateful for the indulgence of my colleagues and students in the Department of Film and Media at the University of Wales, Lampeter. Due credit must also go to the staff of BFI Publishing, especially Rebecca Barden.

This volume was read, reviewed, reread and frequently held together by Cerri Shail – cariad fawr.

Notes on Contributors

Ruth Barton lectures in film studies at Trinity College, Dublin. She has written widely on Irish and other national cinemas. Her books include *Acting Irish in Hollywood* (2006), *Irish National Cinema* (2004) and *Jim Sheridan: Framing the Nation* (2002).

James Chapman is Professor of Film at the University of Leicester. He has wide-ranging research interests in the history of British popular culture, especially film and television, and his recent books include *Past and Present: National Identity and the British Historical Film* (2005), *Inside the Tardis: The Worlds of 'Doctor Who' – A Cultural History* (2006) and *Licence to Thrill: A Cultural History of the James Bond Films* (1999; second edition 2007).

Ian Conrich is Director of the Centre for New Zealand Studies, Birkbeck, University of London. He is an editor of the *Journal of British Cinema and Television* and an advisory board member of *The Journal of Horror Studies*. He has written for *Sight and Sound* and the BBC. The author of the forthcoming book *New Zealand Cinema*, he is an editor or co-editor of eleven books, including *The Technique of Terror: The Cinema of John Carpenter* (2004) and the forthcoming *Horror Zone: The Cultural Experience of Contemporary Horror Cinema*.

Wheeler Winston Dixon is the James Ryan Endowed Professor of Film Studies at the University of Nebraska, Lincoln, and, with Gwendolyn Audrey Foster, editor-in-chief of the *Quarterly Review of Film and Video*. He has written widely on British horror films and his latest books include *Visions of Paradise: Images of Eden in the Cinema* (2006), *American Cinema of the 1940s: Themes and Variations* (2006) and *Lost in the Fifties: Recovering Phantom Hollywood* (2005).

Christophe Dupin is Post-doctoral Research Assistant on the *AHRC History of the British Film Institute Research Project* at Queen Mary, University of London. He previously worked for the BFI while writing a PhD on the history of its Experimental Film Fund and Production Board. Recent publications include essays for *Screen* and the *Journal of Media Practice*. He is currently researching the relationship between the National Film Archive and the Cinémathèque Française.

Steve Gerrard is currently completing his PhD thesis examining the cultural impact of the *Carry On* films on British society at the University of Wales, Lampeter, where he is also a part-time lecturer.

He has given a number of conference papers on 1970s British film comedy and written an entry on *Carry On up the Khyber* for Routledge's *Fifty Key British Films* (2008).

Sheldon Hall is a former film journalist and is currently Senior Lecturer in Film Studies at Sheffield Hallam University. He is the author of *Zulu: With Some Guts Behind It – The Making of the Epic Movie* (2005), the co-author (with Steve Neale) of *Epics, Spectacles and Blockbusters: A Hollywood History* (forthcoming) and the co-editor (with John Belton and Steve Neale) of *Widescreen Worldwide* (forthcoming). He has contributed articles on British cinema to a number of other publications, including *The British Cinema Book* (ed. Robert Murphy, third edition, forthcoming).

I. Q. Hunter is Principal Lecturer and Subject Leader in Film Studies at De Montfort University, Leicester. He edited *British Science Fiction Cinema* (1999) and co-edited *Pulping Fictions* (1996), *Trash Aesthetics* (1997), *Sisterhoods* (1998), *Alien Identities* (1999), *Classics* (2000), *Retrovisions* (2001) and *Brit-Invaders!* (2005). He has published widely on exploitation, horror and cult films and is currently writing a British Film Guide to *A Clockwork Orange* for I. B. Tauris.

James Leggott lectures in film and television studies at Northumbria University. His PhD was concerned with traditions of realism in British cinema and he has published articles on aspects of realist practice. His research interests also include the work of the Amber Film Collective and the representation of children in contemporary film and television.

Claire Monk is Senior Lecturer in Film Studies at De Montfort University, Leicester, and a critic and writer who contributed regularly to *Sight and Sound* in the 1990s. She has written widely on cultural politics and film in post-1970s Britain, is co-editor of *British Historical Cinema* (2002) and has completed a study of British audiences for period films focusing on the debate around 'heritage cinema'. Her interest in Derek Jarman's *Jubilee* dates from the 1980s when she was the writer and publisher of the fanzine *Psychotic Snark*.

Paul Newland is Lecturer in Film at Aberystwyth University. He has published on British cinema and contemporary British literature. His monograph, *The Cultural Construction of London's East End*, was published by Rodopi in 2008.

Dan North is a lecturer in film in the Department of English at the University of Exeter, where he was responsible for archiving the Don Boyd papers at the Bill Douglas Centre for the History of Cinema and Popular Culture. He is the editor of *Sights Unseen*, a collection of essays on unfinished British films, and the author of *Performing Illusions: Cinema, Special Effects and the Virtual Actor* (2008).

Robert Shail is Head of the Department of Film and Media at the University of Wales, Lampeter. He has written widely on masculinity and stardom in cinema, and on aspects of British film history. His recent publications include *British Film Directors: A Critical Guide* (2007) and *Stanley Baker: A Life in Film* (2008).

Justin Smith is Principal Lecturer in Film Studies at the University of Portsmouth. A cultural historian with a specialism in British cinema, his research interests cover film fandom, reception and exhibition, identity and memory. He has published journal articles on the advent of the multiplex in Britain and the cult films *Withnail & I* and *The Wicker Man*. His essay 'British Cult Cinema' will appear in the third edition of Robert Murphy's *British Cinema Book* (forthcoming, 2008).

Sarah Street is Professor of Film at the University of Bristol. Her publications include *British National Cinema* (1997), *British Cinema in Documents* (2000), *Transatlantic Crossings: British Feature Films in the USA* (2002) and *Black Narcissus* (2005). Her latest book is *Film Architecture and the Transnational Imagination: Set Design in 1930s European Cinema* (2007), co-authored with Tim Bergfelder and Sue Harris. She is currently researching the introduction of colour to British cinema, with a particular interest in British Technicolor.

Introduction: Cinema in the Era of 'Trouble and Strife'

During the last thirty years, the scholarly study of British cinema has undergone a startling transformation. The extent of this change was neatly summarised by Alan Lovell who, after a similar period of time had elapsed, responded to his own earlier seminar paper 'The British Cinema: The Unknown Cinema' by describing this development as a move from 'scarcity to abundance'.[1] Appropriately, his updated essay was called 'The British Cinema: The Known Cinema', as Lovell charts the wide array of British cinema topics that have now been explored by cinema historians, including the analysis of 'important historical "moments"'. It can, however, be reasonably asserted that these 'important historical moments' have not generally included the 1970s, and neither does this decade feature in the list of further subjects that Lovell suggests remain to be explored. A curious topography of the landscape of British cinema has emerged from this process of opening up and expanding British cinema studies. This undulating historical map tended to indicate that some eras were of more interest than others, so that even a cursory examination of the existing bibliography of British cinema shows how the 1940s have remained a key focus for historical examination. Nonetheless, most other periods have seen at least some coverage, with even the 'doldrums era' of the 1950s (as described by Raymond Durgnat[2]) coming in for reassessment. The one period that seems to have remained 'unknown' is the 1970s.

It's useful to take a brief tour of some of the relevant literature on British cinema, particularly those volumes where we might expect to find an analysis of the 1970s. There are currently only two books that specifically devote substantial coverage to the period: Alexander Walker's *National Heroes* and John Walker's less well-known *The Once and Future Film*, although it is telling that both of these group the 1970s with the 1980s as an area for study. In addition, John Walker's volume is quite slight, so that Alexander Walker's book, written in 1985, remains the principle point of reference for those wanting to read an account of the cinema of the decade. For some time, the only single-volume histories of British cinema were Roy Armes's *A Critical History of British Cinema* and George Perry's more journalistic *The Great British Picture Show*. Armes's book was written in 1978 and inevitably offered only a brief review of the 1970s that looked for optimistic signs for the future, finding them principally in the 'alternative' cinema of Nicolas Roeg.[3] George Perry's book, written six years later, devotes just two of its twenty-six chapters to the 1970s, with one entitled 'Seventies Stagnation'.

More recent single-volume histories such as Amy Sergeant's *British Cinema: A Critical History* at least privilege these years with the same level of coverage given to the other decades, although her choice of film to represent the 1970s, Nicolas Roeg's *The Man Who Fell to Earth*

(1976) is revealing.[4] Robert Murphy's choice of film for the decade in his collection *The British Cinema Book* is yet another Nicolas Roeg film, *Bad Timing* (1977). Most striking is *A Night at the Pictures: Ten Decades of British Film*, a volume published in 1985 to celebrate British Film Year.[5] This presents two long essays, the first a historical overview by Gilbert Adair that includes one entirely dismissive paragraph on the 1970s, and the second an analysis by Nick Roddick of the 'British Revival', which apparently only started with the dawn of the 1980s, the 1970s having seemingly disappeared into a cinematic black hole.

The reasons for this neglect are not difficult to identify. The popular perception of the 1970s as 'the decade that taste forgot' unquestionably includes a broad critical consensus that British cinema of the period was 'generally of little interest apart from a few isolated films'.[6] This is the era that witnessed the decline and fall of such key British film cycles as the *Carry On*s and the Hammer horrors (whose demise is described by Steve Gerrard and Wheeler Winston Dixon in their respective chapters in this book). Major film-makers like Lindsay Anderson, Tony Richardson, John Schlesinger, Jack Clayton, Karel Reisz and John Boorman either seemed to dry up creatively or found themselves driven to Hollywood in order to keep their careers afloat. The lively experimentation of the 1960s was forced to the margins, while popular mainstream cinema became dominated by cheaply produced exploitation horror films, tawdry sex comedies and uninspired spin-offs from television sitcoms. With declining cinema attendance, British films appeared to be aiming for the lowest common denominator in trying to win back audiences. The middle ground was then, according to the critical consensus, given over to the production of glossy but vacuous period dramas aimed at the American market. One such example, the cycle of Agatha Christie adaptations, is re-evaluated here by Sarah Street. An air of desperation hangs over the period, exacerbated by the fact that the 1970s seemed, in retrospect, to sit in a hollow between the colourful exuberance and optimism of the 1960s and the incendiary antagonisms and defiance of the 1980s. As Andrew Higson puts it, 'the 1970s can be regarded as a transitional period for cinema, caught between two more significant moments'.[7]

Clearly, such an impression of the period owes a good deal to the critical imperatives that have governed some of the accounts we have of the decade. Roy Armes's insistence on the primary value of an auteur history of British film-making means that the popular cinema of the 1970s is simply not on his radar at all. Much of the genre film-making of the era is sorely in need of a properly balanced consideration that goes beyond easy prejudice. Even adopting Armes's own auteurist approach would reveal a decade in which the *Bill Douglas Trilogy* appears, along with significant early work by Derek Jarman, Terence Davies, Peter Greenaway and Stephen Frears. A quick scan of the British releases in 1971 alone reveals a startlingly diverse range of work, from *Get Carter* to *The Abominable Dr Phibes*, by way of *Tales of Beatrix Potter*, *The Go-Between* and *The Devils*. The need for dispassionate reappraisal seems self-evident.

Setting the Scene

A first step in examining the cinematic landscape of the 1970s is to place it in a wider socio-historical setting. A good deal of the turbulence that beset British film-making in these years can be related directly to the political and economic climate of the decade. This context created parameters that conditioned the way that films were made, distributed and shown, as well as the kinds of films that were actually produced.

In 1974, the American-based Hudson Institute published a report called *The United Kingdom to 1980* that suggested that Britain's economic health was the worst in Europe outside of the eastern communist bloc. It declared that Britain's plight stemmed from a 'decline in both governmental competence and economic performance: a universal loss of dynamism'.[8] This underlying decline was attributed to the 'archaic' nature of British society, from its outdated class divisions, to its careless business practices and poor industrial relations. The crisis besetting the economy was centred on low levels of productivity, rising unemployment and the increasing cost of living (by 1974, inflation had reached its highest level since the Second World War, standing at more than 28 per cent).[9] This situation was worsened by the international oil crisis that followed the war between Israel and Egypt in October 1973. The solution arrived at by successive Conservative and Labour governments was to curb inflation by controlling wages, particularly through the public sector. Unsurprisingly, this strategy proved less than popular with a trade union movement emboldened by successes in industrial disputes in the early part of the decade and by high levels of public support. Tory Prime Minister Edward Heath's attempts to confront the unions, and specifically the National Union of Mineworkers (NUM), ultimately failed and this, along with the imposition of a three-day working week in December 1973, led ultimately to his electoral defeat in February 1974. For those who experienced this period, an abiding memory is of the power cuts brought in to conserve energy that regularly reduced the country to candlelight. The subsequent Labour administrations of Harold Wilson and James Callaghan fared little better. Although they preferred to negotiate with the unions a 'social contract' in which wage restraint was central, the end result was still the 'winter of discontent' of 1978–9 when more than a million public service workers came out on strike and the press reported stories of streets piled high with uncollected rubbish and the dead being left unburied in council mortuaries.

One feature of the industrial disputes of the 1970s was the violent confrontations that sometimes occurred. This seemed to mirror an increasing mood of strident militancy and radicalism affecting a number of areas of society. Political and ideological lines had hardened. This took many forms, from the increasingly vocal factions of the far left and far right in politics (represented by Tony Benn on one side and Enoch Powell on the other), through to second wave feminism (given its most public expression in Germaine Greer's *The Female Eunuch* that received its paperback publication in 1971). Much of the decade was marred by racial tensions between police and immigrant communities in Britain's major cities, further heightened by the activities of the far right National Front. The problem was aggravated, as Arthur Marwick points out, by the economic discrimination that many ethnic groups had had to endure.[10] These festering resentments were to ignite in the next decade in a series of inner-city riots that began in the St Paul's area of Bristol in April 1980. The most visible and shocking manifestation of this increased mood of confrontation was the re-emergence of violence in Northern Ireland. Any sense that this was a distant conflict was shattered by the IRA bombing campaign in England in 1974 and by the murder of leading Tory politician Airey Neave in 1979. Marwick suggests that such were the levels of violence and antagonism in Britain that the key political and public debates of 1973–4 focused on whether the UK was governable at all.[11] Britain's postwar consensus, let alone the optimism of the 1960s, seemed a rather distant memory.

The chaotic and miserable political narrative of the decade was brought to a suitably stark ending in the spring of 1979 when the election of a Tory government under Margaret Thatcher heralded the beginning of a very different era. As political commentator Andrew Marr recently put it, the country was about to take a bitter dose of economic medicine: 'it was time for Britain to grimace and open her mouth'.[12] The turbulence of the decade that was ending was more than just a historical backstory for British cinema; it had very real consequences for the industry itself. The volatility of the wider economic and social scene was to be mirrored in the equally unpredictable fate of British film-making.

Making the Films

Filmgoing in Britain continued to decline during the 1970s as it had done throughout the previous decade, so that by 1980 a record low of 102 million admissions for the year was reached (see Justin Smith's chapter for a full discussion of trends in production, distribution and exhibition in the period). The number of screens available remained relatively constant despite the continuing decline in actual cinemas. This was due to the redevelopment of many single-screen cinemas into 'studio' complexes housing three or four screens. These, often unsympathetic, conversions were a painful blight on filmgoing in the period, remembered bitterly by audiences who endured their uncomfortable facilities, and were a world away from contemporary multiplexes. The increase in the price of tickets actually improved the amount of box-office take in pure cash terms, although this has to be seen in the light of the rampant inflation infecting the whole UK economy.

Along with the declining audience, the other major cause for concern was the drop in film production. During the 1960s, British film production had been bolstered by a huge injection of capital from the United States (by 1968, more than sixty of the seventy-six features produced in the UK received American financial backing[13]). During the course of the 1970s, the level of production more than halved from eighty-four features to forty-one.[14] The principle reason for the fall in production levels lay in the loss of confidence that had been brought about by the wholesale withdrawal of American funding, a process that had already started by 1969. By the end of the 1960s, the American majors had seemingly fallen out of love with a Britain that no longer appeared to be 'swinging' and, in addition, they had major financial problems of their own to face at home. Without the bandage provided by American producers, the vulnerable state of the British cinema's infrastructure was rapidly revealed.

During the 1960s, British film production had retracted into a virtual duopoly between the Rank Organisation and the Associated British Picture Corporation (ABPC), resulting in an unsuccessful referral to the Monopolies Commission.[15] During the 1970s, Rank's interest in film-making seemed to wane as they diversified their business into other areas. As John Walker describes it, there was 'little coherent policy in their film production, with the company shunning expensive movies and making little attempt to break into the American market, preferring to back a mixed bag of films'.[16] ABPC was taken over by EMI in February 1969 and Bryan Forbes installed as Head of Production at their Elstree Studios. Forbes announced an ambitious slate of productions, but his tenure was to be very brief; he resigned in March 1971. By the mid-1970s, the company was in stagnation, a situation only partially alleviated when they took over another ailing outfit, British Lion, in 1976 and appointed British Lion's management team of Barry Spikings and Michael Deeley at the helm of EMI. Their policy of 'making American films for the Americans',[17] perhaps inevitably was followed by the departure of Deeley for Hollywood.

Spikings continued to invest heavily in American-based films to the detriment of intrinsically British subjects. A number of the films he was responsible for made substantial losses, most notoriously *Honky Tonk Freeway* (1981), so that EMI's profits dropped from £65 million in 1977 to a mere £11 million in 1979.[18] In 1980, they were taken over by Thorn and by 1983 Barry Spikings had quit.

These developments illustrate two key features of the period. First, production tended to centre on either expensive films aimed at the American market (with consequently high levels of financial risk) or low-budget efforts of limited ambition directed at the domestic market. The middle ground for commercial production largely fell away. The dangers of overambition were most spectacularly epitomised by Lord Grade's ITC company whose plans for a programme of twenty big-budget spectaculars came to grief with the commercial disaster of *Raise the Titanic* (1980).[19] The other end of the spectrum was typified by the plethora of cheaply made exploitation horrors and sex comedies that appeared all through the decade (and which are described here in chapters by I. Q. Hunter and Ian Conrich). The second factor is the level of volatility that is indicated by the succession of management regimes at EMI. British Lion itself had undergone similarly traumatic transformations when a collapse in the British stock market led to the share value of its parent company plummeting from 254p to 24p overnight.[20] Volatility was also endemic in government policy towards the industry during the decade. Christophe Dupin's chapter on the vicissitudes of the British Film Institute's production wing under successive Tory and Labour administrations indicates the degree to which film production was a political football during the 1970s, with levels of support fluctuating markedly and the emphasis shifting backwards and forwards between bolstering commercial productions or fostering a burgeoning art-house sector.

Any period is going to see the demise of individual production companies and of key personnel, but the 1970s seems to have been particularly a time of endings. Along with the final throes of the much-loved Hammer films and the *Carry Ons*, there was a sense that the British studio system itself was unravelling (with two-thirds of Shepperton Studios sold off to property developers[21]). In 1977, the industry's premier elder statesman, Sir Michael Balcon, died and an era appeared to have closed. Film-makers brought up under more stable conditions struggled to maintain their output, but a new breed of creative personnel was emerging. This included a new generation of directors whose background was not in the cinema but in commercial advertising; Ridley Scott and Alan Parker both made their feature debuts during the decade and Hugh Hudson and Adrian Lyne made theirs in 1980. The most significant new producer to emerge, David Puttnam, came from the same background. New, and sometimes unlikely, sources of funding were also to be found. Cinema's old enemy, television, was a source of both finance and creativity, as exemplified by producer Verity Lambert and Euston Films, as well as the avalanche of television spin-offs on the big screen. The pop music industry, for years underutilised by British cinema, was similarly influential, whether through producers like ex-Beatle George Harrison and his business partner Denis O'Brien with their company HandMade, who stepped in to fund the Monty Python film *Life of Brian* (1979) when fainter hearts lost their nerve, or via new film stars like David Essex or Roger Daltrey, or through the substantial number of films made as vehicles for British rock and pop acts of the period.

New forms of film finance: *Life of Brian* (1979) was backed by ex-Beatle George Harrison

Alongside these areas, there was a new breed of independent producer who adapted well to the rapidly changing context of 1970s production, from the film-making team of Clive Parsons and Davina Belling, to the 'boy wonder' Don Boyd whose meteoric rise is examined in Dan North's chapter. A lively independent sector fed into the growing diversity of British art cinema. Here the early work of Jarman and Greenaway sits alongside such individual, quirky talents as Bill Forsyth or the little recognised Barney Platts-Mills (the vision of these new auteurs is recognised here in chapters by Claire Monk and James Leggott). The 1970s also saw the development of more politically radical groups like the London Film-makers' Co-op and the London Women's Film Group, as well as avant-garde and experimental work by theorists/film-makers like Laura Mulvey and Peter Wollen. The extraordinary variety of work that appeared certainly seems to justify Andrew Higson's assertion that, contrary to popular opinion, 'cinema itself was not in decline, but was going through a complex process of diversification and renewal'.[22]

Re-viewing 1970s British Cinema

One hazard confronting anyone attempting to re-examine British cinema of the 1970s is the low reputation of a good deal of its commercial output during the period. The sexist, racist and homophobic attitudes that casually appear in some of these films, particularly the comedies, horror and sexploitation vehicles, seem to have placed them beyond critical examination. Nonetheless, a proper consideration of the era can no longer skate delicately around the subject in the manner of Alexander Walker, George Perry, *et al.* As Andrew Higson says, '*Carry On Emmannuelle*, with its articulation of some dominant desires and anxieties concerning sexuality,

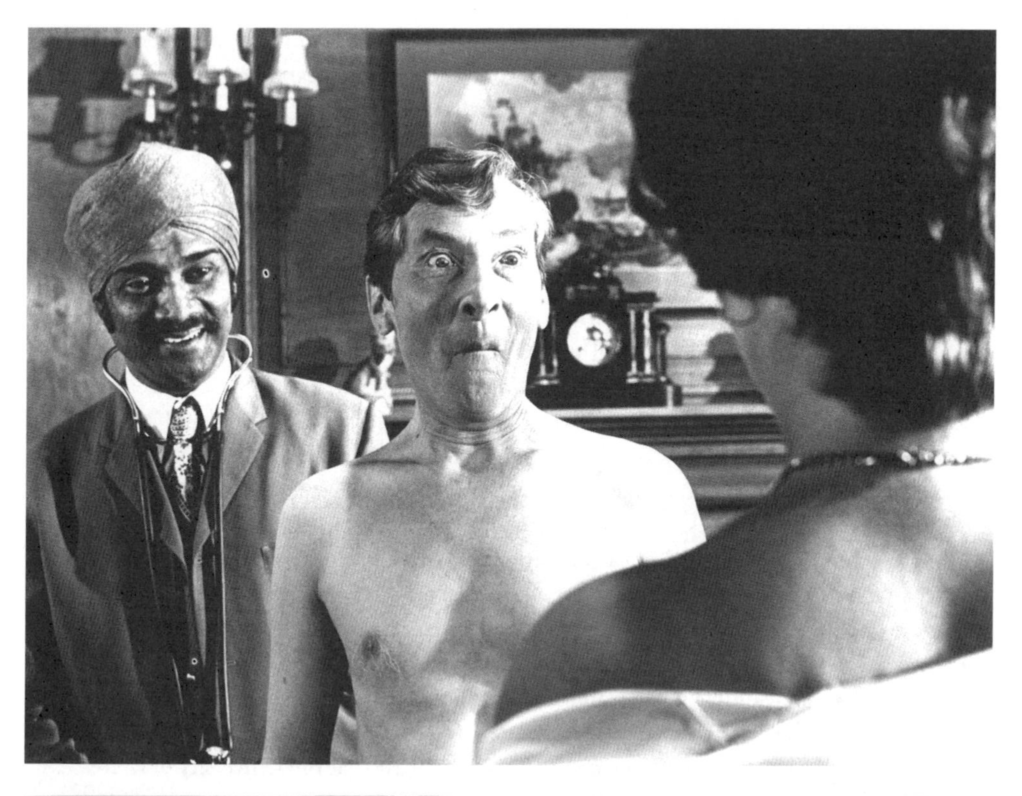

The extremes of 1970s British cinema, from *Carry On Emmannuelle* (1978) to *Jubilee* (1978)

may tell us as much about the condition of Britain as *Jubilee*.'[23] It might even be possible that these films have intrinsic merits of their own, beyond their sociological value. As a result, the first of the three sections into which this collection is divided addresses itself unapologetically to reconsidering the reviled popular genre cinema of the 1970s. Section two presents a selection of essays that address key contextual issues or look at dominant styles such as realism, the punk aesthetic or an emerging Heritage cinema. The final section collects together individual case studies ranging across film stars, producers and specific films.

The 1970s has invariably been seen as an era of decline for British cinema. A brief survey of chapters or essays from previous publications covering the period encapsulates this with titles like 'Seventies Stagnation', 'Decline and Fall' and 'The Bubble Bursts'.[24] This impression is certainly borne out in wider trends such as cinema attendance and production levels, but it clearly does not give a full picture. If 'decline' is a keyword for the period, then 'volatility' and 'polarisation' should also be on the list. This was a decade in which the fortunes of a producer or distributor could alter radically overnight, and where institutional policies were barely more stable. British cinema was driven to extremes, sometimes in an attempt to attract new audiences, any audiences, but just as often to give expression to voices that had often been previously marginalised. It is easy to see this as a depressing picture, but it was also one that was rich with opportunities. New spaces opened up and film-makers as startlingly diverse as Pete Walker and Peter Wollen could find themselves with an outlet that had, up to then, been largely denied. The results are certainly fragmented, but rarely dull. The re-examination of British cinema of the 1970s is a process that is only just beginning, as witnessed by the research project currently underway at the University of Portsmouth and by a conference held in the summer of 2007 at the University of Exeter. This volume is offered as a contribution to that new beginning.

Notes

1 Alan Lovell, 'The British Cinema: The Known Cinema', in Robert Murphy (ed.), *The British Cinema Book, Second Edition* (London: BFI, 2001), p. 200.
2 See Raymond Durgnat, *A Mirror for England* (London: Faber and Faber, 1970).
3 Roy Armes, *A Critical History of British Cinema* (London: Secker and Warburg, 1978), pp. 315–20.
4 Amy Sergeant, *British Cinema: A Critical History* (London: BFI, 2005), pp. 288–92.
5 Gilbert Adair and Nick Roddick, *A Night at the Pictures: Ten Decades of British Film* (Bromley: Columbus Books, 1985).
6 Andrew Higson, 'A Diversity of Film Practices: Renewing British Cinema in the 1970s', in Bart Moore-Gilbert (ed.), *The Arts in the 1970s: Cultural Closure?* (London: Routledge, 1994), p. 217.
7 Ibid.
8 The Hudson Report is examined in both David Childs, *Britain Since 1939: Progress and Decline* (Basingstoke and London: Macmillan, 1995) and David Coates and John Hillard (eds), *The Economic Decline of Modern Britain: The Debate between Left and Right* (Brighton: Harvester, 1986). Childs's section on the 1970s is typically entitled 'Trouble and Strife' and gives this introduction its title.
9 Brian Spittles, *Britain Since 1960: An Introduction* (Basingstoke and London: Macmillan, 1995), pp. 28–38.
10 Arthur Marwick, *British Society Since 1945* (London: Penguin, 1996), pp. 216–22.

11 Ibid., pp. 222–3.
12 Andrew Marr, *A History of Modern Britain* (London: Macmillan, 2007), p. 377.
13 The full story of the 'American invasion' is detailed by Alexander Walker in *Hollywood, England: The British Film Industry in the Sixties* (London: Orion, 2005).
14 In addition to Justin Smith's chapter in this book, a useful digest of statistics produced by Patricia Perilli can be found in the appendix to James Curran and Vincent Porter (eds), *British Cinema History* (London: Weidenfeld and Nicolson, 1983).
15 See Walker, *Hollywood, England* – 'Appendix: An Industry Chronology' provides a succinct history of these developments.
16 John Walker, *The Once and Future Film: British Cinema in the Seventies and Eighties* (London: Methuen, 1985), pp. 32–3.
17 Ibid., p. 30.
18 Ibid., p. 31.
19 See George Perry, *The Great British Picture Show* (London: Pavilion, 1985), p. 286 and Alexander Walker, *National Heroes: British Cinema in the Seventies and Eighties* (London: Harrap, 1986), pp. 201–4.
20 An account of this is provided in Robert Shail, *Stanley Baker: A Life in Film* (Cardiff: University of Wales Press, 2008), chapter six. Baker was involved in a buy-out of British Lion in partnership with Spikings and Deeley.
21 Perry, *Great British Picture Show*, p. 285.
22 Higson, 'A Diversity of Film Practices', p. 237.
23 Ibid.
24 In order, these are drawn from George Perry's *The Great British Picture Show*, John Walker's *The Once and Future Film* and Duncan Petrie's 'British Cinema: The Search for Identity', in Geoffrey Nowell-Smith (ed.), *The Oxford History of World Cinema* (Oxford and New York: Oxford University Press, 1997).

Part One: Popular Genres

1 Take an Easy Ride: Sexploitation in the 1970s

I. Q. Hunter

When I see a couple of kids
And guess he's fucking her and she's
Taking pills or wearing a diaphragm,
I know this is paradise

Everyone old has dreamed of all their lives –

Philip Larkin, *High Windows*[1]

'From now on it's going to be fanny, blow jobs, big tits and beer – that's the kind of lifestyle I want.'
Dave (Johnny Vegas), *Sex Lives of the Potato Men* (2004)

Low-budget sex comedies, 'permissive' dramas, sex education films (known in the trade as 'white-coaters') and sexploitation documentaries sustained the British film industry in the 1970s. Unabashedly populist, they explode the assumption that the mainstream of British cinema means only literary adaptations and 'miserablist' social dramas. While the fly-by-night productions of leading 1970s sexploitationeers like Stanley Long and Derek Ford are still comparatively unknown, films like *Come Play with Me* (1976) and *Confessions of a Window Cleaner* (1974) ran for months or even years at Soho sex clubs and provincial theatres.[2] The sexploitation industry collapsed in the early 1980s because of the arrival of video, tighter censorship, inflation and the end of the Eady Levy in 1985, but today the films offer valuable insights into the tastes, values and frustrated desires of ordinary filmgoers at a period of rapid social and moral change, when exploitation was one of the few thriving areas of indigenous cinema.

This essay provides a brief overview of the British sex film in the 1970s, a genre whose first historian, David McGillivray, described as having no redeeming features whatsoever.[3] Indeed, not so long ago very little critical work existed on sexploitation; perhaps the most overlooked stretch of the 'lost continent' of British cinema. Since the late 1990s, however, in addition to McGillivray's insider account and the BBC 2 documentary adapted from it, there have been a number of useful overviews of British sex films, ranging from Ian Conrich's synoptic discussion in the *Journal of Popular British Cinema*, Matthew Sweet's journalistic account in *Shepperton Babylon*, Simon Sheridan's two exhaustive books for FAB Press on Mary Millington and sexploitation, a handful of video reviews and pioneering interpretations of individual sexploitation films such as *Queen Kong* (1976), and, most impressive of all, Leon Hunt's definitive *British Low*

Culture.[4] At the same time, many previously obscure films (*Zeta One* [1969], *Au Pair Girls* [1972]) have emerged on DVD labels such as Jezebel and Medusa, while the ironic cult of the political errors and fashionable excesses of the 1970s (see, for example, *Life on Mars* [2006–2007]) has reclaimed, among others, Robin Askwith, the star of the *Confessions* films (1974–7), as an icon of unembarrassed Anglo-masculinity.[5] In short, a field of study once wholly beneath contempt is now not only visible but reasonably well served by both academia and fandom, and rough agreement has emerged about British sexploitation's role in trickling down the ideology of 'permissiveness' from the elite and middle classes to suburbia and the working class.

As McGillivray and Conrich authoritatively demonstrate, the British sexploitation film can be dated from 1957, when the first nudist films were released, to 1981, when production petered out with barrel-scraping efforts such as *Emmanuelle in Soho*. The term exploitation refers, in the general sense it has accrued since the 1950s, to low-budget films on sensational subjects, tailored to be appetising to specific audiences. But so-called 'classical exploitation films' during the studio era in the United States can be more tightly defined, being a distinctive mode of sub-B-movie production of independently made and distributed films on lurid topics banned by the Production Code. Films like *Child Bride* (1938), *Reefer Madness* (1936) and *Mom and Dad* (1947) were a tabloid mixture of voyeurism, mock-exposé and self-righteousness. Their salacious moralism was defined by the 'square up', a title crawl at the start of the film that announced the producers' educational purpose in order to appease censors and legitimate the audience's curiosity. Classical exploitation's crudity and emphasis on spectacle over narrative coherence distanced them from the products of the classical Hollywood style. The result, as Eric Schaefer has remarked, is that classical exploitation is more like an alternative mode of film production than simply the 'bad' film-making it has come to represent:

> The classical exploitation films made between 1920 and 1950 had a unique style that set them apart from movies produced by the major production companies such as MGM and Universal and even those of many of the minor companies such as Republic and Monogram. . . . We can chuckle at the incompetence of classical exploitation films, but it is important to understand these 'problems' as the product of a specific mode of production.[6]

Classical exploitation waned in the 1950s and 'exploitation film' became an all-purpose label for cheap sensational movies that were intensively promoted, distributed to a sectionalised market and produced in cycles and subgenres such as the nudist film and soft-core sexploitation, which is usually dated from Russ Meyer's 'tits and ass' extravaganza, *The Immoral Mr Teas* (1959).

British sexploitation, similarly, began with cautious 'A'-rated nudist films in the 1950s that posed as propaganda for naturism, and then diversified into subgenres that responded to social trends, changing audiences, the vagaries of censorship and the financial success of key films. The key subgenres, with their dates of maximum impact, were these:

- The naturist/nudist film (1958–63)
- Sexploitation documentaries (1963–71, peaking with four films in 1971)
- Sex education films (1969–71)

- Permissive drama (1968–79; twenty-nine were produced in total in the 1970s)
- Erotic horror (1970–6)
- Sex comedies (1967–9, and by far the largest category. They peaked in 1975. Six were made in 1971, seven in 1972, eight in 1973, ten in 1974, twelve in 1975, eight in 1977, five in 1978 and two in 1979).

The development of these subgenres must be understood within the context of British film censorship, which until recently was the most stringent in Europe. Unlike in the United States, films could not be screened without the approval of what was then called the British Board of Film Censors; there was, for example, no equivalent to American classical exploitation's traditions of 'four walling' (renting cinemas for one-off screenings of films made outside the Production Code). British sexploitation was constrained by censors who rigorously distinguished between 'serious films' and exploitation, and who disapproved of gratuitously arousing nudity and sex scenes.

The 'high point' of the British sex comedy, *Eskimo Nell* (1974)

Consequently, sexploitation subgenres, such as sex comedies and documentary exposés, flourished in Britain long after the legalisation of hard-core had marginalised them in the USA and continental Europe. British sex films in the 1970s were either mildly titillating soft-core romps or, in the spirit of classical exploitation, disguised as something other than attempted pornography – as social realism, for example, or documentary reports on emerging subcultural trends. It is true that there was some small-scale British hard-core production in the 1970s that, thanks to police corruption and a loophole in the Obscene Publications Act, could be seen in licensed sex cinemas.[7] But, in regard to domestic consumption, because the BBFC simply banned explicit material, British sexploitation film-makers had to find ways to attract audiences with extremely mild fare.[8]

The most popular solution to this enforced castration was the sex comedy, which combined simulated sex scenes with saucy humour in the tradition of the *Carry On* films. Titles such as *Percy* (1971), *Confessions of a Sex Maniac* (1974), *Can You Keep It up for a Week?* (1974), *Penelope Pulls It Off* (1974), *I'm Not Feeling Myself Tonight* (1975), *Adventures of a Taxi Driver* (1975) and, generally reckoned the high point of the cycle, *Eskimo Nell* (1974) have come to define the British contribution to erotic cinema – 'ghastly British cinematic abominations', as Julian Petley dubs them, '. . . the majority of which were neither sexy nor comic'.[9] These films were in the music-hall, naughty postcard tradition of farcical low comedy – 'a harder, cinematic version of Brian Rix losing his trousers at the Whitehall Theatre', as one of sexploitation's key producers, Stanley Long, put it.[10] Their unglamorous vulgarity is that of the ever-popular British take on the 'real wives' genre of pornography, which offers a proletarian (or, more pretentiously, Bahktinian) focus on the body's low pleasures. In the sex comedies, as in soft-core magazines like *Fiesta*, there was, in Feona Attwood's words,

> a particular brand of carnival in which ordinary life becomes a fiesta because of the endless opportunities that can be filched from the routine of life for physical pleasure – for sex and laughs; a utopian and vulgar practice of everyday life.[11]

The sex comedy played not so much on the audience's fascination with sex as on its embarrassment about it, and lived up to the national stereotype of the British as a sniggeringly repressed people, who, to paraphrase George Mikes, had hot water bottles instead of sex lives. As Ian Conrich has noted, 'the British male's sexual fantasies about the provinces are of the ordinary, recognisable and available woman and her libidinous neighbour'.[12]

Key – indeed now iconic – films such as *Confessions of a Window Cleaner* record the farcical exploits of a working-class young man taking advantage of the new 'permissive society'. Leon Hunt has traced how the discourse of 'permissiveness', which was articulated in 1970s sex comedies, embodied a consumerist attitude to sex typified and popularised to the working classes by the *Sun* newspaper under Rupert Murdoch's ownership from 1969.[13] Unlike the *Carry Ons*, which centred on the impossibility of sexual fulfilment, the sex comedies gazed yearningly at a male-centred paradisaical world of instantly available 'dolly birds' and carefree serial copulation. The women were sex objects, the men permanently randy and the attitude to sex firmly consumerist – something you got whenever the opportunity arose. The *Confessions* comedies 'celebrated the joys of laddish abandon and zipless, post-Pill hedonism' and contrasted Robin Askwith's proletarian dynamism with his customer's pretence of bourgeois rectitude.[14] By the

Robin Askwith became one of the most popular stars of the era, seen here in *Confessions of a Window Cleaner* (1974)

early 1970s, most sexploitation films were changing from cautionary tales of the effects of unrestrained pleasure-seeking to cautious condemnations of the effects of sexual repression. As permissiveness filtered down to the ordinary punter, they managed to reflect something of the liberated pleasures newly available to their working-class and suburban audiences.

The sex comedy crossed over from the niche of sexploitation to mainstream success among mixed audiences. This is not entirely surprising, since it mostly elaborated on the sexual themes of sitcoms of the period, such as *On the Buses* and *Mind Your Language* and their feature-film spin-offs, which Julian Upton has described as 'the only domestic cinematic trend to see the decade through'.[15] But there were other important strands of sexploitation, such as the dramatic vice exposé film, which had first emerged in Britain in the late 1950s. While in the 1960s, films such as *The Yellow Teddybears* (1964) had explored sexual themes and youthful misdemeanours, the subgenre really took off in 1970 with films such as *Permissive* (1970) and *Groupie Girl* (1970) cashing in on the rock scene and its exploitable hangers-on such as groupies and drug addicts. Like counter-culture exploitation film in the USA (*The Trip* [1966], for example), these 'permissive dramas' offered snapshots of both changing mores and the pleasurably reprehensible behaviour of the liberated young.

After the success of *Emmanuelle* (1974), a few sex films, such as *Erotic Inferno* (1975), *Emily* (1976) and the De Sade adaptation *Cruel Passion* (1977), ignored the prevailing style of seedy realism and had pretensions to be glossy erotic dramas. Set in country houses, a fantasy space isolated from the everyday world, these films depicted obsessional fantasies being played out in a self-enclosed 'pornotopia' unhindered by law, social ties and middle-class restraint.[16]

The most popular subgenre, however, aside from the sex comedy, was the sexploitation documentary, of which the most straightforward and apparently instructional version was the handful of British-made sex education films that began with *Love Variations* (1969) and *Love and Marriage* (1970). *Love Variations*, one of the first British films to show nudity in the UK, consisted entirely of alternating scenes of a 'family doctor' showing diagrams of sex positions and illustrative tableaux of posed figures faking coition in increasingly unlikely and back-breaking postures. The producers, of course, stressed their good intentions to the censors. The press book for *Love Variations* stated, a little disingenuously:

> The film does not seek to entertain – only to inform. The producers wish to point out that although the film is frank, comprehensive and explicit it will almost certainly prove unrewarding to those looking for titillation or sensation and will be of interest only to those motivated by a sincere desire to be informed.

The BBFC, indecisive about how to treat sex education films, accepted this but nevertheless at first rejected *Love Variations* on the splendidly perverse grounds that since the film was not entertaining it was unsuitable for cinemas, which were essentially places of entertainment. When finally released, *Love Variations* smashed house records at the Jacey Tatler cinema in London, taking £19,309 in the first three weeks and achieving seventy-one capacity houses out of eighty-five performances.[17]

The sexploitation documentary emerged in the 1970s as a fascinatingly impure, hybrid and often haphazard style of realism, which voyeuristically depicted forbidden worlds of sexual pleasure and the interpenetration of subcultural, counter-cultural and suburban practices. Usually presented as drama-documentary exposés, they awkwardly combined a semi-documentary look at emerging sexual trends with moralistic disapproval and a campaigning condemnation of Victorian prudishness. This kind of reportage derived from the so-called 'mondo film', after an Italian film of 1962, *Mondo Cane* ('a dog's life'), which was a sarcastic journalistic compilation of exotic sights, startling incidents and staged curiosities from global locations. Its worldwide success led to numerous sequels and imitations, usually focusing on sexual material and mapping the emerging sexual counterculture. British efforts, beginning with Stanley Long and Arnold Lewis Miller's *London in the Raw* (1964), *Our Incredible World* (1966) and *Primitive London* (1965), which combined footage of childbirth, striptease, hair transplants and intimations of a hidden subcultural London, were followed by films such as *Extremes* (1971), which reported on sensational aspects of the counterculture, and *The Pornbrokers* (1973), a semi-autobiographical documentary by the hard-core film-maker John Lindsay about the fledgling porn industry. Consisting mostly of vox pops, the film is partly a defence of porn (it ends with the voiceover declaring, 'In the final event porn is rather like television. If you don't like it you can simply turn off') and partly, and more curiously, an indictment of its own audience as sad punters who embody typical male weakness – 'Men are such suckers when they look at pretty birdies,' Lindsay remarks, adding, 'Men are nuts, they like to see this crap.'

Naughty!, a report on porn made by Stanley Long, typified both the sexploitation documentary's promiscuity of style and its ideological commitments. A political, albeit self-serving film, it took the side of the younger generation and the 'average man in the street' against the oppressions of the old order and appropriated the discourse of permissiveness in the name of popular sexual liberation. Like the sex comedies, *Naughty!* was enraged by Victorian values and what its press book describes as 'structures imposed by moralising law-making sections of society', and emphasised the difference between healthy permissiveness and the supposed hypocrisy and repression of the Victorian era out of which Britain was now emerging. Like the British horror film in the 1970s, sexploitation films were addressed to audiences understood to be either sympathetic to, or at least tempted by, alternatives to repressive middle-class hypocrisy.[18]

While the sex comedies tracked working-class sexuality, the documentaries contrasted the boredom of suburban living with the promise of permissive sex. The penetration of a new sexual morality into 'the sexual desert of suburbia', as *Suburban Wives* (1971) called it, particularly agitated a remarkable series of sex documentaries made by Derek Ford and Stanley Long. These were vignette films in a variety of documentary techniques, whose multiple storylines, held together by sardonic voiceovers, worked through the impact of permissiveness on the suburban middle class and the proliferation of tempting new alternatives to married convention. The first of the series, *The Wife Swappers*, directed by Ford in 1969, was a cautionary tale that depicted swinging as 'a game of increasing risk and diminishing returns' even as it revelled in the opportunities for nudity. According to McGillivray, it cost only £16,000 but became one of the most successful British sex films ever made.[19] It broke the daily house record at the 450-seat Cinephone movie house in its opening week with £3,723[20] and was still consistently making nearly £1,500 in its twentieth week at the same cinema.[21]

Suburban Wives was followed by *Commuter Husbands* (1972), *Sex and the Other Woman* (1972) (about adultery), *On the Game* (1973) (prostitution) and *It Could Happen to You* (1975) (VD). Despite their often baffling confusions of style, tone and moral address, these films coherently articulated ideological positions that justify permissiveness as reviving the 'natural man' repressed by suburban life, and take for granted the battle of the sexes as an eternal state of affairs. 'A woman is a completely different creature from the male', *Suburban Wives*'s voiceover wearily intones, while in *Commuter Husbands*, over a shot of a bowler-hatted gent, the narrator languidly declares, 'At first sight the commuting man is a peaceful law-abiding creature, placidly accepting the dullness of his nine-to-five routine and the burden of his thirty-year mortgage', but inside he 'blazes into breathtaking fantasy'. *Commuter Husbands* is explicitly organised by a theory of man as a hunter, his natural self damped down by contemporary work, and consists of six stories told by a woman in order to support its pseudo-anthropological homage to Desmond Morris's *The Naked Ape*: 'MAN, when off the leash, reverting to his natural role as the HUNTER, a predator with an appetite not for food, but for a more tasty dish called WOMAN', as the press sheet puts it.

Exploitation becomes avant-garde in *Take an Easy Ride* (1976)

The sexploitation documentary's fragmented style, ideological commitment and fascination with spectacle harked back to the outmoded practices of classical exploitation, not least to what Schaefer describes as its challenge to classical Hollywood narrative:

> Exploitation films relied on forbidden spectacle to differentiate themselves from classical Hollywood narrative films and conventional documentaries. As such, they were related to the cinematic tradition Tom Gunning has called 'the cinema of attractions.' The impulse to display spectacle was relied on almost exclusively in some exploitation films or served up in others in such a way as to disrupt the conventions expected in classical Hollywood cinema.[22]

This is perfectly demonstrated in *Take an Easy Ride*, a short programmer directed by Kenneth Rowles in 1976, whose chaos of documentary styles and indifference to narrative render it all but avant-garde. To tell its story of the dangers of hitchhiking, the film combines found footage, dramatisations, flashback reconstructions, allusions to multiple unrelated genres (from the rock film to the *giallo*) and as many exploitable topics as could be crammed into and stretched out to forty-four minutes: drugs, rape, threesomes, runaway youth and the abiding social problem of homicidal hitchhiking lesbians. Production strategies directly comparable to those Schaefer isolates in classical exploitation include 'padding' (interminable scenes of cars winding through country roads for no purpose other than to fill up the running time), 'recycling' (found footage that would turn up in numerous other films) and 'the square up', where the film is presented, with an entirely straight face, as an exercise in public information.[23] Hence Rowles's insistence, having cut sections from two rape scenes and a threesome, that

> this film will give the opportunity for the public to see the dangers in hitchhiking and as this film will be viewed in the West End cinemas, where there will be a large proportion of young people, I expect it will be taken in a more serious light.[24]

In retrospect, films like *Naughty!* or *Take an Easy Ride* sum up all the problems of the British sexploitation film in the 1970s, quite apart from the low-budget, impoverished acting and disorientating editing, which to fans of 'paracinema' scarcely count as flaws at all.[25] Although the producers, with the exception of David Sullivan, who perpetrated *Come Play with Me*, appear not to have been anxious to move into hard-core production, the films were, to some extent, pathetic substitutes for the unavailable real thing. Doomed to euphemism, British sex films offered mild comic thrills and redundant instruction to punters eager for altogether juicier meat. Nevertheless, the style of British sexploitation continues, albeit in different contexts and guises. The square-up lives on, dedicated to convincing censors that sexual material is really educational, as with *The Lover's Guide* video in 1991 and, more recently, the TV series *A Girl's Guide to 21st Century Sex* (Five, 30 October–18 December 2006), in which, as in the whitecoater, jaw-droppingly explicit renditions of real sex were legitimised by the 'educational' context and, just as in classical exploitation, any excitement immediately deflated by thin-lipped warnings about venereal disease. The sex comedy format has also been revived, still harping on repression and hypocrisy, but now invigorated by the examples of *Viz* magazine's reclamation of working-class bawdy, the continuing popularity of unreconstructed northern comics like Roy 'Chubby' Brown, and American gross-out comedies such as *American Pie* (1999). Cosily transgressive farces such as *Personal Services* (1987) and *Preaching to the Perverted* (1997), as well as critically despised bad-taste fests like *UFO* (1993), the underrated and revealing *Sex Lives of the Potato Men*, *Fat Slags* (both 2004) and *I Want Candy* (2007) draw on a populist style of British cinema generally thought best forgotten.[26]

But perhaps the most direct link to 1970s sexploitation, or rather the culmination of what those films promised but could never deliver, is the popular porn director Ben Dover (real name, Lindsay Honey). At once laddish chancer, disbelieving the sexual possibilities that come his way, and creepy groomer of a traditional cast of horny housewives and randy secretaries, Ben Dover, in video and DVD releases such *Housewife Hussies* (2001) and *British Housewife Fantasies Volume 4* (2005), updates with grubby authenticity Robin Askwith's working-class conspicuous sexual consumption. Whatever the aesthetic disaster of British sexploitation – and only *Eskimo Nell* really qualifies as a first-rate movie – it embodied a distinctively British take on sex still relevant and commercial today.

I wish to thank the BBFC, the BFI Library and Steve Chibnall for their help in researching this essay.

Notes

1 Philip Larkin, *High Windows* (London: Faber and Faber, 1974), p. 17.

2 *Come Play with Me* ran for four years at the Classic Moulin in Great Windmill Street, while *Confessions of a Window Cleaner* was the highest grossing British film of 1974. See Simon Sheridan, *Keeping the British End Up: Four Decades of Saucy Cinema* (London: Reynolds & Hearn, 2001), p. 29.

3 David McGillivray, *Doing Rude Things: A History of the British Sex Film* (London: Sun Tavern Fields, 1992), p. 19.

4 Ian Conrich, 'Forgotten Cinema: The British Style of Sexploitation', *Journal of Popular British Cinema*, no. 1, 1998, pp. 87–100; Leon Hunt, *British Low Culture: From Safari Suits to Sexploitation* (London: Routledge, 1998); Simon Sheridan, *Come Play with Me: The Life and Films of Mary Millington* (Guildford: FAB Press, 1999); Sheridan, *Keeping the British End Up*; Matthew Sweet, *Shepperton Babylon: The Lost Worlds of British Cinema* (London: Faber and Faber, 2005), pp. 250–317; I. Q. Hunter, review of video titles released by Jezebel, *Journal of Popular British Cinema*, no. 1, 1998, pp. 168–70; I. Q. Hunter, 'Deep Inside Queen Kong: Anatomy of an Extremely Bad Film', in Ernest Mathijs and Xavier Mendik (eds), *Alternative Europe: Eurotrash and Exploitation Cinema since 1945* (London and New York: Wallflower Press, 2004), pp. 32–8. The documentary based on McGillivray's book is *Doing Rude Things*, BBC 2, 29 May 1995.

5 Robin Askwith, *The Confessions of Robin Askwith* (London: Ebury Press, 1999).

6 Eric Schaefer, *'Bold! Daring! Shocking! True!': A History of Exploitation Films, 1919–1959* (Durham, NC, and London: Duke University Press, 1999), pp. 42–3. See also Jeffrey Sconce, 'Esper the Renunciator: Teaching "Bad" Movies to Good Students', in Mark Jancovich, Antonio Lazaro Reboll, Julian Stringer and Andy Willis (eds), *Defining Cult Movies: The Cultural Politics of Oppositional Taste* (Manchester and New York: Manchester University Press, 2003), pp. 14–34.

7 A unique survey of Soho sex cinemas in the early 1980s is Nick Roddick, 'Soho: Two Weeks in Another Town', *Sight and Sound*, Winter, 1982–3, pp. 18–22. The most notable British hard-core director in the 1970s was John Lindsay whose short films, sometimes starring Mary Millington and often on schoolgirl themes, included *Jolly Hockey Sticks* (1974), *Juvenile Sex* (1974) and *Girl Guides Rape* (1976). They were shown at his Taboo Clubs. Lindsay also produced two soft-core sexploitation films, *The Love Pill* (1971) and *The Hot Girls* (1974).

8 Some films were made in alternative versions or had material added to spice them up for foreign markets; *The Sex Thief* (1973), for example, an entirely standard sex comedy, was released on the continent with hard-core inserts as *A Handful of Diamonds*. See Sheridan, *Keeping the British End Up*, pp. 25–6.

9 Julian Petley, '"There's Something about Mary . . ."', in Bruce Babington (ed.), *British Stars and Stardom: From Alma Taylor to Sean Connery* (Manchester and New York: Manchester University Press, 2001), p. 210.

10 *Screen International*, 23 October 1976.

11 Feona Attwood, 'A Very British Carnival: Women, Sex and Transgression in *Fiesta* Magazine', *European Journal of Cultural Studies*, vol. 5, no. 1, 2002, pp. 91–105.

12 Conrich, 'Forgotten Cinema', p. 97.

13 Hunt, *British Low Culture*.

14 Steve Chibnall and I. Q. Hunter, *A Naughty Business! The British Cinema of Exploitation*, Festival Programme, Leicester, 1995, p. 4.

15 Julian Upton, 'Carry on Sitcom: The British Sitcom Spin-off Film 1968–80', *Bright Lights Film Journal*, no. 35, January 2002 <www.brightlightsfilm. com/35/britishsitcoms1>. Hammer's film of *On the Buses*, for example, was the most successful British film of the year (1971), grossing over £1 million in domestic rentals in the first six months of release.

16 I. Q. Hunter, 'Deadly Manors: The Country House in British Exploitation Films', in Paul Cooke, David Sadler and Nicholas Zurbrugg (eds), *Locating Identity: Essays on Nation, Community and the Self* (Leicester: De Montfort University Press, 1996), pp. 45–55.

17 *KineWeekly*, 8 August 1970.

18 'In the absence of detailed audience research, it is reasonable to assume that by cashing in on the permissive society, sexploitation films helped to spread rumours of metropolitan licence to suburbia and the tantalised provinces. While middle-class sophisticates thrilled to *Blow-up* (1967) and *Last Tango in Paris* (1973), working-class and suburban "men-in-macs" encountered the sexual revolution in the shabby guise of *Au Pair Girls* (1972).' Hunter, review, p. 169.

19 McGillivray, *Doing Rude Things*, p. 56. He puts the film's success down to its appeal to couples. Ford said it was intended for audiences of about thirty-five years old, *Premiere*, no. 3.

20 *KineWeekly*, 5 September 1970.

21 *KineWeekly*, 4 July 1970.

22 Schaefer, '*Bold! Daring! Shocking! True!*', p. 77.

23 Ibid., pp. 56–75.

24 Letter from Kenneth Rowles to Stephen Murphy dated 3 December 1973 in BBFC file for *Take an Easy Ride*. Sheridan, in *Keeping the British End Up*, suggests that the film was made in 1974 but the BBFC received a 16mm version of it for certification in November 1973. The film subsequently took two years to get passed, which might explain why it seems so out of date for 1976. The BBFC cut elements of a rape scene and pubic close-ups in 1973 and 1975, the examiner noting that the film 'which supposedly shows the perils of hitch hiking becomes an exercise in "tongue-licking" sex in Reel 3'.

25 Paracinema is Jeffrey Sconce's term for '[S]eemingly disparate subgenres as "bad film", splatterpunk, "mondo" films, sword and sandal epics, Elvis flicks, governmental hygiene films, Japanese monster movies, beach party musicals and just about every other historical manifestation of exploitation cinema from juvenile delinquency documentaries to soft core pornography', Jeffrey Sconce, 'Trashing the Academy: Taste, Excess and an Emerging Politics of Cinematic Style', *Screen*, vol. 36, no. 4, 1995, p. 372. British sex films are certainly recuperable as intrinsically British but lack those qualities of excess, outrage and unhinged auteurism that often define paracinema for its connoisseurs.

26 Moreover, as in the 1970s, films posing as art manage to smuggle into the 18 certificate category far more explicit material than is conventionally allowed in mere exploitation: *9 Songs* (2004) and *The Great Ecstasy of Robert Carmichael* (2005), for instance.

2 The End of Hammer

Wheeler Winston Dixon

The end of Hammer Films as a production entity came slowly and inexorably, much like the dramatic arc of a classical horror film. Hammer, which had been one of the most profitable and commercially successful companies in British film-making, and indeed the whole of the 1960s, seemed poised for the same success in the 1970s. Instead, the company saw its fortunes dwindle into nothingness by the end of the decade, releasing its last theatrical horror film, Peter Sykes's *To the Devil, a Daughter*, in 1976, followed by a comic remake of *The Lady Vanishes* (Anthony Page, 1979) and several desultory television series in which Hammer stalwarts attempted in vain to recapture the glories of the past. For all intents and purposes, the studio, which was still a significant force in British cinema in 1969, saw the 1970s as a period of decay and terminal collapse.

What happened? How did this hyper-commercial studio lose its footing in the marketplace, as well as its audience? This essay will trace the decline of Hammer from 1967 through to the end of the 1970s, demonstrating how other British film-makers, such as Pete Walker and Michael Reeves, as well as the American directors John Carpenter and Tobe Hooper, moved horror into a new phase of graphic violence against which Hammer's films seemed positively quaint. There are also other factors that contributed to the studio's decline, such as the move from Bray Studios and the departure of Terence Fisher and Freddie Francis, two of Hammer's most prolific directors. But the key factor seems to be that Hammer, the most cost-conscious and even mercenary production entity in UK film history (with the exception of the Danziger Brothers), finally lost touch with audience demand and failed to understand the cultural shift that the end of the 1960s in cinema represented. By the end of the 1970s, the company that had once been one of the most robust British film producers in history was reduced to being little more than a holding company, a shadow of its former glory.

Although the studio would rise to international prominence in the late 1950s, Hammer was founded in 1934. The name 'Hammer' came from the studio's co-founder, William Hinds, a businessman who ran a theatrical agency on the side. Hinds, an energetic impresario, would occasionally appear on stage under the name 'Will Hammer' and decided that the pseudonym was a perfect name for his fledgling company.[1] The first true Hammer film was a comedy, *The Public Life of Henry the Ninth* (Bernard Mainwaring, 1935), a take-off of Alexander Korda's 1933 production *The Private Life of Henry the Eighth*. At sixty minutes, the film was a 'second bill' proposition and was released through MGM's British offices. In 1936, Hammer took its first shot at a horror film with the atmospheric *The Mystery of the Marie Celeste*, directed by Denison Clift and starring Bela Lugosi.[2] Watching this with interest from the sidelines was Enrique Carreras, father of future Hammer executive James Carreras, who was, in turn, the father of Michael Carreras who would run Hammer during its most prolific and influential era. In 1932, Enrique Carreras had founded Exclusive Films, which by the late 1930s had carved a comfortable niche as a distributor. Sensing an opportunity, Hinds asked Carreras to join forces with Hammer to distribute its product and Hammer/Exclusive was born. The new company released the smaller films of minor production companies, as well as reissues of Korda products and the first Hammer films. Carreras was more accurate and prompt with his accounting than past distributors of Hammer films had been and so the partnership flourished. However, there were no new Hammer/Exclusive productions for more than a decade. The team concentrated solely on the distribution business until well after the Second World War.[3]

From late 1947, Jack Goodlatte, the booking manager of the ABC cinema circuit, became interested in releasing more British-made supporting films in his cinemas. Consequently, Hammer/Exclusive began producing films, as well as continuing to distribute the films of other companies. At that time, the 'quota' system operating in Britain required cinemas to show a certain percentage of British-made films as part of their schedule, rather than relying exclusively on Hollywood products. British cinema managers were caught in a bind. They needed more domestic products to satisfy government requirements and also something that would fill their halls with customers. Hammer/Exclusive thus produced its first new film in eleven years with *River Patrol* (1948).[4] Its most ambitious film of the 1940s, *Dick Barton, Secret Agent* (1948), was based on the then-popular BBC radio serial. Even at this early stage in its history, Hammer/Exclusive was already aiming at a pre-sold public in the production of their films. Despite all this activity, it was not until February 1949 that Hammer Film Productions Ltd was officially incorporated, with Will Hinds, Enrique Carreras, Will Hinds's son, Anthony, and Enrique Carreras's son, James, as chief executives.[5]

In November 1947, Hammer acquired the first of its signature 'house studios', Dial Close, at Cookham Dene in Berkshire. A former furniture store, the Dial Close studio served as the location for the studio's next four projects, including *Dick Barton Strikes Back* (1949).[6] But, as David Pirie, still Hammer's most perceptive biographer, notes:

> After four films had been made [at Dial Close], the sets began to look increasingly familiar and it was necessary to find a new home. For the next sixteen films (over a period of about two years from 1948 to 1950) [Hammer's] base moved at least three times, first to Oakleigh Court, Bray, then to Gilston Park, Essex, and back to Down Place, Bray. The twentieth film, *Stolen Face*, inaugurated the long and fruitful occupation of Bray Studios, a rambling elegant country house near Maidenhead, whose exterior was to double on more than one occasion as part of Dracula's castle. Hammer did not finally vacate Bray until 1968.[7]

During this period, Hammer also consolidated a permanent technical unit that was to become one of the hallmarks of the studio's golden age (roughly 1956–65). Early on, Hammer depended upon Godfrey Grayson and Francis Searle to direct its films, while Tony Hinds served as producer. John Gilling, later a famous Hammer director, began writing screenplays during this time for the company. There was one other important addition to the Hammer 'family' at this point: Jimmy Sangster, who would later write Hammer's most important horror scripts,

joined the company as an assistant director. Terence Fisher, who had worked for Warner Bros. in the UK as an editor and then as an apprentice director at Rank, joined Hammer in 1952 as its key director, effectively replacing Searle and Grayson.[8] He had previously made his mark with *So Long at the Fair* (1950), an extraordinary film that foreshadows his fascination with gothic cinema.[9]

Among Fisher's early films for Hammer was *Four-sided Triangle* (1952). This foray into science fiction was a first for Hammer and paved the way for the space exploration drama *Spaceways* (1953) and signalled towards the generic identity that Hammer would soon adopt, with the 1955 production of *The Quatermass Xperiment*, directed by Val Guest. As with the *Dick Barton* films, *The Quatermass Xperiment* (the 'X' was for the 'X' certificate the film would ultimately receive from the British film censor) was a pre-sold commodity, based on the popular television serial by Nigel Kneale. Much to the shock of Hammer's executives, and despite the restrictive 'X' rating, the film was a massive success both in the UK and America and led to the sequels *X the Unknown* (Leslie Norman, 1956) and *Quatermass 2* (Val Guest, 1956). Though only *Quatermass 2* was an 'official' sequel, *X the Unknown* was clearly inspired by the success of the first film, and both films further identified the studio with the science-fiction genre, with distinct horrific overtones.

Up until 1956, Hammer was essentially a cost-conscious studio in search of an identity, scrambling from one low-budget project to the next with an eye on the public's passing fancy. In addition to detective thrillers directed by Fisher, it also produced a string of comedies and costume dramas, as well as musical shorts. Hammer even produced travelogues. *The Quatermass Xperiment* changed all that. From 1956 onwards, although Hammer would continue to produce the occasional comedy, thriller or big-band short, the company became increasingly identified in the public's mind with one central genre: the horror film. In a typically shrewd move, Hammer's executives polled the public to discover what characteristics of the *Quatermass* films most intrigued them: was it the science-fiction aspect or the horrific overtones that kept them spellbound in their seats? Back came the answer: the audience wanted horror, replete with violent spectacle, colour and high production values. The stage was set for Terence Fisher's *The Curse of Frankenstein* (1957), the first major horror film in colour.

The release of *The Curse of Frankenstein* was the defining moment for Hammer; it made overnight stars of Christopher Lee and Peter Cushing, it launched Terence Fisher into the first rank of British directors and it created a brand identity for the studio that lasted for more than a decade. Realising that it had a palpable hit on its hands, Hammer rushed into production with *Dracula* (1958), directed by Fisher and starring Christopher Lee as Dracula and Peter Cushing as Van Helsing. As with *Curse of Frankenstein*, the film was lavishly produced in blood-drenched colour, although *Dracula* took this strategy to new extremes, with ritualistic stakings, copious quantities of blood and, not least, the revisualisation of Dracula himself as a figure of erotic desire, rather than a ravenous monster indiscriminately thirsting for blood. As Dracula, Lee was the consummate aristocrat and, coupled with Jack Asher's superb cinematography, James Bernard's memorable score and Bernard Robinson's opulent sets (which were nevertheless created for a pittance; indeed, the entire film was budgeted at less than £100,000), the film surpassed the box-office takings of *Curse of Frankenstein* in both the UK and the USA, effectively sealing Hammer's destiny with audiences and critics.

As has been amply detailed in Pirie and other sources,[10] from the first, Hammer was under attack for the supposedly extreme amount of graphic violence employed in its films. The claim has some merit; what made Hammer such a success in the late 1950s and early to mid-1960s was the fact that the studio was constantly pushing the boundaries, trying to see what it could get away with before the censors stepped into the fray. The years that followed produced what would later come to be known as the classic Hammer films, including Fisher's *The Mummy* (1959), *The Curse of the Werewolf* and *The Brides of Dracula* (both 1960). As one can readily see, production at Hammer was now approaching a blistering pace: whereas in 1956, Hammer produced several black-and-white features and a few colour short subjects, just four years later the studio is confidently turning out an average of six features a year, most in colour and most associated with the horror genre. Hammer continued to keep its hand in with comedy films and topical thrillers, as well as a series of psychological chillers beginning with Seth Holt's *A Taste of Fear* (1961) and continuing on through to Freddie Francis's *Hysteria* (1964). As the 1960s progressed, new directors joined the Hammer fold: Francis came on board in 1962 with *Paranoiac*[11] and soon Don Sharp (*Kiss of the Vampire*, 1964), John Gilling (*Pirates of Blood River*, 1962), Silvio Narizzano (*Fanatic*, 1965) and Robert Day (*She*, 1966) were all toiling at Bray, creating a gothic worldview that captivated international audiences and simultaneously revitalised the horror genre with a series of inventive, audacious productions that were entirely in sync with audience expectations. When an audience sat down to watch a Hammer film, they knew exactly what to expect: a violent, vivid, boldly executed film that pushed the acceptable limits of graphic representationalism, coupled with a high production gloss and the presence of the studio's signature stars, Lee and Cushing.

But by 1966, trouble was already looming on the horizon, brought on by the twin exigencies of rising production costs and increasing competition from other companies attempting, with varying degrees of success, to copy the Hammer formula. Universal, realising that *The Curse of Frankenstein* and *Dracula* had revived a genre they had long ago abandoned as moribund, had given Hammer the rights to its stable of cinematic monsters, in addition to throwing the considerable weight of its international distribution mechanism behind Hammer's production efforts. But costs kept rising and in 1965 Hammer instituted a policy of shooting two films back to back on the same sets to save money: Fisher's *Dracula – Prince of Darkness* and Sharp's *Rasputin – The Mad Monk* (both 1966) were shot on nearly identical sets, hastily re-propped and, for the first time, the lack of care in the production is readily apparent, along with a definite air of 'repeating the past', as if Hammer was already running out of fresh ideas. In *Dracula – Prince of Darkness*, Lee, sensing both that the role might typecast him for ever and that the entire production was being thrown together with a minimum of care,[12] refused to speak any lines or dialogue, but rather insisted on playing the role mute, with an occasional hiss of distaste as he dispatches his numerous victims. At almost the same time, Hammer pushed John Gilling through a tight schedule of two more films that were shot back to back on the same sets, *The Reptile* and *The Plague of the Zombies* (both 1966). Even more so than with the *Dracula* and *Rasputin* films, the economies began to show and both films suffered artistically and at the box office as a result. Nor did it help when Hammer enticed ageing horror director William Castle, most famous for thrillers like *The Tingler* (1959), for a dreadful comic remake of *The Old Dark House* (1963), which despite the considerable talents of Robert Morley, Joyce Grenfell, Fenella

Fielding and Mervyn Johns failed miserably at the box office; indeed, although the film was shot in colour, it was released in black and white, as the added expense of making colour prints was seen as throwing away money on a lost cause.

Perhaps most tellingly, Hammer began to exhibit signs of a creative stasis that seemingly compelled it to revisit its past successes with a string of Dracula and Frankenstein sequels that did little to add lustre to the studio's reputation. Indeed, 1965 is possibly the last year in which Hammer's strength as a gothic studio dominated both the genre and the industry; in that same year, a rival studio, Amicus, released Freddie Francis's superb *The Skull*, effectively demonstrating that Hammer's hold on the genre was no longer revolutionary or absolute. In addition, Hammer's output was becoming increasingly formulaic, as the studio seemed uninterested in breaking new ground iconographically or cinematically; it was now enough simply to revisit the past and trade on the earlier glory of the studio. Finally, Hammer seemed disinclined to nurture new talents; when maverick director Joseph Losey turned in his brilliant *The Damned* in 1962, Hammer responded by shelving the film, heavily recutting it and eventually releasing it on the bottom half of a double bill with *Maniac*, effectively dumping the film before it had a chance to find its audience.[13]

In addition, the company turned its back on the most groundbreaking films of its own reliable directors: Terence Fisher's prescient *Stranglers of Bombay* (1960) was far more violent than the usual Hammer film and would eventually pave the way for the 1970s taste for ultra violence, with its ritualistic strangulations, outright blood thirst and vivid sexuality. The film seemed resolutely Sadian compared to the company's other efforts and so Hammer did nothing to protect the film when the censor demanded massive cuts. What emerged was the shell of a film, a film that might have given the company a new direction towards the depiction of more graphic horror on the screen, something that the public clearly demanded.

As the 1960s gave way to the 1970s, Hammer seemed content to cut its budgets with even more brutal abandon, at the same time jettisoning many of its most creative collaborators, either through attrition, old age or a lack of vision; this last had always been the company's strongest point and now it seemed as if management was suddenly bereft of both ideas and imagination. Cheap remakes and sequels of Hammer's old films were hastily cobbled together for an increasingly jaded audience who no longer saw Hammer as the vanguard enterprise it had once been. After the move from Bray, Hammer was forced to rely on a limited supply of sets and existing 'flats' for production design; although Terence Fisher gamely continued, creating some late masterpieces under severe constraints, such as *Frankenstein Must Be Destroyed* (1970), *The Devil Rides Out* (1967, based on Dennis Wheatley's novel) and his last film as a director, *Frankenstein and the Monster from Hell* (1973). The game was clearly over. In a futile attempt to lure audiences to the cinema (much like the *Carry On* series in its waning years), Hammer decided that generous amounts of female nudity and sexual violence would help to sell its films, all to no avail. Thus, at the last minute, a completely gratuitous rape scene was added to *Frankenstein Must Be Destroyed* despite the objections of the actors; although Terence Fisher and Peter Cushing protested vehemently, the scene was shot, undermining the integrity of the entire production.

(Opposite page) Terence Fisher's late masterpiece *Frankenstein Must Be Destroyed* (1970)

Other 1970s Hammer films, such as Roy Ward Baker's *The Vampire Lovers*, Jimmy Sangster's *The Horror of Frankenstein*, Baker's *Scars of Dracula* and Sangster's *Lust for a Vampire* (all shot in 1970 and released in 1970–1), seemed shabby and dated. With the studio's final and definitive move to MGM's Elstree Studios at Borehamwood, such films as Baker's *Dr Jekyll and Sister Hyde* (1972), Alan Gibson's *Dracula AD 1972* (1972) and Peter Sykes's *To the Devil, a Daughter* seem threadbare both intellectually and in their physical production. For the record, the last Hammer film shot at Bray was John Gilling's *The Mummy's Shroud* (1967),[14] but much to Hammer's dismay, the world had moved on and what was once fresh and original was now being cynically recycled for the demands of the marketplace, with little concern for the quality of the final product.

Terence Fisher, not a well man in 1973 when he retired, was the last true visionary the studio possessed; Freddie Francis, never genuinely attracted to the horror genre, made several more horror films for other companies (including his son's company, Tyburn) and then went back to working as a much-in-demand director of photography on such films as David Lynch's *The Elephant Man* (1980) and Edward Zwick's *Glory* (1989), for which he won his second Academy Award for Best Cinematography.[15] In 1968, the American film-maker George Romero turned the accepted conventions of the horror film on their collective heads with his groundbreaking low-budget film *Night of the Living Dead*, which he shot in 35mm black and white at weekends with a miniscule budget, using a small crew and actual locations to tell the story of a doomsday scenario in which the dead rise from their graves to menace the living. Violent, unabashedly gory and resolutely nihilistic, *Night of the Living Dead* did for the horror genre exactly what Hammer had done in 1957; it made everything before it look dated, formulaic and predictable. In Hammer's films, even as the bodies pile up, there is usually a heterotopic ending in which at least some of the more attractive cast members survive; in *Night of the Living Dead*, the hero, an African-American male (another first for the genre), is killed by vigilantes after successfully defending himself during an all-night siege by the living dead, during which every other member of the cast meets a violent end. Romero's film looked like a newsreel, with its grainy black-and-white cinematography and sparse sets; economy was turned into an artistic virtue. Hammer, still largely stuck in a Victorian world of vampires, werewolves and mummies, lacked any connection to contemporary existence.

In addition to the shot of adrenaline provided by Romero's film, in the UK the tragic figure of Michael Reeves was busy reshaping the horror film with *The Sorcerers* (1967) and *Witchfinder General* (1968), which took the competing Roger Corman/American International/Edgar Allan Poe format (which had flourished in the 1960s as Hammer's only serious competition in the genre) and revitalised it with doses of sadism and a brutal naturalism that extended to a surprisingly subdued performance from *Witchfinder*'s star Vincent Price, coupled with meticulous location shooting and attention to detail.[16] When Reeves died of an overdose of barbiturates at the age of twenty-five in 1969, he left behind a brief but influential legacy that inspired other British mavericks like Pete Walker to bring a new level of intensity and immediacy to their genre films. Walker's violent horror films, especially *House of Whipcord* and *Frightmare* (both 1974), paved the way, for better or worse, for the 'splatter' films or 'nasties' that would dominate the genre in the 1970s and 1980s. Again, Hammer's films, once on the bleeding edge of cinematic discourse, looked badly dated.[17]

Just how out of touch Hammer was with current trends was particularly evident in *Dracula AD 1972*, which attempted to mix vampirism with 'Swinging London', an idea that might have had some credence in the mid-1960s but that was by now outdated. In a last-ditch attempt to regain some box-office traction, Hammer made a deal with the Shaw Brothers Studios in Hong Kong for two films in 1973: Roy Ward Baker's *The Legend of the Seven Golden Vampires*, a mixture of kung fu and vampirism, with a dispirited Peter Cushing pressed into service, and the action thriller *Shatter*, directed by Monte Hellman and Michael Carreras during a trouble-plagued shoot and sporadically released in 1974.

In 1978, John Carpenter wrote, directed and composed the music for the groundbreaking horror film *Halloween*, an enormous critical and commercial success that again reimagined the 'rules of the game' for horror films with a degree of flair, stylishness and assured self-referentiality. In the same year, Hammer abandoned horror altogether for a stolid remake of *The Lady Vanishes*, a film utterly lacking in imagination or vitality. Rather than looking forward, Hammer's version of *The Lady Vanishes* is a throwback to the British cinema of the 1930s and a rather tepid homage to Alfred Hitchcock, who had so successfully reinvented himself for succeeding generations for most of his career, especially with *Psycho* (1960), something Hammer no longer seemed capable of accomplishing.

New directions for Hammer: *To the Devil, a Daughter* (1976)

Ironically, as the creative end of Hammer was in sight, the company scored its biggest box-office hit, Freddie Francis's *Dracula Has Risen from the Grave* (1968), after winning the Queen's Award to Industry for its success in conquering both the UK and US marketplace.[18] However, Hammer's next big project, Roy Ward Baker's *Moon Zero Two* (1969), failed at the box office and Hammer suddenly found itself without an international distribution deal.[19] The major creative forces behind the company also began to drift away. Art director Bernard Robinson resigned, and then died of a heart attack at the age of fifty-eight on 2 March 1970, minutes after tentatively agreeing to come back for one last production.[20] In 1971, Roy Skeggs, Hammer's accountant, became the production supervisor for the company and in 1972 was promoted to producer status.[21] Michael Carreras and his father, James, had a personal falling-out that affected their approach to Hammer's production schedule and, after a complex series of negotiations, Michael bought out his father's interest in the company in August 1972, becoming Chief Executive on 31 January 1973. But more heartbreak lay ahead: when all the accounts were settled up, Michael was shocked to discover that the total assets of the company amounted to a mere £200,000 and even the German co-production of *To the Devil, a Daughter* failed to reverse the company's fortunes.[22] As previously discussed, the 1978 production of *The Lady Vanishes*, a co-production with Rank, failed to ignite at the box office and, in February 1979, Hammer was placed in the hands of the bankruptcy lawyers as a result of cost overruns and schedule delays on *The Lady Vanishes*, coupled with the film's lack of success. Michael Carreras resigned on 30 April 1979. He died on 19 April 1994 at the age of sixty-six.[23]

In 1980, Roy Skeggs and Brian Lawrence tried to put Hammer back on the map with two television series, *Hammer House of Horror* and *Hammer House of Mystery and Suspense*, as well as a documentary of classic clips from the past narrated by Hammer stalwart Oliver Reed. But the die was cast; Hammer was history and Brian Lawrence retired in 1985, while Roy Skeggs left the company in 2000 when he sold it to a private group of investors, including advertising executive Charles Saatchi.[24] The end had come at last; Hammer was no more. Ultimately, a combination of factors had brought about the spectacular demise of the company's fortunes. Once in the vanguard, Hammer's approach to horror now seemed timid and out of step with the new level of graphic violence pioneered by Reeves, Walker, Carpenter and other auteurs. The creative talents who had made Hammer the force it once was were all, essentially, Victorians and the concerns of nineteenth-century Britain seemed increasingly remote to twentieth-century audiences as the century neared its close.

Misguided attempts at efficiency took their toll, as the back-to-back films of 1966 began a wave of cost cutting from which the quality of the films never recovered. Rather than seeking new scenarios and new talent, Hammer increasingly relied on old formulas, content to repeat the past rather than forge new ground. But, perhaps, we should acknowledge that the 'newer' horror films of the 1970s now themselves look dated and out of touch with contemporary concerns, in our post 9/11 world of real, rather than imagined horrors. The cinematic stakes of graphic representationalism in horror will continue to push the boundaries of public taste; after all, to truly qualify as a horror film, a film must genuinely 'horrify' its audience. The nihilist brutality of Eli Roth's relentlessly graphic *Hostel* (2005), in which two backpackers stumble into an Eastern European hostel only to fall victim to a gang of cut-throats who offer them as victims to amateur torturers for a price, was once as unimaginable as Peter Cushing's Van Helsing driving a stake through a vampire's heart in *Dracula*.

Everything changes, but the world that Hammer inhabited, and still inhabits, resides firmly in the past and, because of its Victorian roots, resists being brought into the present. Perhaps Terence Fisher was right when he told a reporter from the *Daily Telegraph* on 27 November 1976, 'Please – I never made horror films. They're fairy tales for adults.'[25] We no longer believe in fairy tales, nor do we want to; the present offers us too many proofs that good does not always triumph and that evil cannot always be vanquished. The world of Hammer horror was, in the end, a reassuring zone of escape in which the audience could lose itself for a few hours without any genuine risk attached. Today, we know the risk is all too real, something that Hammer, even in its finest films, resolutely refused to acknowledge. In 2007, the Hammer back catalogue and name were purchased by John DeMol of Endemol Productions, a Dutch firm specialising in reality television programming. Endemol unveiled an ambitious plan of future productions for the studio, but for the moment it seems as if the future of Hammer, if there is to be one, is very much in flux.

Notes

1 Wheeler Winston Dixon, *The Charm of Evil: The Life and Films of Terence Fisher* (Metuchen, NJ, and London: Scarecrow Press, 1991), p. 125.
2 Ibid.
3 Ibid., p. 126.
4 Ibid., p. 127.
5 Ibid., p. 128.
6 Ibid.
7 David Pirie, *A Heritage of Horror: The English Gothic Cinema 1946–1972* (London: Gordon Fraser, 1973), p. 26.
8 Dixon, *Charm of Evil*, pp. 10–11.
9 See Pirie, *Heritage of Horror*, pp. 53–5, for a detailed discussion of this remarkable work.
10 See particularly Wayne Kinsey's *Hammer Films: The Bray Studio Years* (London: Reynolds & Hearn, 2002), for a detailed discussion of Hammer's battles with the censors in both the UK and other sales territories.
11 See Wheeler Winston Dixon, *The Films of Freddie Francis* (Metuchen, NJ, and London: Scarecrow Press, 1991), for a detailed account of Francis's long career.
12 See Pirie, *Heritage of Horror*, pp. 88–92, for a discussion of *Dracula – Prince of Darkness* that highlights these shortcomings.
13 See Pirie, *Heritage of Horror*, pp. 137–8, for more on the troubled history of this project.
14 Kinsey, *Hammer Films*, p. 349.
15 See Dixon, *Films of Freddie Francis*, pp. 142–63, for a discussion of Francis's later work as a director of photography.
16 For a superb discussion of Michael Reeves's films, see Benjamin Halligan, *Michael Reeves* (Manchester: Manchester University Press, 2003).
17 See David McGillivray, *Doing Rude Things: The History of the British Sex Film 1957–1981* (London: Sun Tavern Fields, 1992), pp. 130–1, for a discussion of Pete Walker's work.

18 Kinsey, *Hammer Films*, p. 353.
19 Ibid., p. 354.
20 Ibid.
21 Ibid.
22 Ibid., pp. 354–5.
23 Ibid., p. 355.
24 Ibid.
25 Dixon, *Charm of Evil*, p. iii.

3 The Divergence and Mutation of British Horror Cinema

Ian Conrich

In the 1970s, the British horror film lost its once stable generic identity and split into a variety of directions. Cultural and economic factors pulled the horror film towards sexploitation – seen explicitly in the films *Horror Hospital* (1973) and *Exposé* (1975) – where the sensationalist content of the British sex film was proving to be a formidable and cost-effective box-office attraction at a time when the British film industry was in decline. The continuing rise of the European horror film, with its greater levels of violence and exploitation, was another factor. The British horror film, in the 1960s, had occasionally joined with German co-producers to make low- to medium-budget period and gothic horrors, such as *Vengeance* (1962), *A Study in Terror* (1965) and *The Brides of Dracula* (1966). But in the 1970s, under pressure to compete, the idea of the British–European co-production was extended into imitative and expensive epic horrors such as *To the Devil, a Daughter* (1976), *Holocaust 2000* (1977) and *The Medusa Touch* (1978). The success of the blockbuster American horror film *The Omen* (1976) led to these British imitations, which were drawn to depicting stories of the occult, Satanism, politics and the apocalypse.

In fact, the re-emergence of the American horror film in general, in the 1970s, had a noticeable impact on British horror cinema in the second half of the decade. Driven by a new brutality and a cinema of innovative special effects – as witnessed in films such as *The Exorcist* (1973) and *The Texas Chain Saw Massacre* (1974) – the horror new wave firmly placed the terror within contemporary settings. The British horror film similarly reacted by imitating the contemporary content in films such as *Full Circle* (1976) and *Killer's Moon* (1978). In another attempt to survive, British horror also became transcultural and mutable, absorbing other genres and the distinctive trends in the exploitation films of the period. This resulted in horror hybrids such as the biker horror *Psychomania* (1972), the blaxploitation werewolf whodunit *The Beast Must Die* (1974), the vampire-swashbuckler *Captain Kronos: Vampire Hunter* (1974) and the kung-fu horror *The Legend of the Seven Golden Vampires* (1974).

This essay will explore and consider the panoply of British horror in the 1970s with a focus on the way in which it mutates through exploitation and imitation. The British horror film may have lost its impact by the end of the 1970s, but it did not disappear. It will be argued that in the 1970s, the British horror film diversified, fused with other genres and either sought to compete through big-budget co-productions, or through low-budget independence, a mode of production that provided a refuge until the video age of the 1980s.

An Industry Torn

While the British film industry entered into decline in the 1970s, the British horror film actually continued to flourish in the first six years of the decade, at least in terms of the number of productions completed. According to Linda Wood, between 1971 and 1981 the British horror film was second only to the 'children's film' in terms of total productions.[1] The horror genre had proved to be extremely commercial and able to attract an overseas audience. In fact, with international markets, horror had become synonymous with British film production. It was generally a cost-effective form of production that was able to turn repeatedly to a successful formula, and was therefore likely to be one of the last of the traditional British film genres to be affected by the collapse of the once healthy movie industry. In one way, its attempts to adapt to new developments aided this survivalism, but in another way they precipitated the demise of this cycle in the British horror genre.

By the later years of the 1970s, however, the British horror film was certainly less dominant and one view is that production diminished as a result of the industry crisis. A combination of factors led to the decline of the industry: from the withdrawal of the American studios and film financing from British productions, to the significant drop in audience attendance, as other leisure activities appeared more attractive. Each factor affected the other and the effect was cumulative. As David Docherty, David Morrison and Michael Tracey write in *The Last Picture Show?*:

> The structural changes of the 1950s had undermined the cinema to such an extent that stabilisation, let alone growth, was no longer possible . . . by 1970 only 2 per cent of the population went to the cinema once a week or more, compared to one-third of the population in the late 1940s . . . By 1970 the cinema had become just one more leisure pursuit among a myriad of alternatives.[2]

The authors continue by indicating that as audience numbers decreased so did investment in the infrastructure and the cinema buildings themselves, which led to further reasons why audiences stayed away, as the comfort and quality of the viewing experience was increasingly undermined. With US audiences also in significant decline, the number of US films being produced decreased and in turn led to fewer films being available for British cinemas. Smaller and independent exhibitors consequently found it difficult to screen available films. This in turn, in many instances, created further industry pressure, and as this sector shrunk there were even fewer theatrical options for the UK audience.[3]

There is another position, which argues that the British horror film stumbled and ultimately fell in the first half of the 1970s as a result of the new direction taken by the American horror film, first with *Night of the Living Dead* (1968) and later with *The Exorcist*. Authors such as Barry Keith Grant and Gregory A. Waller see *Night of the Living Dead* as a key production in the emergence of the modern horror film, with its nihilism, reflexivity, realism and contemporary settings.[4] David Sanjek argues that this film in particular 'set in motion the decline of the British horror film and the myth that it embodied. When monsters and human beings could no longer easily be distinguished, the tidy universe of the English horror film was in jeopardy.'[5] Sanjek does note that what he sees as the demise of the British horror film is attributable to

(Opposite page) Victims or monsters?: *Death Line* (1972)

many reasons, but he sees as 'chief among them' the 'exhaustion' of 'artificial horror' and its replacement by 'real horror'.[6] Such developments were not, however, as clear-cut and, as Sanjek identifies in his discussion of both *The Witchfinder General* (1968) and *Death Line* (1972), there was also a blurring of the traditional divide between the victim and the monster.

Sanjek's argument is useful but it presents a narrow terrain for the British horror film of the 1970s, with the discussion of a number of key films masking the fact that the genre was at this time much richer and diverse in content. Leon Hunt writes that 'Sanjek's approach is limited by a certain prescriptiveness about what British horror should have been doing', and that later in following certain British productions he 'is overly concerned with credentials and authorship'.[7] There is also the argument presented by Peter Hutchings that modern horror films such as *Psycho* (1960), *Night of the Living Dead* and *Rosemary's Baby* (1968), which according to critics and writers marked the start of generic change in the horror film, 'look like isolated outposts of activity rather than like the actual beginning of anything'.[8] As Hutchings writes, 'none of them . . . lead directly and immediately to sustained horror production of the type that would later be labelled "modern"'.[9] Comparing US horror film production of the period 1968–73 with horror films emerging from the UK and continental Europe, Hutchings correctly identifies a 'more tentative' approach from the former as opposed to 'an unruly but intriguing mix of different horror approaches and styles' from the latter.[10] There were fewer American than European horrors produced in this period and within the context of both the genre as a whole and the local industry, British horror films remained a dominant force.

Unruly British Horrors

It is perhaps odd to label a particular form of horror film as unruly when in order to be an effective part of this genre it must often appear to present itself as inherently turbulent, assaultive and disobedient. There was, however, a distinctive development in the British horror film of the 1970s, with style and content influenced by a number of key external factors: increasing screen depictions of sexual permissiveness, relaxed censorship, a lingering counter-culture and increased economic demands on an industry that was pushed into experimenting beyond traditional boundaries of genres. Hutchings sees the horror genre as unruly in terms of its mix of different film styles and approaches, as well as identifying a number of British films that exhibit an 'anti-father' theme.[11]

Certainly, the horror film displayed an acute hybridity at this time. *The Legend of the Seven Golden Vampires* was a marriage between Hammer and the Shaw Brothers studio of Hong Kong, which resulted in a vampire-martial arts horror. With fight scenes choreographed by Liu Chia-Ling, the film depicted Count Dracula and Chinese vampires, supported by an army of the Undead, attacking poor Chinese villagers, who are aided in their defence by Professor Van Helsing (played once again by Peter Cushing). There is a novelty to the film, despite its exploitation of the popular interest in kung fu – filming began on 22 October 1973, two months after the release of Bruce Lee's *Enter the Dragon* on 19 August 1973. *Enter the Dragon* had been a significant box-office success in the USA and was credited with being the key commercial text to popularise kung fu Stateside, but despite this *The Legend of the Seven Golden Vampires* could not pick up an American distributor. Hammer films had a distinct presence at American cinemas, with its gothic horrors a recognisable screen product. *The Legend of the Seven Golden Vampires* had appealed to audiences in Britain and the Far East, where the hybrid nature of the film allowed it to function successfully as a transcultural production, but the hybridity of Hammer, or its unruly appearance compared to its earlier productions, may have made it more difficult sell in the USA. The film was not released in the USA until 1979, when it was retitled as *The Seven Brothers Meet Dracula* and was cut by seventeen minutes.

The Satanic Rites of Dracula (1973) similarly failed to gain an immediate release in the USA and was eventually distributed in 1978 as *Count Dracula and His Vampire Bride*. Hammer's struggles to release its horror movies in the USA in the 1970s were one of several significant factors in its collapse as a film studio in 1978. The horror films made by Hammer in this decade were on the whole much weaker productions, structurally flawed and unsophisticated, and its failure to capture a US audience was not due to a change in the nature of the horror film as Sanjek argues. *The Satanic Rites of Dracula* was made by the same director-writer team of Alan Gibson and Don Houghton as *Dracula AD 1972*, with both productions attempting to modernise Dracula by bringing the story into present-day London. With *Dracula AD 1972* (working titles *Dracula Chelsea '72* and *Dracula Chases the Mini Girls*), Hammer made a late attempt at conjoining horror with the youth and hedonism of 'Swinging London'. *The Satanic Rites of Dracula* (working title *Dracula Is Dead and Well and Living in London*) likewise drew on the notion of a 'cool' London and partly on a current popularity for espionage stories and James Bond, depicting the British intelligence, high security homes and Dracula as a penthouse-residing tycoon whose aim (in the style of a good Bond villain) is to spread globally a deadly plague virus.

Such modernising of Dracula could not disguise the growing repetition of the Lee–Cushing vampire films and Hammer's *Captain Kronos: Vampire Hunter* marked a conscious attempt by writer Brian Clemens to reinvigorate British horror production. Foregrounding the heroic qualities of the vampire hunter into a sword-wielding, horse-riding young male, accompanied on his travels by a hunchbacked sidekick, the film merged elements of the Western, swashbuckling adventures and the weekly serials with a rustic mythology on vampirism that included the placement of a toad in the path of a suspected vampire. In an interview with *The Monster Times*, Clemens said that '[t]he basic concept behind *Kronos* is a very deep one: to liberate horror pictures'. Clemens had been frustrated by previous Hammer horrors: 'by the time I got to the third Dracula, I couldn't distinguish it from the first one'.[12]

Hammer was not alone in hybridising British horror, with the slightly camp *Psychomania* another notable example. The film focused on a gang of bikers who terrorise a small community and who, following a pact with the devil, commit mass suicide and return as the motorcycle-riding living dead. The biker film was an American exploitation subgenre of the early to mid-1970s following the indie success of *Easy Rider* (1969). In its wake, the American-produced *Werewolves on Wheels* (1971) was one of several movies of the time to mix Satanism and motorbikes. Of greater camp value was *Theatre of Blood* (1973), which brings Shakespeare, Grand Guignol, a superbly gothic Vincent Price and an impressive cast of thespians (including Jack Hawkins and Robert Morley) to a revenge-on-a-theme horror in the style of the Dr Phibes films (*The Abominable Dr Phibes* [1971] and *Dr Phibes Rises Again* [1972], produced by AIP and starring Price). And Amicus, a key studio in 1960s and 1970s British horror production, made *The Beast Must Die*, a werewolf horror-whodunit that advises the audience at the beginning that they

Camp horror with Vincent Price in *Theatre of Blood* (1973)

are detectives searching for clues within the film as to the identity of the lycanthrope. Just before the film's end and the revealing of the monster's identity, the film pauses giving the viewer a moment to make their decision as to who they believe is the killer. Released in the USA as *Black Werewolf* (on the back of *Blacula* [1972] and *Blackenstein* [1973]), and starring Calvin Lockhart, who earlier had a leading role in *Cotton Comes to Harlem* (1970), the film was one of the few British productions to be influenced directly by the American blaxploitation movies of the early 1970s.

Film as a cultural product, and genre films in particular, very often reflect the period in which they were made and the horror film as a form of exploitation can connect easily with issues relevant to a specific moment in contemporary society, irrespective of the period in which the story is set. A key component of horror's new exploitation in the 1970s was the emphasising of sex and nudity. The new salaciousness that emerged in British horror in the late 1960s – *Corruption* (1967) is a key early example – quickly became a central part of the genre, with sexploitation and horror openly related. Such productions were numerous and I have referred to them elsewhere as Flesh Films.[13]

Horror's Exploitation of Sex

Perhaps the best known of British cinema's union of sex and horror is Hammer's female vampire films of the early 1970s: *Countess Dracula* (1970) and the Karnstein trilogy of *The Vampire Lovers* (1970), *Lust for a Vampire* (1971) and *Twins of Evil* (1971, also known as *Virgin Vampires*). The importance of scenes of female nudity and sexuality to these films can be seen overtly in mainstream publications of the time such as *Film and Filming* and, moreover, *Continental Film Review*, in which the flesh content of the productions was extracted and promoted within the magazines as a blinkered interpretation of the movie content. Perhaps this could not be avoided when a film such as *Twins of Evil* starred the Collinson twins, sisters who posed as *Playboy*'s first twin centrefolds. The manifold nature of these productions was revealed by director Peter Sasdy in 1970, who saw the audience split into three groups: 'One: the large number of people who go to the films to be frightened; Two: those who go for a certain kind of laugh; and Three: the type of audience that goes for sexual thrills.'[14]

The low-budget European horror films of the early 1970s – which included erotic vampire movies such as Jean Rollin's *Le Frisson des vampires* (*Sex and the Vampire*, 1970) and *Requiem pour un vampire* (*Requiem for a Vampire*, 1971), Jess Franco's *Vampyros Lesbos* (*Lesbian Vampires*, 1970) and José Luis Madrid's *El Vampiro de la autopista* (*The Horrible Sexy Vampire*, 1970) – were both competition and a bad influence on the British horror film in the first part of the decade. Working within the British film industry, Spanish-born director José Larraz firmly engaged with horror and sexuality to the point where his third British horror film, *Vampyres* (1974), was seen by many critics as pornography; Larraz's previous horrors, *Scream – And Die!* (1973, also known as *Psycho Sex Fiend*) and *Symptoms* (1974, also known as *The Blood Virgin*), were independently made erotic exploitation films, with the former foregrounding its sensational content and the latter, a more psychological exercise, chosen as the official British entry at the Cannes Film Festival in 1974.

Vampyres was for a long time a neglected British horror. It was not until the mid- to late 1990s, when writers began to reassess British horror and sexploitation films of the 1970s, that the film rightly gained greater attention.[15] The fanzine *Flesh and Blood* described *Vampyres* as '[b]rutal, erotic, unique, inspirational and bizarre', while Tim Greaves devoted an entire booklet to the production, in which Larraz was interviewed and approached on the subject of the film's ferocity and excessiveness: Larraz responded that he imagined his two lesbian vampires (played by soft-core pin-ups Marianne Morris and Anulka) like 'panthers, two wild animals . . . I can't imagine someone coming to suck my blood gently'.[16] Leon Hunt sees the film's pornography as ambivalent, placing a question mark over 'what kind of fantasy it is offering to the audience'.[17] The inability and disposability of the male (whose 'body becomes little more than a prop' for the vampires' sex) make *Vampyres* a complex and challenging film.[18] As Hunt writes '[t]he male heterosexual narrative of *Vampyres* (the one which would sell the film) is an explicitly masochistic one'.[19]

European influences in British horror: José Larraz's *Vampyres* (1974)

With film censorship relaxed in the early 1970s, more explicit movies – both British and foreign productions – were allowed through the system. The secretary and chief censor of what was then the British Board of Film Censors, was Stephen Murphy. He was in office between 1971 and 1975, when low-budget genre films such as *Tower of Evil* (1972), *Horror Hospital* and *The House of Whipcord* (1974), as well as mainstream British films such as *The Devils* (1970), *A Clockwork Orange* (1971) and *Straw Dogs* (1971), were allowed through amid great concern from moral campaigners. Murphy resigned in 1975 as the moral backlash against the films of the period intensified, but by then there had already been significant traffic in the relationship between British sex and horror films. While British directors such as Peter Sasdy and Roy Ward

Baker, who had been associated with the horror film, were compelled to inject sexual scenes into their productions, film-makers such as Pete Walker, Antony Balch and Norman J. Warren switched from sexploitation to making horror movies, and they 'brought with them a willingness to foreground sensational elements'.[20] Such was the industry's drive to make more graphic horror films in the 1970s that some film-makers turned away from production. As I have written, director Basil Dearden, whose career ended with the relatively restrained horror film *The Man Who Haunted Himself* (1970), seemed to be a film-maker out of time and disconnected from the new approaches and demands of the industry.[21] Elsewhere, I have considered producer and distributor Tony Tenser, a cinema manager who in the 1960s turned to distributing sexploitation films as part of the Compton Group, and in 1967 set up Tigon, a company that made the British horrors *Blood on Satan's Claw* (1970) and *The Beast in the Cellar* (1971). Tenser sold Tigon in 1972, 'tiring of the explicit violence he was having to inject into his films'.[22]

Imitation

The decline in British horror film production began around 1975. From 1973 to 1974 thirty British horror films were produced; during 1975–6 there were ten, and 1977–8 saw twelve.[23] The films made in the second half of the decade included a curious mixture of half-horrors, such as the murder-mystery *The Cat and the Canary* (1977), the Sherlock Holmes thriller *Murder by Decree* (1978) and the chilling art film *The Shout* (1978), directed by Jerzy Skolimowski. Most noticeably, production in the second half of the decade often seemed split between low-budget independents and ambitious co-productions with blockbuster desires. Ranging from Warren's first horror, *Satan's Slave* (1976), to Hammer's expensive last horror, *To the Devil, a Daughter*, thematically, many of these films were drawn to the occult, Satanism, possession and the apocalypse, themes that were circulating in American films. This was a decade in which other films had exhibited themes of paranoia, suspicion, political mistrust and a fear of the unknown.

Imitation within film genres was far from being a new development, but what is significant is that by the mid-1970s, British horror was searching for fresh ways of surviving and gaining Stateside theatrical release, and was seduced by recent American horror films, which it copied. The American new wave of horror did not really commence until the late 1970s with films such as *The Hills Have Eyes* (1977), *Halloween* (1978), *Dawn of the Dead* (1979), *Friday the 13th* (1980) and *The Howling* (1980). The rush of productions that followed, which was fuelled by independent film-makers who could see the financial and creative benefits of low-budget special-effects-filled movies with a rapidly growing new fan-base, is a strong indication of the impact made by this new cycle in the horror genre. Prior to this period, American horror films in the 1970s were produced less frequently, though a handful of crucial movies were made by the major studios – *The Exorcist* (Warner Bros.), *Jaws* (1975, Universal), *The Omen* (20th Century-Fox) – that inspired imitation. These studio horrors enjoyed huge commercial success at the box office and have become associated, among other films, with Hollywood's increasing concentration on the production of the blockbuster or event movie.

The British horror film declined in the mid-1970s partly because it tried to copy the American horrors of the time and felt that in order to compete it also had to invest in big-budget productions. The exploitation-horror *I Don't Want to Be Born* (1975), directed by Peter Sasdy, mixed sex with horror (the film is set around a strip club), but also borrowed from the American horrors *The Exorcist* and *It's Alive* (1974), with its story of possession and a monstrous birth. The more expensive Lew Grade-financed British–French co-production *The Medusa Touch*, with a bed-confined Richard Burton exerting his psychokinetic powers, conjoined elements of *The Exorcist*, *Carrie* (1976) and *The Omen*, even casting Lee Remick from the latter film in another leading role. Hammer's British–German co-production *To the Devil, a Daughter*, like *The Medusa Touch*, was an expensive failure that copied *The Exorcist* and *The Omen*. The British–Italian co-production *Holocaust 2000* was more overt in its copying of *The Omen* (made the year before) with another story of the Antichrist, who is the son of a wealthy American.

The occasional bloated, big-budget British horror did continue with films such as *The Awakening* (1980), but its once stable identity had fragmented too much. In the main, British horror film production became increasingly low budget, independent and reliant on the scope, openness and opportunities for exploitation within the new film market provided by the video age and home entertainment. For a period between 1984 and 1993, with no remaining recognised studios or producers of British horrors, it looked as if Palace Pictures – with the films *The Company of Wolves* (1984), *Dream Demon* (1988), *Hardware* (1990) and *Dust Devil* (1993) – could fill the void, but there was increasingly a lack of a marketable national identity within the genre. In a 1992 interview that I conducted with Daniel Battsek, then Managing Director of Palace Pictures, he stated that for a movie such as *Hardware*, which was promoted initially as if it were an American production, 'there is no point from a marketing point of view in selling a horror film as British, at least not in the beginning'.[24] As the British horror movie had mutated and diversified to compete and exist within the challenging industrial climate of the 1970s, it had lost a generic identity that had arguably been the British film industry's most stable throughout the 1960s.

Notes

1 Linda Wood (ed.), *British Films 1971–1981* (London: BFI, 1983).

2 David Docherty, David Morrison and Michael Tracey, *The Last Picture Show? Britain's Changing Film Audience* (London: BFI, 1987), p. 29.

3 Ibid., p. 30. For a brief overview of the social and economic context of the period, see Sarah Street, *British National Cinema* (London: Routledge, 1997), pp. 92–3.

4 Barry Keith Grant, 'Taking Back the *Night of the Living Dead*: George Romero, Feminism and the Horror Film', in *The Dread of Difference: Gender and the Horror Film* (Austin: University of Texas Press, 1996); Gregory A. Waller (ed.), *American Horrors: Essays on the Modern American Horror Film* (Champaign: University of Illinois Press, 1988).

5 David Sanjek, 'Twilight of the Monsters: The English Horror Film 1968–1975', in Wheeler Winston Dixon (ed.), *Re-viewing British Cinema, 1900–1992: Essays and Interviews* (Albany: State University of New York Press, 1994), p. 196.

6 Ibid., p. 196. 'Artificial horror' and 'real horror' are terms Sanjek borrows from James B. Twitchell, *Dreadful Pleasures: An Anatomy of Modern Horror* (New York: Oxford University Press, 1985), p. 8.

7 Leon Hunt, *British Low Culture: From Safari Suits to Sexploitation* (London: Routledge, 1998), p. 146.

8 Peter Hutchings, *The Horror Film* (Harlow, Essex: Pearson, 2004), p. 172.

9 Ibid.

10 Ibid., pp. 180 and 178.

11 Ibid., p. 178.
12 Quoted in Tom Johnson and Deborah Del Vecchio, *Hammer Films: An Exhaustive Filmography* (Jefferson, NC: McFarland, 1995), p. 359.
13 See Ian Conrich, 'Traditions of the British Horror Film', in Robert Murphy (ed.), *The British Cinema Book* (London: BFI, 1997), pp. 226–34.
14 Johnson and Del Vecchio, *Hammer Films*, p. 334.
15 See, for instance, *Flesh and Blood*, 3, October 1994, pp. 51–3; and Hunt, *British Low Culture*, pp. 158–9.
16 *Flesh and Blood*, no. 3, p. 52; Tim Greaves, quoted in *Flesh and Blood*, no. 3, p. 52.
17 Hunt, *British Low Culture*, p. 158.
18 Ibid., p. 159.
19 Ibid., p. 158.
20 Conrich, 'Traditions of the British Horror Film', p. 231.
21 Ian Conrich, '*The Man Who Haunted Himself*', in Tim O'Sullivan, Paul Wells and Alan Burton (eds), *Liberal Directions: Basil Dearden and Post-war British Film Culture* (Trowbridge, Wiltshire: Flicks Books, 1997), pp. 222–30.
22 Mike Wathen, 'For Adults Only! Home Grown British Crud, 1954–1972', in Stefan Jaworzyn (ed.), *Shock Xpress* 2 (London: Titan, 1994), p. 102. For an excellent overview of Tony Tenser's film career and productions, see John Hamilton, *Beasts in the Cellar: The Exploitation Film Career of Tony Tenser* (Godalming, Surrey: FAB Press, 2005).
23 See L. S. Smith, 'Filmography of British Horror Films of the Sound Era', in Steve Chibnall and Julian Petley (eds), *British Horror Cinema* (London: Routledge, 2002), pp. 221–7. These totals do not include the Mary Millington sexploitation vehicle *The Playbirds* (1978), which Smith strangely categorises as a 'British horror film': a production with one of its 'primary intentions [being] . . . to evoke fear or horror', p. 196.
24 Ian Conrich, 'The Contemporary British Horror Film: Observations on Marketing, Distribution, and Exhibition', in Harvey Fenton (ed.), *Flesh and Blood*, Book One (Guildford, Surrey: FAB Press, 1998), p. 30.

4 What a Carry On! The Decline and Fall of a Great British Institution

Steve Gerrard

> Oh, what can you say at the end of the day?
> Was the plot so sound? Or the lines profound?
> Was there rather less grain than chaff?
> Oh, what can you say at the end of the day?
> You can say that you made them laugh.[1]

> If I had to think why the *Carry Ons* matter so much, it's because they really aren't recuperable for proper culture . . . they display a commitment to bodily functions and base desires that will always render them irreducibly vulgar, inescapably Not Art.[2]

On 16 July 2003, the British tabloid newspaper *The Sun* printed a series of photographs under the characteristic headline 'Danni gets her Babs out'. These images of former *EastEnders* actress Danniella Westbrook masquerading as ex-*Carry On* (and also *EastEnders*) star Barbara Windsor in various states of undress were to advertise the fact that a new *Carry On* film entitled *Carry On London* was due to begin filming over the coming months. Almost three years later, on 16 May 2006, the same newspaper printed the headline 'Carry On Victoria'. This time the photograph was of Swedish supermodel/actress Victoria Silvstedt. The story concerned the announcement at the Cannes Film Festival that *Carry On London* was still gearing up for production to commence sometime in the near future. In an interview in January 2007 with Peter Rogers, the founder of the *Carry On* films, I was informed that 'We are very close to starting shooting soon.' It would seem that, despite the fondness with which the *Carry On* series is still regarded by audiences (the satellite television channel UK Gold devotes entire weekends to repeat screenings), production companies and distributors are viewing this latest reincarnation with a wary eye. After all, films in the main are made to make money and the last *Carry On* movie, *Carry On Columbus* (1992), failed at the box office, pleasing neither critics nor audiences. In these days of such 'gross-out' comedies as *American Pie* (Paul Weitz, USA, 1999) and the legion of similar, mostly American, fare, would a British farce really succeed in the cinema marketplace?

This pattern of difficulty in finding distribution, or even an audience, has happened before with the *Carry On* cycle. But before examining why this might be, it would be useful to set the films into a wider historical and social context. In 1958, producer Peter Rogers and director Gerald Thomas (who were both to occupy the same roles throughout the main series run of thirty films) brought to the screen a small-scale ('No more than £72,000'[3]) adaptation of R. F. Delderfield's romantic drama *The Bull Boys*. Screenwriter Norman Hudis modified the story to a topical one about life as a National Service conscript in the British Army. The film (*Carry On Sergeant*) became a huge (and surprise) success at the British box office despite being 'treated with derision' by most reviewers.[4] Like the Ealing comedies before, the film engaged with social tensions of the day by poking fun at bureaucracy, and the foibles and customs of the British class system. Almost the exact same team of technical crew and cast was reassembled to make a follow-up, *Carry On Nurse* (1959), which examined that other great British institution, the NHS. The film was another box-office hit, and in America it ran for a full two years. From this moment, the *Carry On* series began to take shape, forming the longest-running series of comedies in British film history.

The films were not presented as anything vaguely approaching accepted standards of 'good taste' or even in most cases as satire. They gained their place in the British cinematic pantheon by the very fact of their longevity and their popularity with British audiences. As Andy Medhurst attests, the comedies were viewed as 'Not Art', but instead embodied the standpoint of the common man, offering a proletarian, democratic version of what cinema might provide. This approach invited the audience to enter the double-entendred world of the Donald McGill seaside postcard, a style of humour based around sexual innuendo that left the audience with a feeling of contentment that all was safe with the world. Through thirty-one movies (one was a compilation of highlights), the *Carry On* team utilised a variety of themes and comic treatments that were reassuringly familiar in order to lure the audience into the theatre. Whether they were hospital-based escapades such as *Carry On Doctor* (1967), which was, thematically at least, a ribald extension of the more timid Betty Box and Ralph Thomas *Doctor* movies of the 1950s and 1960s, or (literally) camp comedies, as found in the 'daring' *Carry On Camping* (1969), which mocked both the hippie movement and 1960s naturist films such as *Naked – as Nature Intended* (Harrison Marks, 1960), the movies were almost always successful with the paying public but hardly ever with the critics. The reasons for the hostile critical reception of the films then (and now) could have been far-reaching for the series,[5] but the production team largely ignored them, simply wanting to continue making a profit for the least possible outlay of expense.

Despite this critical disregard, the *Carry On* series is possibly the last major incarnation of a key historical movement within British cinema, following on, as it does, from the traditions of the music hall and acts such as Max Miller, George Formby and Will Hay. Medhurst argues that, like music hall, the principal reason for the hostile critical reception aimed at the films is that

> Low comedy has consistently been culturally undervalued because those who tend to have the power of valuing are the very opposite of its target audience: they're pasty-faced, alienated, solitary bookworms who would flinch in horror from the warm, boozy, communal embrace of *Carry On* togetherness.[6]

This sense of affinity with the working-class populace, away from highbrow critical circles, helped the series. After all, audiences clearly find pleasure in the familiar; it enables them to identify with and become part of the film's narrative structure. Familiarity through character and genre identification, despite any inherent conservatism that this incurs, allows the audience to become enveloped within a recognisable environment, to become immersed in the subject's

The *Carry On* team pose for a publicity still for *Carry On Abroad* (1972)

appeal. By using the same actors to reprise almost identical roles from film to film (Sid James as proletarian rogue, Kenneth Williams representing the supercilious middle classes, Charles Hawtrey as effeminate eccentric, Joan Sims as sexpot or harridan and Kenneth Connor or Jim Dale as the likeable romantic bumbler), and by calling the characters by the actors' first names, the combination of persona/character became so ingrained in the national consciousness that the actors were iconographically typecast.

As the series 'progressed' in the hands of its second principal writer, Talbot Rothwell – who took as his influence the work of Max Miller – the films began to submerge themselves in innuendo-laden deconstructions of such populist and contemporary genres as the James Bond franchise (*Carry On Spying*, 1964) and the ghoulish delights of Hammer horror (*Carry On Screaming*, 1966). Rothwell even debunked the collapsing British Empire in what is arguably the zenith of the series with *Carry On up the Khyber* (1968), which, while simultaneously parodying *Zulu* (Cy Enfield, 1964), finally found the canon lending itself a degree of satirical respectability.[7] And here lies an ironic problem for the *Carry On* sequence as a whole. *Khyber* was produced in the middle of the most successful period for the series as a whole. The production values for these films belied their low budgets and the cast had become cemented as iconic figures with the public. The films had hit their stride during the height of the Swinging Sixties phenomenon, when the Beatles took the world by storm, England won the World Cup and Carnaby Street ruled the fashion world. The joyful irreverence of the films was perfectly in keeping with the exuberance of the moment, but that moment was quick in passing.

Bearing in mind the popular and critical fascination with the film-making developments of the 1960s, it has at least been suggested by Leon Hunt that the 1970s, despite being dubbed 'the decade that taste forgot', might be worthy of closer critical analysis than has hitherto been the case. Hunt refers to Bart Moore-Gilbert's assessment of the period in his study *The Arts in the 1970s: Cultural Closure*, where he describes the decade as 'a crisis in the grand narrative of progressive, politically and aesthetically enlightened culture'.[8] Hunt effectively reverses the negative connotations of this description by offering his own treatise on the 'permissive populism' of the 1970s, seen here as a vital strand in British cinema culture. He describes it in terms of a 'low' counterbalance to Moore-Gilbert's narrative of 'high' art achievement. Hunt offers the decade up as 'a particularly cruel parody of the 1960s'.[9]

The consequence of this change in the cultural landscape can be seen in a shift in the tone of the *Carry On* films towards something approximating a social realist mode. While the 1960s had witnessed the series' genre parodies at their height, the 1970s outings contain a more definable sense of visual realism (albeit in a caricatured form). In light of Andrew Higson's suggestion that the British realist tradition offers 'a serious, committed, engaged cinema'[10] and Benedict Anderson's well-known concept of nationhood as an 'imagined community',[11] series entries such as *Carry On Girls* (1973) use realist strategies to their own particular ends. By grounding the plot in the 'real' contemporary world rather than a historical or generic one, realistic traits become a means with which to reflect the cultural morés of the early 1970s. For example, in *Girls* the opening shots are of a typical British holiday: it's raining, a family sit huddled in a broken-down pier's shelter and a sign behind them reads 'Come to Fabulous Fircombe' with graffiti commenting 'What the hell for?'. Following this, we see the Mayor's downtrodden wife, Mildred Bumble (Patsy Rowland), sitting in her house dressed in her nightie and dressing gown, smoking a fag, slopping her husband's tea out of the pot, listening to the radio and reading the paper. Just from these two examples, we can see how the film has a grounding in everyday believability. The repressed British view of sex so endemic in the 1960s *Carry Ons* is not alluded to any more – people have sex and they get married, and through this end up as a dour commentary upon the probable real-life fate of the Donald McGill postcard caricatures of yesteryear.

However, this realism was to lead to the first major commercial mistake for the series, with the result that Anderson's 'imagined community' stayed away in droves. *Carry On at Your Convenience* (1971) is now regarded as one of the key texts of the cycle,[12] but is arguably a turning point in the *Carry On* story. With this film, the culturally transgressive strain that had been central to their appeal seemed diminished. *Convenience* (its original title was to have been *Carry On Comrade*) parodies the trade union movements of the early 1970s, setting the narrative in a toilet

VICTORIA BAR
TAKE COURAGE

factory run by W. C. Boggs (Kenneth Williams) and his son, Lou. The union leader, Vic, constantly leads the workers out on strike while trying to court Myrtle Plumber (Jacki Piper), the daughter of Sid (Sid James), the works foreman. In the film's central set piece, the gang travels on the annual works outing from the factory to Brighton, historical venue for saucy seaside fun. At the end of the film, the workers are back in situ. Sid has become a partner in the firm and Myrtle has married Boggs Jnr. Despite the anarchy of the Brighton sequence, the narrative openly embraces a cosy conservatism that was always an undercurrent in the series but that here has come defiantly to the fore, leaving the exuberant irreverence of the 1960s behind. This reversal of cultural positioning did not bode well for the film at the box office. As Robert Ross summarises, 'the working-class, beer and chips audience who were the films' chief admirers were not so chuffed with the treatment of the unionists as bumbling, idiotic, mini-dictators with attitude problems'.[13]

Yet, the Brighton sequence remains the film's chief pleasure. It is a culmination of the series' celebration of the ethos of British working-class culture, indicating that the seaside trip, however mundane, offers a respite from the toils of suburbia and work, and, most importantly, allows free-wheeling anarchy to become the order of the day. While Vic and Lou fight for the attentions of Myrtle, the older characters ignore the film's wider endorsement of class division, with fun as their priority. James, Williams, Hawtrey and Sims embark on a tour of destruction encompassing a hotel, the pier, the promenade and an arcade shooting gallery ('skinheads' shouts the owner); all get the *Carry On* treatment. At the sequence's climax, the film becomes a zany parody of working-class traits: through a montage of speeded-up scenes accompanied by a medley of popular tunes (including 'Trish Trash Polka', 'She'll Be Comin' round the Mountain', 'Little Brown Jug', various melodies from *Worker's Playtime* and 'Merrily We Roll Along'), the gang visit a succession of local hostelries. When the pubs eventually curtail the gang's drinking, a crate of pale ale is brought out from the boot of their coach. In juxtaposition to this, the closing sequence sees the mood change to melancholy and a return to reality. With Sid and Joan walking home, framed in a wonderful two-shot that amply demonstrates the skill of the actors, they discuss how they want each other but recognise that this can never happen. When Joan says that the neighbours may gossip about them sharing 'a cup of tea', Sid looks skywards and mutters 'Bloody neighbours'. The sequence puts the film directly into the British realist tradition. Despite being critically neglected, this moment is as significant in the representation of the British working classes as the melodramas of the 'kitchen-sink' school of film-making.

Due to the film's box-office failure, Rogers, Thomas and Rothwell headed back to the formula that audiences had always previously preferred, with a return to the hospital wards in *Carry On Matron* (1972); as Kenneth Williams noted in his diaries, 'the hospital jokes are unending'.[14] This is where the *Carry On* franchise began to seriously fail. Despite some excellent one-liners, inspired character names such as Dr Prodd, Sir Bernard Cutting and Dr Francis A. Goode, and a welcome return to the fold for Kenneth Connor, the film falters in a tired, rehashed plot that attempts to critique such 1970s novelties as the 'pill' and the collapse of the NHS. One of the most striking elements of the film is the role given to Williams and Hawtrey. While both can be seen as an indication of relaxing attitudes to homosexuality during the

(Opposite page) Celebrating working-class culture: *Carry On at Your Convenience* (1971)

1960s, where they are usually depicted warmly and with affection, in the 1970s they seem almost to reverse this position. For example, Hawtrey plays a psychiatrist who calls his wife Hamlet ('She thinks she's a Great Dane'), while Williams, again pursued by Matron (the wonderful Hattie Jacques), thinks that he is transforming into a woman. The level of stereotyping seems to have hardened.

The later films attempt, with varying degrees of success, to broaden the scope of the franchise. With *Carry On Abroad* (1972), the team are shipped to 'foreign' shores but seem all at sea, becoming increasingly caricatured in their notions of Britishness. What is particularly interesting here is that with the collapse of their Spanish resort hotel, the British holidaymakers can only find solace in Sid and Joan's structurally sound, typical East End pub. Rothwell seems well aware that the *Carry On* franchise could only relate successfully to British audiences when firmly entrenched in representations of recognisable British life. Anything outside that familiar domain wouldn't work. Furthermore, it became increasingly apparent that the films could only offer notions of Britishness that were no longer in tune with audiences themselves.

Meanwhile, their genre parodies seem like tired reruns of earlier films. *Carry On Dick* (1974), which revisited the Gainsborough melodramas of the 1940s, is indicative of how the series had to rely on recycling past subject matter. Hence, *Carry On Behind* (1975) and *Carry On England* (1976) both hark back to the earlier successes of *Camping* and *Sergeant*. Herein lay another problem for the production team. They were rapidly running out of ideas. With Rothwell retiring after *Dick*, other writers failed to recapture the zest of the older movies. Despite some good jokes, *Behind* reeks of staleness. Even an attempt to inject more risqué gags flounders in an effort to recapture past glories. The cast were ageing and in 1976 the team was dealt a major blow when Sid James, arguably *the* face of the series and its main embodiment of their working-class ethos, died. The loss to the series was all too evident. While Hawtrey was dropped after *Abroad* for his apparent drunkenness, and Williams was left out of the odd film here and there, it became apparent that Sid James could not easily be replaced. Although the idea had been toyed with, Rogers realised that James was so emblematic of the ethic of the series that it was almost impossible to carry on without him. Admittedly, *Behind* did not feature James due to a clash of working engagements, and his replacement, Windsor Davies, does an adequate job. But it is not Sid James at the head of the team, and the audience remembered this, staying away from both *Behind* and *England*.

It must be remembered that the film industry in Britain was altering. While American money was withdrawn, the rising popularity of film spin-offs from television sitcoms meant that the audience could see their contemporary comedy heroes on the big screen. The *Carry On* style is one of gentle sexual innuendo, but the late 1960s and 1970s saw the rise of the British sex film. Movies such as *Come Play with Me* (Harrison Marks, 1977) and the direct competitors to the *Carry Ons*, the *Confessions* films, took advantage of the relaxing of censorship, playing to large audiences around the country. These films had begun to usurp the cosiness of the *Carry On* films, presenting bare breasts, bums and even full-frontal nudity (at least of the female performers). While Barbara Windsor's bra had spectacularly sparked into life, flying towards Williams's Doctor Soaper, in *Camping*, and her bottom was seen in *Abroad* ('You haven't got any soap on that bit,' says James as the camera pans down, accompanied by a swannee-whistle on the soundtrack), that was as far as the production team were usually willing to go.

However, in trying to keep up with the *Confessions* films, *England* attempts but fails to emulate their success, and the employment of nudity seems gratuitous and out of place with the approach that the series had come to represent. Two scenes depict female soldiers in a state of undress: the first occurs in the dormitory, where the women sit up in their bunks, the bed sheets falling to reveal their breasts; in the second, the troupe comes to the parade ground topless. Both scenes add nothing to either narrative or character development within the film and seem grossly out of keeping with the mild suggestiveness that the series was famous and loved for. In their biography of Peter Rogers, Bright and Ross come to the conclusion that this nudity 'was not what *Carry On* audiences had come to expect' and record that the film was 'hastily re-edited and re-released to slightly better audiences'.[15] On enquiry, the British Board of Film Classification was able to tell me the following:

> This is a curious case. The film would appear to have been classified 'AA' uncut on 29 June 1976. However, this category was a change to previous *Carry Ons*, and proved, according to our *Monthly Bulletin* for 1977, 'difficult to accommodate at the box office.' The film was re-submitted to the BBFC in December 1976 for advice on cuts required to reclassify it to 'A'. It was re-classified 'A' on 11 January 1977, with the following cuts:
>
> Reel 6
> Joke about Heinkels and Bristols replaced with cover material which omits the utterance of 'Fokker'. Shots of bare-breasted women replaced by flash shots of bare breasts to establishment only.[16]

With another box-office failure on their hands, the team issued a last-ditch attempt to resurrect the series with *That's Carry On!*, a celebration of the finer moments of the series. This proved to be a success due to the reassuringly familiar faces on display. Yet, the final film in their remarkable run saw the *Carry Ons* branching out into far more risqué territory. With their target audience still staying away, a further rethink was in order. *Carry On Emmannuelle* (1978), which added an extra 'n' for 'naughtiness' (and to avoid any possible litigation) to its spelling,[17] was designed not only to parody Just Jaekin's French 1974 soft-core sex film, but to open up new avenues for the production team. However, the market for sex comedies had already all but evaporated, with even the *Confessions* movies running out of steam. Even though old members of the gang had been recruited, the film is ramshackle at best. Poorly made and badly paced, with great comic actors looking embarrassed, the film's only notable addition to the cycle is allowing the audience to witness Kenneth Williams finally, in his twenty-seventh *Carry On*, getting 'it'. The film suffered from not being risqué enough for its target audience, while simultaneously offending those who expected to see the usual cosy farce. The *Carry On* films consequently came to an inglorious end, failing to adapt to the changing tastes of both audiences and film distributors.

At the beginning of this essay, I referred to how difficult it seems to be to get a new *Carry On* movie made. Despite the belated *Columbus* failing to ignite the box office, Peter Rogers seems confident that at least the brand name – if not the product – will survive. While the original run of films reached its peak in the mid- to late 1960s, the fact that they survived until 1978 is a testament to their resilience in the marketplace. Britain in the 1970s was anything but united, with the re-emergence of the IRA, lightning strikes and rising inflation, all impacting upon notions

The inglorious demise of a great British institution: *Carry On Emmannuelle* (1978)

of Britishness, but the *Carry Ons* did carry on regardless. In doing this, they were often at odds with their own audience as they vacillated between attempts to reflect changing attitudes and their more instinctive desire to remain the same. While the series as a whole still has its critics, it deserves to be recognised as part of the British film canon, placed alongside other populist strains such as the Gainsborough melodramas or Hammer's horrors. If the films finally lost their audience in the 1970s, their ability to engage that same audience for the best part of twenty years should be celebrated.

Notes

1 Russell Davies (ed.), *The Kenneth Williams Diaries* (London: HarperCollins, 1994), p. 447, diary entry for 11 April 1973.

2 Andy Medhurst, 'Carry On Camp', *Sight and Sound*, vol. 2, no. 4, August 1992, p. 19.

3 John Walker, *The Once and Future Film: British Cinema in the Seventies and Eighties* (London: Methuen, 1985), p. 56.

4 Morris Bright and Robert Ross, *Mr Carry On: The Life and Work of Peter Rogers* (London: BBC, 2000), p. 76.

5 Alexander Walker's *National Heroes* (London: Orion, 2005) and *Hollywood England* (London: Orion, 2005) examine British cinema from the 1960s to the 1980s without a single reference to the *Carry On* films, while Robert Murphy's *Sixties British Cinema* (London: BFI, 1992) devotes just two pages to them.
6 Medhurst, 'Carry On Camp', p. 19.
7 *Carry On up the Khyber* was recently voted ninety-ninth in the BFI poll of the 100 Greatest British Films.
8 Leon Hunt, *British Low Culture: From Safari Suits to Sexploitation* (London: Routledge, 1998), p. 1; Bart Moore-Gilbert (ed.), *The Arts in the 1970s: Cultural Closure* (London: Routledge, 1994).
9 Hunt, *British Low Culture*, pp. 1–2.
10 Andrew Higson, *Waving the Flag: Constructing a National Identity in Britain* (Oxford: Oxford University Press, 1997), p. 188.
11 Benedict Anderson, *Imagined Communities: Reflections on the Origin and Spread of Nationalism* (London: Verso, 2006), p. 16.
12 Robert Ross awards the film a 'Four Sids' rating in his *The Carry On Companion* (London: B. T. Batsford, 1996), p. 96.
13 Ibid.
14 Davies, *Kenneth Williams Diaries*, p. 399.
15 Bright and Ross, *Mr Carry On*, p. 187.
16 J. L. Green (Chief Assistant on Policy at the BBFC) in personal correspondence with the author, 2 February 2007.
17 Bright and Ross, *Mr Carry On*, p. 189.

5 When the Chickens Came Home to Roost: British Thrillers of the 1970s

Ruth Barton

> An early hero of mine was John Buchan, but when I re-opened his books I found I could no longer get the same pleasure from the adventures of Richard Hannay. More than the dialogue and the situation had dated: the moral climate was no longer that of my boyhood. Patriotism had lost its appeal, even for a schoolboy, at Passchendaele, and the Empire brought first to mind the Beaverbrook Crusader, while it was difficult, during the years of the Depression, to believe in the high purposes of the City of London or of the British Constitution. The hunger-marchers seemed more real than the politicians. It was no longer a Buchan world.
>
> Graham Greene, *Ways of Escape*

The thriller is arguably the pre-eminent genre in British fiction, crossing the boundaries between the popular and the literary, the local and the international, the novel and the film. It has traversed time and generation, with the origins of its most identifiable incarnation, the spy thriller, conventionally being traced back to the imperial novel and its more amorphous 'other', the crime thriller, arising out of the Victorian shocker. Definitions of the thriller vary: Michael Denning combines a formalist analysis of the structure of the spy thriller with a social and historical reading of the genre, distinguishing between the 'realistic' (Ambler, le Carré) and the 'romantic' (Fleming), and between amateur and professional protagonists.[1] Published in the same year, John G. Cawelti and Bruce A. Rosenberg's *The Spy Story* reprises certain of Denning's structuralist concerns while exploring in greater depth questions of individuality and authorship.[2] Both focus, as I will here, on the international spy thriller as the most definable form of the genre and both acknowledge the pre-eminence of the British literary tradition in establishing its parameters. Both too were written in the wake of the Watergate revelations and in a period of mounting public concern about the relationship between the state, particularly the American imperialist state, and law enforcement agencies such as the CIA and the FBI.

What most writers agree on is that the contemporary thriller thrives in an atmosphere of social and political uncertainty. Where once, as the opening quotation from Graham Greene asserts, it was a straightforward celebration of the values of Empire, the genre swiftly became a tool with which to critique those very values and to explore the cracks in the social fabric occasioned by the end of imperialism, the relationship between materialism and morality under capitalism, and the shifting definitions of national identity that accompany social and historical change. On the face of it, therefore, there was no better moment for the thriller to flourish than in Britain in the 1970s. As is documented elsewhere in this volume, this was a decade of extreme instability: the oil crisis of 1973 onwards reminded the country that control over its economy lay in territories that had little regard for the British nation. The alternative, the development of local nuclear power, was widely viewed with alarm. The miners' strike of 1974 and the 'winter of discontent' of 1978–9 highlighted social and economic divisions, further based on a north/south geographical divide that had lain submerged in the 1960s, while the 1976 Race Relations Act, with its assertion of racial equality, convinced the increasingly impoverished white working class that it was at threat from internal as well as external 'foreigners'. The Sex Discrimination Act of 1975 formalised advances in equal rights for women initiated in the 1960s, even if it further alienated the conservative working-class male. A concrete threat to the nation came in the shape of the revitalised IRA campaign that accompanied the re-emergence of the Troubles in Northern Ireland and spilled over into outbreaks of terrorist activity in mainland Britain.

Internationally, the Cold War continued to throw up fears of communist infiltrators, double agents, deception and betrayal. It was no wonder that the decade closed with the election of Margaret Thatcher and her promise of a return to Victorian values. By this stage, however, as I will argue, the sense of alienation between the individual and the machinery of the state that had been let loose by the 1960s counter-culture was so deep-rooted that it was entrenched in popular cultural representation and, specifically, popular film. In particular, I am interested in exploring how the British cinematic thriller of the 1970s returned to the settings of the past, particularly those of the Second World War, in order to reassess the old certainties of good and evil, right and wrong, that structured what now appeared as an overly complacent social order. As I will argue, this permitted it to critique the rhetoric of privilege that underpinned order while questioning its myths.

If these thrillers were primarily funded by British (television) money, a secondary model was the European co-production, a formally and thematically variable cycle that often seemed to reflect confusion over coherence. At the back of any discussion of the cinematic thriller lies the dominant model of the literary thriller and, by the late 1970s, its successful transfer to the small screen, notably with the 1979 BBC mini-series *Tinker, Tailor, Soldier, Spy*, adapted from the 1974 novel of the same name. I want to finish, therefore, with a discussion of a film that attempted to reproduce the essence of the British literary thriller, Otto Preminger's 1979 version of Graham Greene's 1978 novel, *The Human Factor*. Most successful of all these models was, of course, the Bond film, with an extraordinary five releases during the 1970s: *Diamonds Are Forever* (Guy Hamilton, 1971), *Live and Let Die* (Guy Hamilton, 1973), *The Man with the Golden Gun* (Guy Hamilton, 1974), *The Spy Who Loved Me* (Lewis Gilbert, 1977) and *Moonraker* (Lewis Gilbert, 1979).[3] As these are dealt with elsewhere in this volume, I shall lay them to one side in order to focus on the less discussed British thrillers of the decade, although many of the points made here could also be transferred to the Bond cycle.

Winning the War

Many of the literary thrillers of the 1960s and 1970s drew on the defining real-life British spy story of the era, Kim Philby's defection in 1963 to Moscow and the earlier defections of Guy Burgess and Donald Maclean. As Michael Denning has written, 'the narrative of Kim Philby is one of the betrayal of the service and the idea of service; it is the riddle and cover-up of the question "who killed Great Britain?"'.[4] It is this question too that, at a subtextual level, underpins the thrillers discussed in this chapter. Whether as a revision of the historical narrative of British greatness, or located within the framework of an oedipal conflict between a disenchanted male investigator and a paternalistic state organisation, the search for a culprit on whom to pin the blame for the demise of the wartime values of community, decency and incorruptible leadership informs the otherwise diverse collection of 1970s films that can be loosely clustered together under the rubric of the political or spy thriller. Only in a few instances did the thriller pander to nostalgia, producing the somewhat curious remakes of *The Thirty Nine Steps* (Don Sharp, 1978) and *The Lady Vanishes* (Anthony Page, 1979), two obvious made-for-television productions that have more in common with the Agatha Christie cycle (discussed in Sarah Street's chapter). Nostalgia for an uncomplicated past in which problems of national importance could be solved by gifted amateurs is in itself symptomatic of the general malaise that the thrillers of the 1970s exploited. What further connects these two films to a number of other productions in the cycle is their wartime setting. Thus, for instance, *The Riddle of the Sands* (Tony Maylam, 1978) and *The Eagle Has Landed* (John Sturges, 1976) are set respectively in the First and Second World Wars and share many of the traits of the war film.

The Riddle of the Sands, an adaptation of the novel by Erskine Childers that is often cited as the prototype for the British literary spy thriller of the twentieth century, cannot simply be classified as a nostalgia film. Although the activities of its two amateur heroes, Carruthers (Michael York) and Davies (Simon MacCorkindale), in defeating a German plan to invade Britain (in 1901) locate it within an older model of thriller production, the film's look and pacing give it a contemporary feel quite lacking in the self-consciously period *mise en scène* of *The Thirty Nine Steps*. Where the latter revels in its adumbration of items of clothing, furnishing and personal effects of the time, inviting its audience to feel that they are really 'back' in the teens, *The Riddle of the Sands*, although observing period detail, is played as if it were in the present. The point is that Carruthers and Davies must act more like contemporary (1970s) spies and abandon their amateur blundering if they are to defeat the machinations of Captain Thompson/aka Dollman (Alan Badel), a British officer turned traitor; nor can Carruthers maintain his gentleman's club hauteur if he is to participate in an effective counter-intelligence operation. In their case, they can expect little assistance from a British establishment that is quite unaware of the threat about to be launched by the Kaiser on its territory. At the same time, there is an elegiac feel to *The Riddle of the Sands*, a sense of conclusiveness in Carruthers's final words as he spells out the ending of a yarn in which good and bad were identifiable elements and traitors could be guaranteed their comeuppance, ideally, as here, at the hand of those to whom they sold their services.

The Riddle of the Sands intersects with a number of themes articulated in the thrillers discussed in this chapter. Its concern with the paralysing effect of old-school Britishness is one that is not restricted to this genre but is an important part of it. It is also a key to understanding certain of the wartime films of the 1970s, productions that share much of the same ideological territory as the thriller. The revisionist direction of the war film, exemplified in Lamont Johnson's critically overlooked *The McKenzie Break* (1970), invited audiences to reconsider the cinematic inheritance of Britain's 'golden era' of film production.[5] This film, with its gung-ho Irish commander, Captain Jack Connor (Brian Keith), and its ineffectual British chain of command ranged against a troupe of well-drilled German POWs suggested that the heroic stereotype of Allied individualism versus German parade-ground conformism derived from an outdated myth.

The revisionist war thriller: *The McKenzie Break* (1970)

Johnson's film reverses the usual perspective of the prisoner-of-war escape drama by pitting Connor against a more than capable, if ruthless, German leader, Captain Willi Schleuter (Helmut Griem), in a contest that reveals the strategic superiority of the German and the blustering incompetence of the Irish captain. It is never made quite clear in *The McKenzie Break* why an Irishman should be in command at a Scottish POW camp or indeed whether Connor's failings are a consequence of his national identity; certainly, he drinks too heavily.

The introduction of an Irishman into the narrative of another film from this period that again intersects with the war film provides one of the more disconcerting casting choices of the productions surveyed here. In *The Eagle Has Landed*, Donald Sutherland plays Liam Devlin as a charming but feckless IRA sympathiser who has thrown in his lot with the Nazi

Michael Caine as the sympathetic German officer in *The Eagle Has Landed* (1976)

regime. S. P. MacKenzie has noted that *The Eagle Has Landed* (both book and film) is a remake of the classic British war film *Went the Day Well?* (Alberto Cavalcanti, 1942). Discussing the changing ideological climate that separates the two films, MacKenzie relates the shift in sympathy away from a simple binary of good Britons versus evil Germans to a general movement within British popular culture that distinguished between average Germans and Nazis. The former were treated with some sympathy, as victims of their own political system, while the rhetoric of British wartime flagwaving was positioned as fair game for comic subversion.[6]

In *The Eagle Has Landed*, a conspiracy to kidnap Winston Churchill is hatched by German intelligence officer Lieutenant-Colonel Max Radl (Robert Duvall) in tandem with Admiral

Canaris (Anthony Quayle) and Heinrich Himmler (Donald Pleasence), with the connivance of local villager Joanna Grey (Jean Marsh), and executed by maverick officer Lieutenant-Colonel Kurt Steiner (Michael Caine) and his crack team of German paratroopers. Steiner has been educated in England, hence his perfect accent. His humanity is established in an early scene where he attempts to rescue an escaping Jewish woman from a convoy; he is, according to Himmler, 'intelligent, ruthless, a brilliant soldier, but above all a romantic fool'. It is this romanticism that proves Steiner's undoing – his men wear their German uniform under their Polish disguise so that in the end, if they must, they can fight and die as German paratroopers. When one of the men rescues a village child from the weir, he is trapped in the waterwheel, his rotating body revealing his German uniform. Thereafter, the Germans hold the villagers to ransom in the church; the ineffectual American commander, Colonel Clarence E. Pitts (Larry Hagman), leads a disastrous attack to release the hostages, but the Germans are eventually overcome and Steiner alone escapes. Making his way to Churchill's residence, he assassinates the leader only for it to be revealed that the man he shot was a double.

Joanna Grey, we are informed in the early stages of the narrative, has turned traitor in revenge for the treatment of her family by the British in South Africa; her mother died in a British concentration camp, a reminder that such institutions were not invented by the Germans. Devlin's motivation for participation equally derives from a national sense of grievance: 'My fight is with the bloody British Empire . . . my aim is a united Ireland.' Despite being referred to as a university lecturer, Devlin speaks in a stage Irish brogue that sees him greet the Colonel with a bibulous 'Top o' the morning to you'. Later he admits to Steiner that his motivation is dependent on which side cuts him the best deal. Close to the film's ending, the American, Captain Harry Clark (Treat Williams), will remind Steiner that 'there is no such thing as death with honour, only death'; yet his men die with honour, holding off the American forces long enough for Steiner to make his getaway to assassinate Churchill. Loyalty and honour in *The Eagle Has Landed* are the preserve of the German paratroopers and their leader; not by chance, one of them also plays the village organ exquisitely. Radl too is a man of honour and one whose days in high command are numbered; at the film's end he is executed for exceeding his orders. Yet the film is careful to balance romanticism against realism. The assassination attempt ultimately fails because the British have made provision against such an eventuality by hiring a variety artist to impersonate Churchill and thus act as a decoy, so Steiner's bravery has been in vain. If romanticism is laudable, it may be equally anachronistic in the new order of military affairs, *The Eagle Has Landed* suggests.

The foregrounding of Irish characters in both this film and in *The MacKenzie Break* permits these plots to revisit earlier concerns about Irish collaboration with the Nazis in the Second World War. Treated comically in *I See a Dark Stranger* (Frank Launder, 1946) and more seriously in *The Man Who Never Was* (Ronald Neame, 1955), it is not surprising to see this theme re-emerge in the 1970s as IRA paramilitarism became identified as a new threat to mainland Britain. Whether this was to be seen as the return of the repressed on a par with the treatment of the Boers by the British military is an issue on which *The Eagle Has Landed* remains undecided. The decision to cast Donald Sutherland as Devlin is emblematic of the ideological indeterminacy of the role. While Michael Caine is awarded a backstory (his English education) that permits him some credibility playing a German, and Duvall's acting history allowed him to perform a believable Radl, Sutherland's hammy interpretation of Devlin verges on the absurd and undermines much of the film's integrity. It also underlines a problem that I will explore further, that of identifying Britain's external enemies in the present.

The revisiting of wartime narratives chimed with a popular interest in 'secret histories' such as those explored in Len Deighton's *SS-GB* (1979), set in German-occupied Britain, and Ken Follett's *Eye of the Needle* (1979), about the deception of the Allies on D-Day. These were, according to Denning, 'haunted by the sense that the war was really lost, that the West German "economic miracle" was not matched by a British "miracle"'.[7] If *The Eagle Has Landed* falls into the secret history category, another reason for returning to the events of the Second World War is established in *The Odessa File* (Ronald Neame, 1974). The film's premise is that Allied victory in the Second World War did not result in the eradication of fascism. Set in 1963, the film concerns freelance journalist Peter Miller's (Jon Voight) efforts to uncover the identity of the ODESSA organisation. In so doing, he reveals the existence of an underground Nazi group operating to protect its members' identities, but also committed to the restoration of National Socialism in Germany and globally. Repeatedly, as he digs further into the conspiracy, he is told by the older generation, including his own mother, that the past should be left alone. Meanwhile, old Nazi Roschmann (Maximilian Schell) demands that Miller recognise the validity of Nazi history. Ultimately, the confrontation between the two men is shifted from the political to the personal as Miller reveals that Roschmann killed his, Miller's, own father, a dissenting German officer. The film ends on an upbeat note, which distinguishes it from indigenous German films of this period that deal with similar material, if in less generic form. The conspiracy is laid bare and key members of the Nazi organisation are arrested.

The European Factor

The Odessa File was a pan-European co-production that included British financing, as was another similar part-British thriller, also adapted from a novel by Frederick Forsyth, *The Day of the Jackal* (Fred Zinnemann, 1973). Although neither was financed by Hollywood, both made overt connections to the international Hollywood thriller through casting (Jon Voight) and direction (Austrian-born Hollywood director, Zinnemann). Other pan-European productions of the era include *The Cassandra Crossing* (George Pan Cosmatos, 1976), while British-financed films such as *Ransom* (Casper Wrede, 1974) used European settings to explore issues of international terrorism.

Although it is reductive to treat all these films as one, they do share similar concerns and, more obviously, confusions. Foremost among these is a general inability to identify the enemy. Where, unusually, *The Odessa File* was able both to name and eliminate its terrorist figures, many of the other productions were less certain. The resolution of the best known of these British co-productions, *The Day of the Jackal*, hinges specifically around the anonymity of its central assassin for hire, played by Edward Fox. Concerning a plot to assassinate General de Gaulle, *The Day of the Jackal* reprises many of the themes already outlined above: the blurring of the boundaries between factual and fictional characters; a sense that present troubles are the outcome of past injustices (in this case the French colonial policy in Algeria); and, technically, the use of newsreel footage to add authority to the screen images. *The Odessa File* went as far as to cast the celebrated Nazi hunter Simon Wiesenthal in one of its roles and subsequent claims for its authenticity made much of the part it played in trapping a leading former Nazi. Again, in *The Cassandra Crossing*, very little is revealed about the nature of the subversive activity (stealing radioactive materials) that initiates the plot, but much of the dramatic and ultimately tragic tension is derived from the consternation of the Jewish character, Hermann Kaplan (Lee Strasberg), who realises that the diverted train will lead him back to Poland, where his wife perished. In fact, as the ending reveals, all the passengers are being led to their death as the authorities plan to dispose of them by manufacturing a fatal crash on a disused bridge; one massive return, in other words, to the concentration camp, this time planned by the Americans.

The overall effect of these thrillers is a hiatus between their sense of place, character and narrative. Visually they play on the fetishistic display of glamorous European locations as a kind of vicarious tourism, a phenomenon more usually associated with the James Bond cycle. Another common production trick was to cast unlikely actors in lead and, particularly, secondary roles – one thinks here of the appearance of O. J. Simpson and Ava Gardner alongside Sophia Loren and Richard Harris in *The Cassandra Crossing*, or Voight performing with a German accent in *The Odessa File*. This disconcerting trait is a distraction from the drive towards verisimilitude and seems to reflect a desire to 'perform' stardom in a manner that can compete with Hollywood. Diegetically, the films tend to throw up more than they can resolve, with their shadowy terrorists and indecipherable political machinations casting a potency over the narrative that lingers on well after their ostensible eradication at the films' conclusion.

The exigencies of co-production contracts may be blamed for the unevenness of these films, and the race from setting to setting is partially a consequence of having to shoot in a number of territories. A secondary, and we may assume deliberate, effect is the decentring of Britishness as the central point of concern in the narratives. Where the classic British thriller located the British investigator/hero at the heart of the conspiracy and relegated its European characters to the margins, where they were often viewed with some derision, in these co-productions the heroes were as likely as not to be continental Europeans and the British characters were forced to compete for their share of the diegetic cake. Even though all the films listed in this pan-European category were made with partial British funding and in English, they reflect a sense that the balance of power (and conspiracy) was located on mainland Europe even if the exact identity of the enemy was never quite revealed. It's not unreasonable to see parallels here with the national divisions and anxieties caused by Britain's initial entry into the European Economic Community in 1973 and the subsequent referendum held in 1975.

The Human Factor

Only at the close of the decade was a film made that responded to the interrogation of Britishness that so identified the writings particularly of John le Carré, but also of Graham Greene and the other key British thriller writers of the decade. Dismissed by the author of its source novel as 'outstandingly bad', Otto Preminger's production of Graham Greene's *The Human Factor* was dogged by financial difficulties and received with critical indifference.[8] This was to be Preminger's final film before his death and much of the blame for its failure has been ascribed to his waning professional capabilities. The screenplay, by Tom Stoppard, is characteristically wordy and its literariness was also seen as a fault, indicating a failure to adapt from book to film. Although the direction of *The Human Factor* is undeniably languid, an alternative position is to

Nicol Williamson and Iman in *The Human Factor* (1979)

view the film as a tribute to the literary tradition from which it sprang. Running counter to the majority of the 1970s thrillers discussed above, the cast of *The Human Factor* is exclusively British, with Richard Attenborough playing the new Head of Security, Colonel Daintry, whose role is to sweep the cobwebs from the Secret Service, personified here by the ageing Brigadier Tomlinson (John Gielgud). When a mole is suspected, Daintry is led to believe that it might be a young man, Arthur Davis (Derek Jacobi), and is aided in his offhand disposal of the suspect by the corrupt Doctor Percival (Robert Morley). The cast of central characters is completed by Davis's colleague, Maurice Castle (Nicol Williamson), whose performance is a constant reminder of the dreariness of any functionary's life, be it in the Secret Service or any other government department.

It is this insistence on understatement and deglamourising that creates the film's aesthetic. Even the extended flashback sequences, in which Castle's romance with his Bantu wife, Sarah (Iman), is outlined, are shot in an Africa so far removed from the conventional romanticisation of its landscapes that it ends up looking as dull as the suburb in which the two finally settle with Sarah's son, Sam (Gary Forbes). The film ends with the revelation that the mole is Castle and that he has been cornered into selling secrets to the Russians in order to rescue Sarah. In the closing sequences, in an obvious nod to the Philby story, Castle sits alone in the Moscow apartment promised to him should he need to defect, waiting for Sarah to join him, though it is evident that she never will. As Cawelti and Rosenberg write:

> there is a definite connection between the clandestine protagonist as a symbol of everyman in the twentieth century and an aspect of modern culture which has often been discussed in contemporary works of sociology, both popular and academic: the alienation of the individual from the large organizations – corporations, bureaucracies, professions – which dominate our lives.[9]

It is this alienation that defines the mood of *The Human Factor*; but underlying it is a feeling that the film shares with the majority of the thrillers discussed in this chapter, that the inadequacies of the present are a consequence of the hubris of the past. In the most optimistic of these films, a new hero emerges to right those wrongs; in the least, the train hurtles into the ravine, taking with it the innocents who trusted in the invisible machinery of a corrupt state to preserve them.

Notes

1 Michael Denning, *Cover Stories: Narrative and Ideology in the British Spy Thriller* (London and New York: Routledge and Kegan Paul, 1987), p. 12.
2 John G. Cawelti and Bruce A. Rosenberg, *The Spy Story* (Chicago and London: University of Chicago Press, 1987).
3 See James Chapman, *Licence to Thrill: A Cultural History of the James Bond Films* (London and New York: I. B. Tauris, 1999).
4 Denning, *Cover Stories*, p. 121.
5 Not all war films were as progressive as *The MacKenzie Break*. Guy Hamilton's *Force 10 from Navarone* (1978), for example, simply rehashes the old stereotypes of the conventional war film.
6 S. P. MacKenzie, 'Nazis into Germans', *Journal of Popular Film and Television*, vol. 31, no. 2, Summer 2003, pp. 83–92.
7 Denning, *Cover Stories*, p. 148.
8 'Greene Criticizes Film Adaptations of His Books', *New York Times*, 6 September 1984, p. C17.
9 Cawelti and Rosenberg, *The Spy Story*, p. 32.

6 From Amicus to Atlantis: The Lost Worlds of 1970s British Cinema

James Chapman

The most persistent metaphor of recent British cinema historiography has been the notion of 'the lost continent', coined by Julian Petley to describe 'the repressed side of British cinema, a dark, disdained thread weaving the length and breadth of that cinema, crossing authorial and generic boundaries, sometimes almost entirely invisible, sometimes erupting explosively, always received critically with fear and disapproval'.[1] The exploration of this lost continent has become one of the main intellectual projects of British film studies in recent decades as once-despised traditions of popular cinema have been accorded their place in the sun. The chief beneficiaries of this cultural revisionism, the Gainsborough costume melodramas and the gothic horrors of Hammer, have now become part of the official canon of British cinema, lauded for their transgressive narratives and expressive visual style that is the antithesis of traditional notions of 'realism' and 'quality', while more recently the barnstorming antics of Tod Slaughter and the postwar cycle of 'British film noir' have also been subject to critical scrutiny.[2] This essay sets out to explore another area of the lost continent in the form of a cycle of fantasy adventure films produced in the 1970s: *The Land That Time Forgot* (1975), *At the Earth's Core* (1976), *The People That Time Forgot* (1977) and *Warlords of Atlantis* (1978). These films constitute a distinct production cycle in so far as they all shared the same producer (John Dark), director (Kevin Connor) and star (the American actor Doug McClure). The first three films, moreover, were all based on novels by Edgar Rice Burroughs, whereas *Warlords of Atlantis* was an original screenplay by Brian Hayles. The cycle has been absent, however, from histories of British cinema of the 1970s and is afforded scant attention even in the popular literature of science fiction and fantasy.[3]

While it is not my intention to make any claim for the 'lost world' cycle as unjustly neglected masterpieces, the films are nevertheless of some significance in understanding the production strategies of the British film industry during the 1970s – a decade characterised by what Andrew Higson has called 'a diversity of film practices'.[4] Those strategies include, on the one hand, expensive productions for the international market (such as the Agatha Christie adaptations *Murder on the Orient Express* [1974] and *Death on the Nile* [1978] and the James Bond films) and, on the other hand, low-budget genre films intended solely for domestic British audiences (television spin-offs, comedies, sexploitation films). The lost world cycle represents a hybrid of those two opposing strategies in that while they did not benefit from the lavish budgets of the Bond or Christie films – *Warlords of Atlantis* was the most expensive film in the cycle at $2 million – they did, nevertheless, exhibit international ambitions, albeit of a limited nature. The casting of American stars in British films is usually taken as an indication that the producers have half an eye on the US market, though Doug

McClure, a beefcake actor whose reputation arose mainly from television (he played Trampus in the long-running series *The Virginian*), could hardly be considered a major box-office name. The first three films were distributed in the United States by American International Pictures (AIP), whose reputation rested largely on 'exploitation' fare. According to the trade press, *The Land That Time Forgot* 'fared so well financially' that its sequel was 'a surefire b.o. attraction'.[5]

The production company responsible for *The Land That Time Forgot*, *At the Earth's Core* and *The People That Time Forgot* was Amicus, a small but significant British studio of the 1960s and 1970s. Amicus, founded by Americans Max J. Rosenberg and Milton Subotsky, has usually been regarded as something of a poor relation to Hammer. Like Hammer, which in addition to the Dracula and Frankenstein pictures for which it is best known also produced fantasy adventures (*One Million Years BC* [1966], *When Dinosaurs Ruled the Earth* [1969]), costume swashbucklers (*Pirates of Blood River* [1961], *The Devil-Ship Pirates* [1963]) and spin-offs of television sitcoms (*On the Buses* [1971], *Love Thy Neighbour* [1973]), Amicus had a mixed production strategy that included pop musicals (*It's Trad, Dad!* [1962]), spy films (*Danger Route* [1967]) and science fiction (*The Terrornauts* [1967], *They Came from Beyond Space* [1967]). The studio is most closely associated, however, with the portmanteau horror film in the tradition of *Dead of Night* (1945), beginning in 1964 with *Dr Terror's House of Horrors* and continuing into the 1970s with *The House That Dripped Blood* (1970), *Tales from the Crypt* (1972) and *From Beyond the Grave* (1973). The latter was the first to be directed by Kevin Connor, a former film editor, who thereafter teamed with producer John Dark to make a series of five fantasy adventure films.[6] To date, Amicus has not received anything like the attention devoted to Hammer, though a strong case could be made that in the early 1970s it was the more creative force at a time when Hammer seemed to have run out of residual cultural and economic energy.[7]

The lost world films are perhaps best understood as late examples of what might best be described as a 'matinée cinema': films produced largely for juvenile audiences. To this extent they can be located within a tradition of popular but critically marginalised production that stretches back to the serials or 'chapter plays' of the 1930s and 1940s and also includes the two cinema spin-offs from the BBC's science-fiction series *Doctor Who* (*Dr Who and the Daleks* [1965]and *Daleks' Invasion Earth 2150 AD* [1966]) produced by Rosenberg and Subotsky in the mid-1960s.[8] An assumed juvenile audience is evident both in the content of the lost world films (undemanding action-adventure fare) and in their release strategies (coinciding with the school holiday periods). *The Land That Time Forgot*, for example, opened in London on 20 March 1975 'with a Rank release over the Easter holidays'.[9] According to its distributor, British Lion, the film had achieved rentals of £280,000 from seventy-six screens: this represented approximately 750,000 admissions, of which 60 per cent were half-price (i.e. children).[10] This was surpassed by *At the Earth's Core*, released during the summer of 1976 and that British Lion reported 'is going great guns in the provinces'.[11] In Glasgow, it took 75 per cent more than *The Land That Time Forgot* and also overtook its predecessor in Birmingham, Sheffield and Liverpool. In 1978, similarly, *Warlords of Atlantis* 'also opened to coincide with the start of the school holidays, [and] netted a very healthy £18,624 at its four screens' in London.[12] *Warlords of Atlantis*, however, fell out of the top ten after only one week, a more rapid decline than its predecessors that can probably be attributed to stiff competition during the summer of 1978, including *Revenge of the Pink Panther*, *Close Encounters of the Third Kind* and *Grease*.

'Matinée cinema': *The Land That Time Forgot* (1975)

John Dark, for his part, claimed that the films were aimed 'somewhere in the middle' of bland 'family entertainment' and the 'AA' category (films prohibited for exhibition to the under-fifteens such as the action-adventure *The Wild Geese* [1978]). He elaborated:

> You see, children today find 'family entertainment' films too tame because they see *Policewoman* and *Kojak* on television, and they also see people being shot dead on the news. So we make robust adventure stories, but we don't have blood spurting all over the place. Sure enough, we have fight scenes – baddie against goodie. But we steer clear of all that marshmallow.[13]

While most critics seem to have accepted the films as 'robust adventure stories', a dissenting note was sounded by Gavin Millar, who thought that *At the Earth's Core* was too frightening for young children. It was, he averred, 'pretty dismal, depressing and frightening for under-sevens. My own six-, eight- and ten-year-olds had their moments of terror, which they didn't enjoy.'[14] This was reflected in the fact that *At the Earth's Core* was awarded an 'A' certificate rather than the 'U' granted to *The Land That Time Forgot*, though whether this was due to its more horrific content or to Caroline Munro's cleavage is debatable.[15]

The critical reception of the lost world films did not, as it happens, exhibit the 'fear and disapproval' that has so often characterised responses to the periodic eruptions of the lost continent. The tone of most reviews ranged from mild condescension to grudging admiration, while the sort of terms used ('nonsense', 'hokum', 'potboiler') suggest that they were not being taken seriously. As with other cycles of popular genre cinema, the first films were the best received, while the later entries tended to be seen as derivative and formulaic. The *Monthly Film Bulletin*, for example, felt that *The Land That Time Forgot* 'is rendered with a fair amount of care and intelligence, in an efficient script that keeps the action moving briskly'. *The People That Time Forgot*, however, was 'a most perfunctory sequel, aimed at capitalising on the success of an earlier, more deftly crafted work'; while in *Warlords of Atlantis* '[t]he formula is evidently wearing thin and, in this loosely scripted sortie into a cut-price Atlantis, the brisk pace of the earlier, intermittently engaging productions is sorely missed'.[16] Most reviewers described the films as 'old-fashioned' and located them in relation to earlier traditions of juvenile entertainment. *Variety*, for instance, felt that *At the Earth's Core* 'harks back to a simple and unabashed kind of adventure formula which unfortunately isn't used much any more'.[17] And in *Films and Filming*, Eric Braun drew parallels with the tradition of the boys' story paper:

> Aeons ago as a schoolboy I used to receive *Boy's Own Paper* and follow the adventures of Captain Justice in the Sargasso Sea: his noble vessel, enmeshed in seaweed, was beset by horrific prehistoric monsters which he and his trusty bo'sun engaged in deadly and ultimately victorious battle. All this was recalled happily at the press show of *Warlords of Atlantis*, minus seaweed, with Peter Gilmore as a studious professor's son standing in for Captain Justice and Doug McClure as his old college chum.[18]

In contrast, Jan Dawson in *The Listener* felt that *Warlords of Atlantis* 'emerges as a slightly lifeless comic-strip in which the actors cast as humans (eccentric Victorian scientists and yo-ho-ho mutinous sailors) often seem more mechanical than the studio-built dinosaurs and jumbo octopus which assail their submarine passage'.[19]

The production values of the films were often a source of some amusement, though to be fair they are no worse than other examples of the genre. The response to this aspect of the films exemplifies the different technical standards expected by British and American critics: while the British trade press averred that the monsters in *The Land That Time Forgot* 'move very realistically', *Variety* complained that some of the prehistoric creatures 'are so big they can barely move, jerking along, often locked in spastic combat'.[20] In contrast to the stop-motion 'Dynamation' process used by Ray Harryhausen for fantasy adventure films such as *The Golden Voyage of Sinbad* (1973) and *Sinbad and the Eye of the Tiger* (1977), most of the prehistoric and other monsters in these films were puppets. Maurice Carter, production designer of *The Land That Time Forgot* and *At the Earth's Core*, confirmed that 'we couldn't work with his [Harryhausen's] animation technique because it's so involved and too long a process'.[21] The first two Amicus films are largely studio-bound and this is reflected in their visual style. As *Screen International* complained about *At the Earth's Core*: 'The customary confrontations with papier-maché monsters and primitive humans might as well be taking place on Mars for all the use that is made of the subterranean locale.'[22] The exteriors for *The People That Time Forgot* were shot in the Canary Islands. *Warlords of Atlantis* was shot largely on Malta, though this did not prevent the complaint that 'the city of the élite seems to consist solely of a Turkish bath peopled by swim-suited beauties'.[23]

While the production and release strategies of the lost world films can be understood in relation to the economics of British film production in the 1970s, their narratives and themes can also be seen as part of an older tradition of popular fiction. The lost world films are best described not as science fiction but as scientific romance, a genre that emerged in late nineteenth-century popular literature exemplified by the work of Jules Verne (*Twenty Thousand Leagues under the Sea*, *Journey to the Centre of the Earth*), H. G. Wells (*The Time Machine*, *The First Men in the Moon*), Sir Henry Rider Haggard (*King Solomon's Mines*, *She*) and Sir Arthur Conan Doyle (*The Lost World*). The themes of scientific romance – much of which featured the discovery of lost worlds or civilisations by groups of intrepid explorers – were informed both by popular Darwinism and the relatively new science of palaeontology. They are often posited on the premise of cultures that due to their geographical isolation had evolved differently: the explorers encounter dinosaurs (the discovery of fossilised skeletons in the nineteenth century had led to a popular fascination with these 'terrible lizards') as well as 'primitive' tribes that represent the 'missing link' between apes and humans. The genre of scientific romance was a natural for the cinema and has been present since its earliest days. Georges Méliès's celebrated 'trick' film of 1902 *Le Voyage dans le lune* (*A Trip to the Moon*), for instance, was influenced by Verne's *De la terre à la lune* and Wells's *The First Men in the Moon*. There were silent film versions of *20,000 Leagues under the Sea* (1916) and *The Lost World* (1925), and later sound films of *20,000 Leagues under the Sea* (1954), *Journey to the Centre of the Earth* (1959), *The Lost World* (1960), *The Time Machine* (1960) and *The First Men in the Moon* (1964). The British lost world cycle maintained the period settings of those films: *The Land That Time Forgot* and *The People That Time Forgot* are set during the First World War, while both *At the Earth's Core* and *Warlords of Atlantis* are set some time in the late nineteenth century. Indeed, the cycle could be said to represent the last flowering of the tradition of scientific romance in popular cinema: later lost world adventures such as *Jurassic Park* (1993) and its sequel *The Lost World: Jurassic Park* (1997) have eschewed period flavour in favour of present-day settings, while their dinosaurs are the genetically engineered products of modern science.

The three Amicus films were in fact adapted from novels by Edgar Rice Burroughs, the American fantasy author best known as the creator of Tarzan. There are some significant differences from the source materials, however, which can be related to the different cultural imperatives of the 1970s as opposed to the early decades of the twentieth century. *The Land That Time Forgot*, for example, follows the survivors of a British merchant ship who succeed in boarding and taking over the German submarine that sank them but who lose their way, eventually arriving at the mythical continent of Caprona, an island in the South Seas surrounded by icebergs and sealed off by an inhospitable coastline. The film is less jingoistic than the novel (which, published in 1918, was characterised by a strong anti-German feeling) and also exhibits more progressive gender politics: the heroine, here called Lisa Clayton (Susan Penhaligon), is given a scientific background (she is a biologist) that her equivalent in the book does not possess. The film rehearses a scientific discourse that might have passed above the heads of its intended audience – Lisa and Captain von Schoenvorts (John McEnery) debate the merits of 'German metaphysics' and 'British empiricism' – that can probably be attributed to the influence of Michael Moorcock, co-writer of the screenplay with James Cawthorne. Moorcock was the former editor of *New Worlds*, the progressive science-fiction magazine that had became the focus of 'new wave' SF in the 1960s. Jonathan Rosenbaum, however, felt that the film was so concerned not to offend modern sensibilities that it lost the essence of the original:

> The major drawback to this kind of cautious piety is a certain scaling down of the more 'primal' emotions appealed to by Burroughs – a kind of sustained sexual and racial hysteria that makes the original a lot closer to *King Kong* than this tamer and more moderate version.[24]

The film version of *The Land That Time Forgot* also includes certain elements from Burroughs's sequels, *The People That Time Forgot* and *Out of Time's Abyss*, particularly the explanation for the coexistence of creatures from different stages of the evolutionary cycle. Von Schoenvorts describes Caprona as 'like a geological exhibit – a world of life outside of time, representing almost all the ages of the Earth'. The film concludes, somewhat unusually for a juvenile adventure story, on an uncertain note: Lisa and Bowen Tyler (McClure) are left stranded on Caprona after the others are all killed during a volcanic eruption. The opening of the film, however, has already suggested the possibility of a sequel with the discovery of the cannister, later revealed to have been thrown into the sea by Tyler, containing a manuscript account of his adventures. *The People That Time Forgot* concerns the effort of Tyler's friend, Major Ben McBride (Patrick Wayne), to find and rescue him at the end of the war.[25] Again it modernises the social and gender politics of the novel: the aristocratic heroine, Lady Charlotte (Sarah Douglas), is a photographer for a newspaper, a profession that seems more apt for the 1960s, while her 'Women's Lib' attitude is clearly a reflection of the second wave feminism of the 1970s rather than an accurate representation of the attitudes of 1918.

At the Earth's Core also revises its source material, though in a rather different way. Here the gender politics are more conservative: the heroine Dia (Caroline Munro) is a fantasy princess whose role is nothing more than an object of desire for competing male suitors. These inevitably include David Innes (McClure), the engineer who has arrived with Dr Abner Perry (Peter Cushing) in the subterranean land of Pellucidar when their excavating machine, the 'iron mole', runs out of control on its first test drilling. The film rehearses the struggle of the human inhabitants of Pellucidar against the tyrannical rule of the Mahars, but its ending is very different from the book. In Burroughs's version, Innes escapes from the underground world to discover that his companion in the iron mole is not Dia but the corpse of a Mahar, placed there by the treacherous Hooja ('the Sly One'). The film eschews this rather ghoulish ending in favour of a comic moment where the mole emerges through the lawn of the White House to the consternation of two Keystone Kops policemen on guard duty. The 'rugged primal emotions' of the novel are again less in evidence, displaced here by an insistence on spoofery, with Cushing reprising his dotty professor act from the two *Dr Who* films and relishing the tongue-in-cheek dialogue: 'You can't mesmerise me: I'm British!'

In certain respects, *Warlords of Atlantis* is the most interesting of the films, perhaps because it was an original screenplay rather than an adaptation of pulp literature. The script has some pretension to seriousness in so far as it suggests an alternative history of the Earth in which the course of technological development has been determined by the survivors of the lost civilisation of Atlantis, who, it transpires, came to Earth on an asteroid from Mars. The Atlantian leader, Atraxon (Daniel Massey), attempts to persuade scientist Charles Aitken (Peter Gilmore) of the desirability of a technocratic dictatorship:

> ATRAXON: This is the future that we intend to create, by every occult means we know. A military state that will not merely set the whole world beneath its heel . . . but one that can – by force of war – release the full creative energies of twentieth-century science.
> CHARLES: Science – creating the new millennium! Utopia – the perfect society![26]

Doug McClure and Peter Gilmore leading the escape in *Warlords of Atlantis* (1978)

Charles is shown a vision of the future, including images of the Nazis and the atomic bomb – a similar sequence would be used to represent the 'brainwashing' of Doctor Zarkov in Mike Hodges's *Flash Gordon* (1980) – though it is cut short by the intervention of Greg Collinson (McClure), who removes the helmet from his friend's head. The suggestion that the entire course of human development has actually been engineered by an alien race is a familiar device of science fiction: it is a potentially subversive idea in so far as it challenges the conventional historical narrative of human achievements in scientific and technological advancement.[27]

Warlords of Atlantis had been produced not by Amicus but by EMI, which in the late 1970s was embarking upon yet another of the British film industry's periodic attempts to conquer the lucrative American market. Its larger budget was partly the result of the inflation that affected film production at the time and partly a response to the extraordinary success of the space opera *Star Wars* (1977), which had redefined both the nature and the expectations of fantasy adventure cinema. Its failure to achieve anything like that level of success (it came a respectable fourteenth at the British box office in 1978, but it was a long way behind *Star Wars* and *Close Encounters of the Third Kind*) signalled an end to the lost world cycle. The Victorian décor and puppet monsters now looked quaint and old-fashioned in the new era of futuristic special-effects-driven spectacle. The vogue in the late 1970s and early 1980s was for cheap and not-so-cheap imitations of

Star Wars – including *Starship Invasions* (1977), *Battlestar Galactica* (1978), *Starcrash* (1979), *The Black Hole* (1979) and *Battle Beyond the Stars* (1980) – which the chronically under-resourced British film industry could not equal for spectacle. To this extent, the lost world cycle represents probably the last indigenous example of a British fantasy cinema: for this reason, if no other, the films deserve to be accorded their place in the sun.

Notes

1 Julian Petley, 'The Lost Continent', in Charles Barr (ed.), *All Our Yesterdays: 90 Years of British Cinema* (London: BFI, 1986), p. 98.

2 This revisionist historiography includes, but is not limited to, Sue Harper, *Picturing the Past: The Rise and Fall of the British Costume Film* (London: BFI, 1994), Peter Hutchings, *Hammer and Beyond: The British Horror Film* (Manchester: Manchester University Press, 1993), Robert Murphy, *Shadows Are My Friends: British Film Noir* (London: BFI, forthcoming), and Jeffrey Richards, 'Tod Slaughter and the Cinema of Excess', in Jeffrey Richards (ed.), *The Unknown 1930s: An Alternative History of the British Cinema, 1929–1939* (London: I. B. Tauris, 1998), pp. 139–61.

3 Alexander Walker, *National Heroes: British Cinema in the Seventies and Eighties* (London: Harrap, 1985), mentions only *Warlords of Atlantis*, and then only as a passing reference to the production schedule of EMI in the late 1970s. The films are listed in the filmography of I. Q. Hunter (ed.), *British Science Fiction Cinema* (London: Routledge, 1999), but are not discussed anywhere in the text, while they are entirely absent from Daniel O'Brien's *SF/UK: How British Science Fiction Changed the World* (London: Reynolds & Hearn, 2000).

4 Andrew Higson, 'A Diversity of Film Practices: Renewing British Cinema in the 1970s', in Bart Moore-Gilbert (ed.), *The Arts in the 1970s: Cultural Closure?* (London: Routledge, 1994), pp. 216–39.

5 *Variety*, 22 June 1977, p. 17.

6 The fifth film, following the four 'lost world' adventures, was *Arabian Adventure* (1979), a virtual remake of Alexander Korda's *The Thief of Bagdad* (1940), also written, like *Warlords of Atlantis*, by Brian Hayles. Connor also directed *Trial by Combat* (1976), an action-thriller about a secret society dedicated to the ritual execution of criminals who have escaped the law. *Trial by Combat* was produced by Fred Weintraub and Paul Heller, though some reviews of the later 'lost world' films mistakenly attribute it to John Dark.

7 See Peter Hutchings, 'The Amicus House of Horror', in Steve Chibnall and Julian Petley (eds), *British Horror Cinema* (London: Routledge, 2002), pp. 131–44. A more celebratory history can be found in Alan Bryce, *Amicus: The Studio That Dripped Blood* (Liskeard, Cornwall: Stray Cat Publishing, 2000).

8 The television series *Doctor Who* was aimed at a 'family' audience, including older children and adults as well as juveniles. The films were altered in order to downplay the horrific elements, changing the characterisation of 'Doctor Who' from a grumpy and mysterious alien to a bumbling, eccentric inventor and turning the teenage 'granddaughter' of the television series into a precocious eight-year-old. This can be seen as a deliberate strategy to appeal to younger viewers, as the received wisdom of juvenile fiction is that children do not identify with child characters younger than themselves. See James Chapman, *Inside the Tardis: The Worlds of 'Doctor Who' – A Cultural History* (London: I. B. Tauris, 2006), pp. 12–48, and John R. Cook, 'Adapting Telefantasy: The *Doctor Who and the Daleks* Films', in Hunter (ed.), *British Science Fiction Cinema*, pp. 113–27.

9 *CinemaTV Today*, 8 March 1975, p. 1.

10 Ibid., 26 April 1975, p. 2.
11 *Screen International*, 24 July 1976, p. 2.
12 Ibid., 29 July 1978, p. 2.
13 Quoted in 'The Greatest Show Beneath the Earth', *Film Review*, vol. 26, no. 7, July 1976, p. 18.
14 Gavin Millar, 'Core Blimey', *The Listener*, 5 August 1976, p. 154.
15 *The People That Time Forgot* was a 'U' and *Warlords of Atlantis* an 'A'. In America, all four films were rated 'PG' by the MPAA.
16 Jonathan Rosenbaum, *Monthly Film Bulletin*, vol. 42, no. 493, February 1975, p. 35; John Pym, *Monthly Film Bulletin*, vol. 44, no. 523, August 1977, p. 172; John Pym, *Monthly Film Bulletin*, vol. 45, no. 534, July 1978, p. 145.
17 *Variety*, 23 June 1976, p. 16.
18 *Films and Filming*, vol. 24, no. 10, July 1978, p. 37.
19 Jan Dawson, 'Escapologies', *The Listener*, 27 July 1978, p. 121.
20 *CinemaTV Today*, 15 February 1975, p. 13; *Variety*, 9 April 1975, p. 20.
21 Quoted in 'The Greatest Show Beneath the Earth', p. 18.
22 *Screen International*, 17 July 1976, p. 13.
23 John Pym, *Monthly Film Bulletin*, vol. 45, no. 534, July 1978, p. 145.
24 Jonathan Rosenbaum, *Monthly Film Bulletin*, vol. 42, no. 493, February 1975, p. 35.
25 There is a marked similarity between *The Land That Time Forgot* and *The People That Time Forgot* on the one hand and *Planet of the Apes* (1968) and *Beneath the Planet of the Apes* (1969) on the other. *Planet of the Apes* follows an astronaut called Taylor (Charlton Heston) to a world where the course of evolution has been reversed: apes are the rulers and humans the primitives. This world turns out to be a post-apocalyptic Earth: the film ends with Taylor and his native companion, Nova (Linda Harrison), finding the remains of the Statue of Liberty. In *Beneath the Planet of the Apes*, another astronaut, Brent (James Franciscus), follows Taylor's path in order to effect a rescue. Heston appeared as a 'guest star' in *Beneath*, just as McClure returns as Tyler in *People*. The parallel is more than the similarity in the characters' names (Taylor/Tyler): both are killed in the sequel.
26 BFI Library Script Collection S15365: '*7 Cities to Atlantis*'. Screenplay by Brian Hayles. Fifth Construction Script, 20 June 1977.
27 This idea informs several *Doctor Who* stories, including 'The Dæmons' (1971) and 'City of Death' (1979). Brian Hayles was an occasional writer for *Doctor Who*, to which his main contribution was the creation of the Ice Warriors. His stories 'The Curse of Peladon' (1972) and 'The Monster of Peladon' (1974) anticipate *Warlords of Atlantis* in their representation of a society caught between feudalism and modernisation.

Part Two: Contexts and Styles

7 Glam, Spam and Uncle Sam: Funding Diversity in 1970s British Film Production

Justin Smith

Cinemagoing in the 1970s

Though it has been only thinly documented until now, the 1970s is widely believed to have been a decade of stagnation and decline in the fortunes of the British film industry. Certainly, the popularity of cinema as a social pastime continued its downward trend, resulting in the outright closure, or double- and triple-screen division, of many exhibition sites up and down the country (see Table 1). It is important to recognise here, however, that while admissions and per capita visits fell, and cinemas did close, the number of screens remained fairly constant and box-office receipts (by dint of increased ticket prices) actually grew. So there was no shortage of films being shown or of exhibition revenue across the decade.

The explanations for the decline in admissions are familiar: specifically, increasing competition from television (now in colour and boasting three channels); and more generally, the draw of other domestic and social consumption (Table 2 shows the growth in ownership of television sets). However, these figures must be treated with caution. The 1960s boom in television ownership is over by this time and there is a noticeable downturn in sales by mid-decade. This may

Table 1: Cinema attendance and related statistics, 1972–80

	1972	1973	1974	1975	1976	1977	1978	1979	1980
Cinema sites	1,314	1,269	1,176	1,100	1,057	1,005	985	978	942
No. of cinema screens	1,531	1,600	1,590	1,576	1,562	1,547	1,563	1,582	1,576
Total admissions (m)	163	142	143	124	107	108	127	112	102
Gross box office (£m)	59.4	58	69.3	71.2	75.8	85.5	118.2	126.8	143
Payments to BFFA (£m)	4.2	3.7	4.4	4.9	4.8	5.4	7.2	7	5.8
Average admission charge (p)	38	43	50	61	73	83	94	113	141
Films registered	386	380	402	341	338	318	286	274	257
British features	89	80	78	70	64	42	50	40	41
Visits per year	2.89	2.47	2.54	2.14	1.91	1.9	2.31	2.05	1.85

Sources: *Business Monitor, Screen Digest* 'British Cinema and Film Statistics', 1990, p. 1.

Table 2: UK television deliveries (000s), 1971–5

Year	Colour		Monochrome	
	Units	£000s	Units	£000s
1971	824	115,583	1,538	61,009
1972	1,446	203,971	1,473	59,102
1973	2,076	292,952	941	36,947
1974	1,770	267,156	574	23,602
1975	1,326	221,178	504	23,475

Source: *Screen Digest*, May 1976, p. 81.

Table 3: UK video recorder imports, 1975–9

		Units	£ Total	£ Unit
1975	Q1	965	715,519	741.47
	Q2	1,150	1,902,527	1654.37
	Q3	1,235	1,113,482	901.60
	Q4	1,861	916,413	492.43
	Year	5,211	4,647,941	891.95
1976	Q1	2,374	1,104,591	465.29
	Q2	2,687	2,069,108	770.29
	Q3	2,984	2,002,005	670.91
	Q4	4,663	4,090,985	877.33
	Year	12,708	9,266,689	729.20
1977	Q1	4,074	2,902,878	712.54
	Q2	5,441	4,023,347	739.45
	Q3	5,251	3,894,459	741.66
	Q4	7,047	3,127,612	443.82
	Year	22,813	12,948,296	611.42
1978	Q1	8,026	5,487,000	683.65
	Q2	16,225	7,679,000	473.28
	Q3	22,240	9,516,000	427.88
	Q4	49,135	17,502,000	362.67
	Year	95,626	40,502,000	423.55
1975–8		136,358	68,364,926	501.36

Source: *Screen Digest*, April 1979, p. 74.

be blamed on economic recession and a temporary failure of consumer confidence. Yet, general trends indicate that consumer spending across a range of leisure pursuits (including cinema and theatre) continued to rise. And, as Table 3 reveals, the import figures for domestic video recorders rose from 1975. Analysis carried out by *Screen Digest* during the 1970s wisely cautions against straightforward correlations between television and video on the one hand and cinemagoing on the other. One consideration is that cinema may have been competing against a wider range of personal and domestic entertainments – figures show, for example, a continued rise in record sales and equipment during the decade. For other explanations, we need to look more closely at cinema itself.

One reason for the falling off in attendance may have been, paradoxically, the rise in admission charges. Yet as early as August 1970, Terry McGrath, the General Manager of the Theatre Division of Rank Leisure Services, warned that in facing increasing competition from alternative entertainment products, the market for cinema 'will continue to fragment into distinct buyer groups . . . with different requirements'.[1] In order to cater for these diverse tastes, he advocated a 'system of multi-auditoria' that would 'allow us to offer choice'. Furthermore, 'if we are able to exhibit the average film for a second week in a small, low-cost cinema . . . nearby or as part of a complex of theatres . . . there is admissions potential to be picked up'.[2] Indeed, the multi-screening of many cinema sites during the decade that followed this assessment is evidence of the fragmentation in the audience constituency.

How, then, was this acknowledged market imperative addressed by British film producers during the 1970s? And what implications did this have for the kinds of films that were made? A *Screen Digest* report of December 1976 predicted that 'as the cinema contracts, there appear to be two poles towards which it can be attracted. It either becomes dominated by aggressively commercial material, be it disaster movies or porn, or it becomes more introspective and national.'[3] Both these broad trends are, as we shall see, discernible in the films of the period. But the key issue here, of course, is how one maps the flow of capital against the measure of popular tastes. Before attempting any answers to those questions, let us outline the constraints upon the financial market for British film production in the 1970s. I want to consider the economic background, film policy and film finance, before offering an overview of film production.

Economic Background

The 1970s brought recession and saw a rapid withdrawal of American funding from British film production. The National Film Finance Corporation's 1971 Annual Report showed that US finance had peaked 'in 1968 when 43 out of 49 British first features or co-features exhibited on the two main circuits were wholly or partly US-financed'.[4] However, as *Today's Cinema* reported, 1969 saw these figures drop to 35 out of 45 films and by 1970 the figure was only 29 out of 44.[5] Several of the Hollywood majors had suffered heavy losses through overzealous speculation at the end of the 1960s. In 1969, MGM lost $35.4m and Warner Bros. $42m. The following year, United Artists lost $45m and Fox $76.4m and, in 1971, Columbia had debts of $28.8m.[6] By 1974, total American funding for British subsidiaries had fallen to £2.9m. Dickinson and Street have produced a table showing patterns of imported capital for runaway production for the 1960s and 1970s (see Table 4). The recession was, these authors conclude, largely financial rather than social or cultural; though the new wave of American youth-oriented pictures at the end of the 1960s (*Bonnie and Clyde* [1967], *The Graduate* [1967], *Easy Rider* [1969] and so on) competed vigorously with imported British films. In fact, as Street notes, the total number of films imported to the US fell at the end of the 1960s to the lowest level since the Second World War.[7] Furthermore, lucrative tax incentives (7 per cent tax relief and deferment of tax on a film's foreign earnings if reinvested in another domestic production for export) and two devaluations of

Table 4: Total receipts by UK subsidiaries of American majors in imported capital, 1968–79

Year	£millions
1968	31.3
1969	20.9
1970	12.8
1971	18.6
1972	14.0
1973	4.8
1974	2.9
1975	4.2
1976	4.8
1977	5.3
1978	7.9
1979	6.0

Source: M. Dickinson and S. Street, *Cinema and State* (London: BFI, 1985), p. 240.

the dollar gave a boost to American exports while making foreign investment in production comparatively less attractive.[8] In the mid-1970s, American investment in Britain did recover somewhat (though nothing in comparison with the heady days of the late 1960s). By this time, the Hollywood blockbuster had established itself as a dominant and extremely lucrative overseas export, with production values on a scale that British producers were unable to emulate on any consistent basis.

However, dependent as the British film industry has always been on American product and investment, the story of the 1970s is by no means one-way traffic. Indeed, as Vincent Porter revealed in a survey published as early as 1979, from 1975 onwards, 'earnings by British film producers from performances overseas have been greater than the money paid out by British exhibitors for screening Hollywood films'.[9] Furthermore, the successful penetration of British corporate interests ACC and EMI into the American market yielded profits of £20m in 1978, before those particular bubbles burst.[10] Sarah Street has tabled figures for the biggest British earners in the American export market (see Table 5), and these titles give a good indication of the type of (mainly big-budget) film product that continued to be successful overseas. But to return for now to the domestic arena, the early 1970s decline in American studio investment in their British subsidiaries represented at the time a major crisis for domestic film production. How did British producers respond? First, in time-honoured fashion, they turned to the politicians.

Film Policy

The Government's film bank, the National Film Finance Corporation, had long since extended its responsibilities beyond the terms of its original remit. Labour's Films Bill of 1970 pledged to increase the NFFC's charter for a further ten years, relieve it of some of the repayments on its crippling debt, and empower it to borrow a further £5m for production.[11] In 1969, the Corporation had lost £149,239 in interest payments on the original loan to British Lion. The following year,

Table 5: US rental earnings of British films of 1970s

Title	Rentals ($millions)
Superman (1978)	82.8
Alien (1979)	40.3
Moonraker (1979)	33.9
The Spy Who Loved Me (1977)	24.4
A Bridge Too Far (1977)	20.4
Return of the Pink Panther (1975)	20.2
The Pink Panther Strikes Again (1976)	19.8
Diamonds Are Forever (1971)	19.7
Murder on the Orient Express (1974)	19.1
Tommy (1975)	17.8
A Clockwork Orange (1971)	17
Live and Let Die (1973)	16
Dracula (1979)	10.7
Monty Python's Flying Circus (1979)	10.5
Barry Lyndon (1975)	9.2
Death on the Nile (1978)	8.8
The Day of the Jackal (1973)	8.6
The Odessa File (1974) **	5.7
Monty Python and the Holy Grail (1975)	5.2
The Eagle Has Landed (1977)	4.2
Straw Dogs (1971)	4
Mary, Queen of Scots (1972)	3.6
The Man Who Fell to Earth (1976)	3
Scrooge (1970)	3
Women in Love (1970)	3
* Britain/France	
** Britain/W. Germany	

Source: S. Street, *Transatlantic Crossings* (London: Continuum, 2002), p. 195.

its losses amounted to £304,786. Yet, as Penelope Houston reflected, the NFFC had lost the taxpayer only an average of £150,000 a year in its twenty-two-year existence; value for money by her judgment.[12] Additional parts of the bill proposed to keep the quota intact, but to advance a small grant from the Film Fund to the British Film Institute Production Board, as well as an amount from the same source to help finance the new National Film School. In a jibe that crystallised the terms of the political debate about public support for the film industry in the 1970s, the Tories' Sir Keith Joseph suggested that such aid should come from the Department of Education and Science rather than in the form of an industry levy.

Joseph was anticipating the questions that dogged film policy during the 1970s: what was the efficacy of state intervention? And was it commercially or culturally motivated? The outgoing Labour Films Minister, Gwyneth Dunwoody, in her role as Director of the Film Production Association, called for more modest ambitions: 'For obvious reasons we are always going to have difficulty in raising finance. I think the future may well lie in more pictures, but at lower budgets.'[13] Her incoming opposite number, Nicolas Ridley, insisted that it was not the new Conservative 'Government's policy to put money into industry of this sort. In the long term it should be able to stand on its own feet in the market.'[14] However, in the short term, and for the duration of the 1970s, successive administrations continued, largely ineffectually, to maintain the existing instruments of state aid for the film business: the quota, the Eady Levy and the NFFC. Specifically, the Tories significantly watered down the terms of Labour's original Film Bill. They cancelled the new £5m loan, agreeing instead to advance up to £1m in public money for every £3m derived from the private sector. A National Film Finance Consortium of private capital interests would be formed for the purpose. These included occasional involvement from merchant bankers Josef Shaftel, Dimitri de Grunwald and Morgan Grenfell. Under these new arrangements, a film 'would receive 50% of its finance from the consortium and 50% from the distributors'.[15] The scheme was symbolically significant, if nothing else, and it produced results that were conducive to encouraging new talent in quality if not quantity of products.

More significant is the type and changing pattern of NFFC-supported films across the decade. Vincent Porter has suggested that, as a cultural pump-primer, this scheme can be said to have achieved some modest success. But as a serious financial investment, it was a disaster. Porter is also right to point out that the type of projects funded changed during the decade from the low-budget horror and domestic comedies to more international-looking ventures such as *The Romantic Englishwoman* (1975), *The Man Who Fell to Earth* (1976), *Jabberwocky* (1977) and *The Duellists* (1977). Clearly, the Consortium also provided valuable assistance to emerging production talents such as Lieberson and Puttnam's Visual Programme Systems and Goodtimes Enterprises and, later, Merchant–Ivory. Furthermore, the NFFC's funding imperatives during the 1970s can be said, as Porter notes, to have advanced a cultural, rather than a purely economic, agenda, as is represented by support for projects such as *Akenfield* (1974) and the work of Ken Loach. These examples should also be viewed within the context of the Corporation's increase in contributions to the National Film School and the BFI Production Board during the decade. Alexander Walker records that the grant to the BFI increased from £750,000 in 1971 to £5,829,000 in 1980.[16] Moves as a result of the 1975 Films Act to give blessing to the newly formed Association of Independent Producers (AIP) and to promote a National Film Development Fund to originate scripts further enhanced this cultural role.

Harold Wilson's Interim Action Committee, established as a result of the Prime Minister's working party report of 1976, set up the British Film Authority, which was assigned the task of distributing in a more targeted manner Eady contributions to the NFFC. Significantly, perhaps, the AIP became a strong voice in championing the case for a fourth television channel, which itself became a powerful and radical force in promoting independent film-making during the 1980s. But the aims of government funding for the film industry remained, in the words of the report, culturally rather than financially motivated: 'We . . . believe that the barriers between industry and art in relation to film are largely artificial and subjective, and that government policy should cater for films as a whole.'[17] To some extent, the ambivalent attitude of successive governments towards the British film industry in the 1970s can be said to have reflected, and exacerbated, the fragmented nature of film funding. For while the Independent Film Makers Association (IFA), founded in 1974, the BFI's Production Board and

Looking to international markets: Ridley Scott's *The Duellists* (1977)

the Regional Arts associations promoted ideologically and geographically diverse film culture, in the commercial marketplace financial practice was equally decentralised, though in rather different ways.

Film Finance and Production

What is interesting about British film production during the 1970s is how little continuity there is. This should not come as a surprise to us, of course, since the market for cinema as entertainment was in steep decline and adverse economic trends made financial speculation an even more precarious business than usual. To begin with, the distribution and exhibition sectors in the UK continued to be dominated by the vestiges of the two vertically integrated combines Rank and EMI. During the 1970s, Rank withdrew almost completely from film production, although it continued showcasing erstwhile successful franchises like the *Carry On* series, which addressed the concerns of the new decade on an annual basis with a quite new attitude of reassurance in matters of sexual pleasure, until it finally ran out of steam in 1978. Meanwhile, EMI continued to expand, despite considerable losses, swallowing up the last ailing independent, British Lion, in 1975. During the first half of the decade, EMI pursued a series of relationships with American studios (MGM being the most important), with varying degrees of profitability. But when Bryan Forbes's ambitious plans to rejuvenate British film production met with only modest success – notably *The Go-between* (1970), *The Railway Children* (1970) and *The Tales of Beatrix Potter* (1971) – he resigned in March 1971. This marked a significant breach of faith: effectively the end of the productive relationship between corporate financiers and their men of vision. Few old-style studio producers and their journeymen directors survived into the 1970s. From now on, the old rules did not apply.

Much film funding was characterised hereafter by one-off projects, often financed from a range of diverse sources (from wider media, entertainment and business concerns). Scratch production outfits were formed and disbanded, new temporary alliances forged on the basis of expediency. This situation, while tenuous, may also be seen to have opened up rare opportunities for creative freedom on the part of enterprising and ambitious talents. Yet the corporate investors were not without policy direction. It is the film historian's task to follow each strand in this tangled web to tease out the origins of money that funded small projects, as well as the larger corporate indifference that (unwittingly) sanctioned gambling at rather higher stakes. The picture is complex and much work remains to be done. Here I have only the space to offer an outline sketch of the landscape. It may be characterised, for these purposes, by three sorts of initiative, which I have labelled 'Glam', 'Spam' and 'Uncle Sam'.

'Glam'

One trend that emerges in British films of the 1970s is their debt to, and engagement with, popular youth culture. Of course this wasn't new, but the money interests from the music business in particular were at last persuaded to invest in product that should have been to their advantage. On a corporate scale, of course, EMI sustained its frequently faltering film production schedule through a combination of its profitable ABC cinema circuit and its record business, just as Bernard Delfont's brother Lew Grade supported his grand cinematic speculation on the strength of his television empire, and just as Rank's rather less ambitious plans were founded on a combination of bingo and photocopying. But at the local, ad-hoc level, the 1970s also witnessed the intervention of music money just as cinema seemed to be becoming aware of the crossover potential of the considerable youth market. Ray Connolly, the writer who, with David Puttnam, conceived *That'll Be the Day* (1973) and its sequel *Stardust* (1974), reflected wrily that

> Although you and I may have known for years that the people who buy records in large numbers tend to be the very same people who enjoy going to the pictures, it appears to have come as a recent revelation to the film industry . . . for 20 years, while rock has been establishing itself as the contemporary music form of the second half of this century, film-makers have continued to view it with suspicion and not a little distaste.[18]

Thus it was that their nostalgic rock 'n' roll story cast David Essex (fresh from *Godspell*) alongside ex-Beatle Ringo Starr. Having failed to persuade EMI to provide the whole budget, Puttnam agreed a deal with the American record label Ronco to part-finance the film in return for an action-packed soundtrack. The sequel, *Stardust*, attracted NFFC support and established the Puttnam/Lieberson partnership of Goodtimes Enterprises beyond the radical speculation of Roeg and Cammell's avant-garde *Performance* (1970). Like many of the new entrants into the film business, Puttnam's background was in other media (he ran a photographic agency), while future collaborators Ridley Scott and Alan Parker had both made a raft of successful television commercials.

Pop star becomes film star: David Essex in *That'll Be the Day* (1973)

In a similar vein, the London stage sensation known as *The Rocky Horror Show* drew its talent from the cast of *Hair* and *Jesus Christ Superstar*, while finding American backing for a film incarnation from the rock impresario Lou Adler (1975). Again, The Who's rock opera *Tommy* (1975), directed by Ken Russell, attracted investment from Robert Stigwood (the Australian music mogul), who went on to produce *Bugsy Malone* (1976), *Saturday Night Fever* (1977) and *Grease* (1978). As *Variety* trumpeted loudly: 'Stigwood, after *Jesus Christ Superstar* (1973) . . . now heads a whole corps of music industry personnel who are looking to get into films.'[19] Perhaps the most surprising (and surprisingly successful) of these interventions was the company formed by another ex-Beatle, George Harrison, and his financial partner Denis

O'Brien. HandMade films was established in 1979 when, again, EMI's Lord Delfont refused to fund the Monty Python team's third feature film, *Life of Brian*. Which brings me to my second theme: 'Spam'.

'Spam'

American Denis O'Brien ran Euro-Atlantic, a financial consultancy, from an unobtrusive house in Chelsea. Harrison put his own home up for mortgage to raise the rest of the capital and the pair were involved in a number of creative changes to *Life of Brian* between the script that Delfont had rejected and the finished film.[20] It was a pattern of financial probity and creative input that sustained the partnership to such notable curiosities as *A Private Function* (1984) and *Withnail & I* (1986). Meanwhile, O'Brien's other showbusiness client, Peter Sellers, saw his career relaunched thanks to Lew Grade brokering a peace with director Blake Edwards, which resulted in a further three reincarnations of the Pink Panther: *The Return of the Pink Panther* (1975), *The Pink Panther Strikes Again* (1976) and *Revenge of the Pink Panther* (1978). But British comedy of the 1970s had risen to these lofty heights of international appeal on the back of a succession of low-budget TV spin-offs that were domestically popular and safe, if modest in ambition and, almost without exception, inferior to their small-screen originals. Of these, perhaps the Frankie Howerd vehicles known as the *Up . . .* series were among the most notable, while *On the Buses* (1971), *Steptoe and Son* (1972), *Ooh . . . You Are Awful* (1972) and *Love Thy Neighbour* (1973) were among the most lamentable. Extraordinarily, the last of these, and the sequel, *Steptoe and Son Ride Again* (1973), attracted NFFC support, as had *Up Pompeii* in 1970. Even, by the decade's end, *Porridge* (1979) still made the top twenty at the British box office.

Whatever the cultural merits of these spin-offs, here is evidence of how television impinges financially in the domestic film industry in the 1970s. Aside from comedy, one could cite the successful *Sweeney* cop flicks (1977 and 1978), made by Thames Television's Euston Films, as specific examples of economic crossover. At the same time, the cultural and aesthetic similarities between film and television of the period (from Loach and Leigh's politically committed social naturalism to *Confessions of a Window Cleaner* [1974]) are a measure of two important facts. First, this is indicative of the powerful place of television in national cultural life and suggestive of the importance of the domestic space at this time. Second, and by contrast, it suggests a lack of confidence in film both financially and culturally, which caused mainstream cinema to fall back upon residual and introspective cultural forms, without the bold financial enterprise required to champion its aesthetic distinction. Perhaps this underlying unease explains the furious and indignant outpourings in the trade press of the time about United Artists selling Connery's Bond adventures to ITV in 1974 and the reduction in the statutory delay between theatrical release and television broadcast for feature films from five years to three in 1976. Not until the 1980s does a sense of rapprochement emerge when both media begin to realise that it is in their interests to work together in producing more imaginative fare than the 1970s 'Spam' denotes. If 'Spam' represents the largely inward-looking, nationalistic flavour of British cinema in the 1970s, its efforts at international appeal (especially to the US market) also operated on two distinct levels. It is these interests that I shall touch upon briefly before attempting any provisional conclusions.

'Uncle Sam'

The international market had long been a necessary target for any but the lowest-budget British film hoping to recoup its costs. Alexander Korda knew this in the 1930s just as well as Puttnam, British Lion, Amicus and the Grade Brothers did in the 1970s. But with the risks of speculation on such a scale so high, casualties are inevitable, and again, as in the late 1930s, so in the late 1970s, some corporate fingers were duly burned, in certain cases spectacularly so. James Bond retained his evergreen appeal, despite (or rather because of) a change of persona. Other contemporary thrillers followed suit: for example, the Frederick Forsyth adaptations *The Day of the Jackal* (1973) and *The Odessa File* (1974), which were West German and French co-productions respectively; and the Alistair Maclean sequence, *When Eight Bells Toll* (1971), *Puppet on a Chain* (1971), *Fear Is the Key* (1972), *Caravan to Vaccares* (1974), *Force 10 from Navarone* (1978) and *Bear Island* (1979, UK/Canada co-production). The historical film remained a typically British staple and achieved considerable success with EMI's two Agatha Christie Poirot films, *Murder on the Orient Express* (1974) and *Death on the Nile* (1978). More seriously, perhaps, literary adaptations at the beginning of the decade from Ken Russell (*Women in Love* [1969]) and mid-decade from Stanley Kubrick (*Barry Lyndon* [1975]) held their own at the box office thanks to American studio backing for their considerable production values. Charles Jarrott's costume dramas for Universal (*Anne of the Thousand Days* [1969] and *Mary, Queen of Scots* [1971]) were notable successes, along with David Lean's *Ryan's Daughter* (1970) and Richard Attenborough's US co-production *Young Winston* (1972).

Sue Harper has begun some very interesting work focusing particularly on the unusual aesthetic manner and arrangements of *mise en scène* that are characteristic of the costume film in this period. Early indications suggest a curiously ironic, sometimes picaresque, detachment from the historical subject, deriving in part from a tendency towards flatness in the picture plane.[21] It appears that the costume film was a more significant strand in British international pictures of the 1970s than has been thought. The other profitable British export of the period remains the war film, and especially those, like *The Eagle Has Landed* (1976), *A Bridge Too Far* (1977) and *The Wild Geese* (1978), that could attract Hollywood personnel as well as finance.

The final trend worthy of note, not to mention lament, in the late 1970s was the ability of the major British producers to overreach themselves in making, financing and distributing films in America, just as some Hollywood studios began a tentative return to production on British soil encouraged by economic exigency and technical expertise: for example, *Superman* (1978) and *Alien* (1979). Barry Spikings and Michael Deeley, formerly of British Lion, who had taken over the reins at EMI when the conglomerate had absorbed the last major British independent, began by speculating with Nicolas Roeg's relatively successful David Bowie science-fiction film *The Man Who Fell to Earth* (a wholly British-funded, British-crewed film, made entirely on location in New Mexico without a distribution deal). They went on to back (with varying degrees of success) *Nickelodeon* (1976), *The Deer Hunter*, *Convoy* and *The Driver* (all 1978). Finally, John Schlesinger's monumentally unsuccessful *Honky Tonk Freeway* (1981), produced by Don Boyd, accrued debts that even a new-found alliance with electrical giant Thorn could not absorb. ACC followed the successes of *The Boys from Brazil* and *Capricorn One* (both 1978) with the infamous *Raise the Titanic* (1980), of which Lew Grade later quipped: 'it would

Raise the Titanic (1980) sinks to financial oblivion

have been cheaper to lower the Atlantic'. In truth, both corporations overreached themselves, especially in attempts to obtain controlling influence in the tightly organised American distribution markets.

At the other end of the financial spectrum, low-budget British horror and sex films continued to do reasonably well in overseas markets, their familiar recipes sustaining their fortunes beyond their limited domestic appeal. It is here that comparison between the production output and British box-office popularity reveals the most marked discrepancy. For while Hammer, in decline, resorted to *On the Buses* (and its progeny) to maintain a production schedule, Tyburn persisted with formulaic exploitation fare, and Amicus branched out into fantasy with *The Land That Time Forgot* (1975), *At the Earth's Core* (1976) and *The People That Time Forgot* (1977). Between them they accounted for a formidable chunk of 1970s British film production. Yet, perhaps unsurprisingly, they scarcely feature in the box-office charts.

Conclusion

For sure, much work remains to be done. Funding streams for individual films need to be traced back to their sources, changing patterns of audience tastes require careful mapping and a study of censorship constraints will reveal much about the place of cinema in the public sphere. What is manifest, from the ground cleared so far, is that the parlous, uncertain state of British film production during the 1970s spawned a wide diversity of trends and some notable fringe innovation. International pictures tend to inflate traditional genres (costume, war, adventure, thriller, comedy) with big budgets and all-star casts. Domestic fare relies on television for its inspiration, and exploitation depends on the lucrative low-budget export market. Meanwhile, independent production outfits cashed in on popular youth culture, or pursued art-house aesthetics or soft-core pornography for minority tastes. The irony remains that while the British film industry in the 1970s boasted some of the best creative talents in international cinema (among writers, directors, producers, actors and technicians), their collective power was dissipated both by economic paralysis and cultural uncertainty. This permitted a colourful assemblage of marginal work to enjoy an unaccustomed position centre stage. When the condition of the economic base has such direct and marked effects upon the cultural superstructure, one can deduce that some important shifts are taking place in the social fabric of the decade.

Acknowledgment

I gratefully acknowledge the support of the AHRC-funded research project on British Cinema in the 1970s at the University of Portsmouth in the development of this work, and would particularly like to thank Sian Barber for her contributions to the finished text.

Notes

1 Terry McGrath, 'The Market Place Changes – So Must We', *Kinematograph Weekly*, 29 August 1970, p. 7.
2 Ibid., p. 9.
3 'CTV Report', *Screen Digest*, December 1976, p. 222.
4 Cited in 'And Still a Vast Market for Movies', *Today's Cinema*, 3 September 1971, p. 1.
5 Ibid.
6 Sarah Street, *Transatlantic Crossings: British Feature Films in the USA* (New York and London: Continuum, 2002), p. 190.
7 Ibid.
8 Margaret Dickinson and Sarah Street, *Cinema and State: The Film Industry and the British Government, 1927–84* (London: BFI, 1985), p. 240.
9 Vincent Porter, 'Film Policy for the 80s: Industry or Culture?', in *Sight and Sound*, vol. 48, no. 4, Autumn 1979, p. 221.
10 Ibid.
11 See Margaret Dickinson and Simon Hartog, 'Interview with Sir Harold Wilson', *Screen*, vol. 22, no. 3, 1981, pp. 9–23.
12 Penelope Houston, 'Films Bill', *Sight and Sound*, vol. 39, no. 2, Spring 1970, p. 72.
13 Rod Cooper, 'More Pictures at Lower Budgets', interview with Gwyneth Dunwoody, *Kinematograph Weekly*, 19 December 1970, p. 5.
14 Quoted by Robin Page, '"Stand on Your Own Feet" Film Row', *Today's Cinema*, 2 July 1971, p. 1.
15 Ernest Betts, *The Film Business: A History of British Cinema, 1896–1972* (London: Allen & Unwin, 1973), pp. 285–6.
16 Alexander Walker, *National Heroes: British Cinema in the Seventies and Eighties* (London: Harrap, 1985).
17 Interim Action Committee, 1979, quoted in Dickinson and Street, *Cinema and State*, p. 244.

18 Ray Connolly, 'Tommy', *Time Out*, no. 265, 28 March 1975, pp. 10–11.

19 '"Tommy" Opera Reverses Flow', *Variety*, 15 May 1974.

20 John Walker, *The Once and Future Film: British Cinema in the Seventies and Eighties* (London: Methuen, 1985), pp. 88–9.

21 Sue Harper, 'History and Representation: The Case of 1970s British Cinema', in James Chapman, Sue Harper and Mark Glancy, *The New Film History: Approaches, Methods and Sources* (London: Palgrave Macmillan, 2007).

8 'Now, what are we going to call you? Scum! . . . Scum! That's commercial! It's all they deserve!': *Jubilee*, Punk and British Film in the Late 1970s

Claire Monk

Introduction: British Punk Versus 'Punk Cinema'

The brief yet resonant eruption of British punk rock from late 1975 (when the first trickle of punk bands appeared in London) to 1979 – rapidly followed by its less confrontational musical successors bracketed under the labels 'post-punk' or 'new wave' – was captured raw in documentary footage shot by observers/participants, both British and non-British. From Derek Jarman's *Jubilee* (1978) onwards, it also provided aesthetic/political inspiration or subject matter for a number of British feature films.

The 'primary' footage capturing the immediacy of British punk as it happened – observing both early live performances and the participatory energy and sartorial innovations of young punk audiences, and, in keeping with punk's ethos, typically shot on Super 8 stock by fans or novice film-makers – would resurface in virtually every later retrospective documentary on British punk. This material, along with key punk features such as *The Great Rock 'n' Roll Swindle* (Julien Temple, 1980) and Temple's more recent revisionist Sex Pistols documentary, *The Filth and the Fury* (2000), all now occupies an important place in British punk's historical/nostalgic documentation and historiography. By contrast, relatively little analytic attention has been devoted to the British punk (and post-punk) films *as films* in the context of late-1970s British cinema.

The exception to date has been Kevin J. Donnelly's 1998 article 'British Punk Films',[1] which offers a survey of those produced and released from 1978 to 1981 – plus, in coda, Alex Cox's 1986 Sid Vicious/Nancy Spungen biopic *Sid and Nancy: Love Kills* – contextualised with reference to the British punk scene, the contemporary socio-political context and the continued flow of non-punk, rock-related films during the same broad period.[2] More recently, the US scholar Stacy Thompson's 2004 essay 'Punk Cinema'[3] has offered formal analyses of *The Punk Rock Movie* (Don Letts, 1978) and *Rude Boy* (Jack Hazan and David Mingay, 1980). However, Thompson's aim is to theorise a more generalised, extended concept of 'punk cinema', defined in terms of a 'dialectical relationship between aesthetics and economics' and ostensibly applicable not merely beyond the British, or 1970s, context but, by implication, to films not directly connected with punk rock or other aspects of punk culture.

For Thompson, punk cinema is 'non-Hollywoodised' and 'must bear, aesthetically and economically, a filmic version of punk's democratising dictum'; it 'employs an open, writerly aesthetic, engages with history, and critiques its own commodification'.[4] One difficulty with this definition is that it does not clarify how (if at all) 'punk cinema' is supposed to be distinct from other oppositional or 'alternative' film practices developed or theorised in other (often European or Third World) contexts. For an analysis of British punk films, it is unhelpful for two further reasons. First, it effaces their cultural specifics – when, as Donnelly rightly observes, *British* punk was striking precisely for 'its sheer Britishness'.[5] This was equally true of the British punk-related films; while they vary considerably in form and style, all are striking for their immersion in the conditions of 1970s Britain, British popular culture and British history, and their attendant indifference to the USA.

Second, the British films conformed rather variably with Thompson's notion of 'punk cinema'. It is notable that he develops his argument with reference only to a documentary (*The Punk Rock Movie*) and a semi-documentary (*Rude Boy*), both filmed in a 'transparent', observational mode, rather than the more radically hybrid, iconoclastic British punk features, notably *Jubilee* and *The Swindle*. In particular, *The Swindle*'s gleeful celebration of the advances and pay-offs notched up by the Pistols' (or rather, their manager, Malcolm McLaren's) management company, Glitterbest, from a succession of major record labels may not be quite what Thompson had in mind when he suggested that punk cinema 'critiques its own commodification'.[6]

This chapter joins Donnelly's article in seeking to address the critical neglect of the British punk (and post-punk) films but with more selective aims. First, I will explore the chronology of these films and seek to highlight significant patterns and connections – but also disconnections – between them. Second, I will crystallise some of the critical, institutional and contextual issues thus raised via a detailed consideration of Jarman's *Jubilee*. A crucial point, however, is that British punk's varied influences and heterodox nature, and the particularities of the films themselves, tend to undermine such neatly stated goals. Even when these films are approached centrally *as films* rather than as spin-offs from punk as a musical or (sub)cultural phenomenon, their influences emerge as by no means exclusively cinematic, while their consequences for subsequent developments in British film are at times enigmatic.

British Punk Films: An Untidy Chronology

As Donnelly notes, despite British punk rock's substantial cultural and – largely sensationalist – media impact, it 'produced very few films',[7] and still fewer that would be released (let alone widely seen) during the 1976–9 period he identifies as 'the white heat of punk'.[8] In view of this difficulty, this chapter takes 'the 1970s' to extend to those films produced and released by the end of 1980.[9] By 1979, only three feature-length films inspired by British punk had been made and released: *Punk in London* (Wolfgang Büld, West Germany, 1977), *Jubilee* and *The Punk Rock Movie*. Of these, two were documentaries, the first was German and only *Jubilee* received more than fleeting, London-only, distribution.

They were joined in 1979 by *Radio On* (UK/West Germany), the directorial debut of (then) *Time Out* film critic Christopher Petit – a downbeat road movie shot in black and white, which was not a punk film (opening with a scribbled quotation from the German electronic group Kraftwerk and drawing much of its soundtrack from artists, such as Ian Dury and the Blockheads and Wreckless Eric, whose roots were more in the pre-punk London pub-rock tradition) but which, Donnelly argues, 'tangibly benefited from punk's spirit'.[10] Evaluated from one perspective, *Radio On* was a hard-to-classify art movie – made with subsidy from the British Film Institute and the National Film Finance Corporation, and the patronage of the New German Cinema auteur Wim Wenders. From another angle, however, it can be viewed as the first – and longest – music promo for the first of the new independent record labels to emerge out of the British punk and pre-punk pub-rock scenes; the superb soundtrack was not only diegetically integrated into the film in ingenious, original ways but drawn centrally from artists signed to Stiff Records.[11]

Although *Punk in London* – shot by twenty-five-year-old Munich film student Büld on 16mm during a two-week visit in September 1977 – was edited in time for a December 1977 German premiere, neither it nor the similarly (un)structured *The Punk Rock Movie* (filmed on Super 8 at the Roxy Club, Covent Garden, by Don Letts, the Roxy's Rastafarian DJ) was screened publicly in London until the second half of 1978 (and then only briefly). This made Jarman's *Jubilee,* premiered in spring 1978, de facto the first British punk feature film. Importantly, it would remain the only wholly *imagined* British film response to the punk moment – given that the later fiction feature *Breaking Glass* (Brian Gibson, 1980) would owe more to post-punk, and *Sid and Nancy* would be a retro biopic. *Jubilee* also remains the most imaginative in grasping the sensibility and creative practices of punk (in the brief phase before it became neutralised into a mass-produced commodity) and in attempting a translation of these to film, as I explore further in the next section.

However, shaped as it was by a (Warholian) underground sensibility, the nature of Jarman's social circle (a self-conscious, gay-inflected glitterati of artists, designers and art-school pop figures from an older pre-punk generation) and lack of money,[12] *Jubilee* not only lacked the big names of British punk,[13] it was structured in a way calculated to frustrate spectators expecting complete or uninterrupted song footage of its featured performers. Not until 1980 was *Jubilee* followed by the release of the two films that most closely approximated to 'vehicles' for Britain's higher-profile punk bands, namely *The Great Rock 'n' Roll Swindle* (the Sex Pistols) and the drama-documentary *Rude Boy* (the Clash). The rapid rise and burnout of punk – and specifically the Pistols – had been such that by the time *The Swindle* went into production in mid-1978,[14] Johnny Rotten had already made his now-iconic walkout from the final gig of the Pistols' only US tour,[15] and both refused to cooperate with the film and held it up through legal action.[16]

One effect of this is that *The Swindle*'s soundtrack album was released a year before the film.[17] Moreover, at least some of the film's formal innovations can be read as a response to the need to find strategies for telling the Pistols' story without Rotten (notably in the animated sequences that narrate the band's trashing of the offices of A&M records during their six-day contract with the label and a street attack on Rotten at the height of their tabloid notoriety). As Donnelly notes, *The Swindle* was a 'fragmented and dislocated' entity, 'bricolaged from new and existing elements . . . to produce a picaresque roller-coaster ride'.[18] These elements extend from a highly anachronistic reconstruction of the 1778 anti-Catholic Gordon Riots (in which the Sex Pistols are burned in effigy) to the casting of British film and TV comedy veterans Irene Handl and Liz Fraser, thus inserting the Pistols into, on the one hand, a long history of English insurrection and, on the other, a lineage of British low culture. However, this 'bricolage' is structured, ostensibly, as a series of lessons from McLaren (billed as 'The Embezzler') – delivered in wheezing, Fagin-eseque tones from inside a rubber fetish hood – in how to manufacture a pop-culture phenomenon, swindle the music industry and dupe the media. The film's knowing,

Punk on film: Sid Vicious in *The Great Rock 'n' Roll Swindle* (1980)

complicit address of its audience fails to mitigate its status as, in Donnelly's words, 'a reorientation of [the Sex Pistols'] story around McLaren that others involved do not sanction'.[19] So much so that Julien Temple's 2000 documentary *The Filth and the Fury* – featuring extensive interview contributions from all the ex-Pistols – explicitly presents itself as a corrective to the McLaren version.

Rude Boy was premiered at the 1980 Berlin Film Festival and reached British cinemas ahead of *The Swindle*. It blends dramatised elements with documentary footage shot (mainly in London) from 1977 to 1979. These range from contemporary events – notably the violent, heavily policed street clashes between National Front supporters and anti-racists that prompted the formation of the Anti-Nazi League and its offshoot Rock Against Racism (RAR) – to onstage and off-duty footage of Clash members (including their performance at the 1978 RAR carnival in Victoria Park, Hackney). In stylistic contrast to *The Swindle*, *Rude Boy* was constructed to produce a comparatively seamless documentary-realist effect, while devoting sufficient screen time to dynamic, well-filmed concert footage to appeal to Clash fans. Yet, paradoxically, where

The Swindle was effectively a commercial production (its producers included the maverick Don Boyd, McLaren's management company and Virgin Films), *Rude Boy* was produced independently by its directors, Jack Hazan and David Mingay, without finance from the Clash or their (major) record label, CBS.[20] *Rude Boy*'s reported budget (£500,000) was, however, ten times that of *Jubilee*, and its UK distributor was the exploitation specialist Tigon. These tensions around the alternative/commercial/exploitation character of both films are at once consistent with the wider context of British film production, distribution and exhibition in the 1970s and characteristic of the wider corpus of British punk-related films.

Rude Boy is a loose, sprawling film characterised by an 'uncommercial' disregard for narrative economics or economy. While *Punk in London* and *The Punk Rock Movie* share a similar shapelessness, they had fewer pretensions – they were straight documentaries, simply alternating live performances of punk bands with interviews and footage of their fans – and were much shorter than *Rude Boy*'s two-and-a-quarter hours. Hazan and Mingay impose a narrative (of sorts) via a fictional storyline in which a Clash fan and aspiring roadie, Ray Gange (who plays himself), is taken up and dropped by the group. This story is temporally defined by bookending the film with footage of two events from the realm of Establishment history: Queen Elizabeth II's procession through London in celebration of her Silver Jubilee in summer 1977 and the election of Margaret Thatcher's Conservative government in May 1979. Everything else in *Rude Boy* operates in a tacit counterpoint to these images and what they signify. A further, submerged narrative strand (no doubt dramatised but with the appearance of documentary) traces the surveillance, arrest and imprisonment of a south London black youth framed by corrupt police. His fate is presumably intended to present a parallel – or contrast? – with that of Gange, but this is never articulated.

Donnelly writes that *Rude Boy* 'has a palpably radical agenda, played out [in part] through onscreen discussions about Socialism', while also seeking to validate the Clash 'as still retaining their vocal social criticism, despite their increasingly corporate status'.[21] But in a film that eschews interpretation, and in which the distinction between (presumably) staged and documentary scenes is constantly effaced, this attempt becomes both problematic and ambiguous. *Rude Boy* over-relies on reaching an already-sympathetic audience predisposed to accept it as radical critique rather than incoherent posturing.

Between *Rude Boy* and *The Swindle* came *Breaking Glass*, an unapologetically mainstream, unpretentious fiction feature tracing the rise, exploitation and crash of a spikily idealistic young female singer-songwriter, Kate (the unknown Hazel O'Connor, who also wrote the songs and enjoyed brief pop stardom as a result of the film). Accounts of punk films (British or otherwise) tend to dismiss *Breaking Glass* or exclude it from the category; O'Connor, 'discovered' for the film, was not a 'real' punk. For Donnelly, *Breaking Glass* 'demonstrates vividly the iconography of post-punk music' but is merely 'a highly conventional backstage musical story . . . dressed up . . . in punk apparel'.[22] Despite such reactions, *Breaking Glass* is worthy of brief consideration, as are the reasons for its dismissal. It lacked the participation of real (extra-diegetically existent) bands on the soundtrack or on screen, but its central problem – from a film-critical and punk perspective alike – was that it operated within well-worn narrative and genre conventions. Its highly conventional style showed no awareness that a punk or post-punk aesthetic might be expressed through film. Its credibility was further compromised by its 'AA' certificate, making it

Radical critique or incoherent posturing: *Rude Boy* (1980)

the first of the punk or post-punk feature films to address – and be able legally to reach – a younger audience who had missed the original punk scene.

In its defence, *Breaking Glass* included Phil Daniels (billed above O'Connor as the star) in one of his fresh, guileless early performances (following *Scum* [Alan Clarke] and *Quadrophenia* [Franc Roddam] in 1979), as Danny, a young record plugger who becomes Kate's promoter and her boyfriend, but is sidelined by record-company sharks. It marked the feature debut of Jonathan Pryce in an affecting performance as the band's deaf saxophonist who becomes addicted to heroin. It also convincingly inhabited the authentic territory of 1970s London's alternative music scene (from vile pubs to renowned venues such as the Music Machine in Camden and the Rainbow Theatre, Finsbury Park). Thus, despite its limitations, it featured engaging performances from a new generation of young actors and belonged to a transitional moment in the move towards a younger, more realist, popular British cinema.

Breaking Glass also gains significance as the only British punk-related film apart from *Jubilee* to centre on a female protagonist. This is strange, given that, as Michael O'Pray notes, 'the role of women in punk was more forceful and provocative than in any previous pop music movement',[23] and punk's liberating impact for women has been widely acknowledged. Simon Frith and Howard Horne observe that punk 'from the start raised questions about sexual codes',[24] opening up a space where women felt unconstrained and able to enter on their own terms. These female punk vocalists and musicians are highly visible and audible – yet rarely commented on – in early documentaries such as *Punk in London*, while women were surprisingly marginal or marginalised in *Rude Boy* and *The Swindle*.

Jubilee as Case Study

Kevin J. Donnelly comments that punk 'shocked Britain through the front pages of the tabloid newspapers, and brought about significant changes in the worlds of pop music and fashion, [but] it was not as influential in the cinema'.[25] It is productive, however, to ask whether punk *should* have been expected to translate to film, and to consider some of the counter-arguments as to why it might not. This section will seek to distil this and other critical, institutional and contextual questions via a consideration of *Jubilee*.

A reality little acknowledged is that film was *not* the productive medium of choice for most of those inspired by punk's DIY ethos and its (Situationist-inflected) emphasis on self-expression rather than being a mere cultural consumer. The expense of the pre-digital film technologies available in the mid- to late 1970s was only one reason: the non-spontaneity and protracted timescale of conventional film-making were fundamentally antithetical to punk's ethic of instantaneous creativity. A related issue is that punk was a verbal and performative medium at least as much as it was a visual one. Much of its impact came from the iconoclasm of its song lyrics and how these were intoned/performed; while both its wider creative practices and its 'look' owed more to graphics, text, print, graffiti and fashion than to cinema. In this context, the thriving independent culture spawned by British punk did not, on the whole, embrace DIY film-making. As we have seen, the British punk films were typically commercial/art cinema/exploitation hybrids and were rarely untouched by financial imperatives. While the early punk documentaries might seem an exception to this, Donnelly notes that even Letts's apparently amateur *The Punk Rock Movie* 'was produced by Peter Clifton, a seasoned pop music filmmaker', director of Led Zeppelin's *The Song Remains the Same* (1975).[26]

The saturation of the (otherwise ailing) 1970s British film industry by the porn and exploitation sectors – alongside the emergence of notions of, and venues for, cult film – arguably had considerable significance in shaping the terms in which the British punk films were promoted and circulated. Interestingly, these porn/exploitation connections extended to films – like *Jubilee*, and even *Radio On* – usually discussed as art cinema. The notoriety that could be milked from the 'X' certificate was crucial to the marketing of *Jubilee* as much as *The Swindle*. *Jubilee* featured much casual nudity, an implied threesome between incestuous gay brothers Sphinx (Karl Johnson) and Angel (Ian Charleson) and artist Viv (Linda Spurrier), a recidivist nymphomaniac named Crabs (Little Nell, aka Nell Campbell) and considerable violence, including the graphic (if visibly low-budget) murder of four men by its core gang of female protagonists.

The actions of *Jubilee*'s pointedly post-sexual female posse (Crabs excepted) were, however, conceived as a deliberate inversion of the gender norms of sexual violence, inspired in part by Valerie Solanas's notorious 1968 anti-patriarchal *SCUM* ('Society for Cutting Up Men') *Manifesto*.[27] This point was understood by the BBFC; despite professed concerns about copycat violence (in the wake of Stanley Kubrick's 1971 *A Clockwork Orange*), they accepted Jarman's argument that *Jubilee*'s violence was 'unglamourized, quite real and seen negatively' and demanded only one cut.[28] In retrospect, this response seems particularly enlightened given the abject sexism still routine in British popular culture at the time and that *Jubilee*'s extreme Swiftean take on gender power relations was ahead of its time in relation to both radical-feminist landmarks such as *A Question of Silence* (Marleen Gorris, Netherlands, 1982) and the rape-revenge exploitation cycle exemplified by *Ms 45: Angel of Vengeance* (Abel Ferrara, USA, 1980).

Where *Jubilee* offered dark satire and sexual subversion, the explicit tendencies of other punk films were more a reflection of the 'pornification' of mainstream 1970s British culture than a counter-reaction.[29] *The Swindle* slung together exploitation ingredients – a nude pubescent girl morphs into early punk 'face' Soo Catwoman; British porn star Mary Millington has public sex with Pistol Steve Jones in a cinema foyer – in a calculated and slightly desperate effort to keep the Pistols' 'brand' controversial after the band's demise. In *Rude Boy*, Gange's employment in a porn shop naturalises this 'pornification' as a fact of life. By contrast, in *Radio On* the darker side of the porno-economy becomes a narrative element, as the protagonist Robert (David Beames) drives to Bristol to investigate the death of his brother. Where virtually all the punk films invoke the social disintegration of 1970s Britain by referencing the National Front, the news bulletins on Robert's car radio oscillate between the conflict in Northern Ireland and the smashing of a porn ring in the West Country.

Jubilee remains the most inventive and subversive of the British cinematic responses to punk, to a great extent because of its intelligent grasp of punk's dissenting rhetoric, preferred modes of expression and resulting aesthetics. Of the other films discussed in this chapter, only the early documentaries (particularly Büld's filmed-in-a-fortnight *Punk in London*) can really be said to embody a 'punk' mode of production, but *Jubilee* achieved this to more creatively ambitious, visionary effect. Jarman's success can be attributed variously to his distinctly English and queer politics of dissent, and his position as a close, yet ambivalent and critical, observer of the punk scene from outside. But perhaps most significant is his (self-described) 'home-movie' approach to film-making and lifelong insistence on his own amateurism.

Jarman's own notes testify to *Jubilee*'s conception as a spontaneous response to punk – and, through this, 1970s Britain's wider malaise – and to his intention that its collaged mode of development should find aesthetic expression in the finished film. An existing script about the Elizabethan alchemist, kabbalist and court adviser Dr John Dee [30] 'was pirated and used as a framing device . . . scrambled with [borrowings from the punk fanzines] *SNIFFin Glue* and *London's OUTRAGE*',[31] and a sequence choppily re-edited footage from Jarman's 1977 short film *Jordan's Dance*, in which female punk icon Jordan[32] performs classical ballet in an urban wasteland of burning books:

> [*Jubilee*] was a determined and often reckless analysis of the world which surrounded us, constructed pell-mell through the early months of 1977. The shooting script is a mass of quick notes on scraps of paper, torn photos and messages from my collaborators, and the resulting film has some of the same quality.[33]

While it is precisely these scrapbook, mixed-media qualities that make *Jubilee* distinctively a 'punk' film, they have presented difficulties for many critics in forming an appropriate response to it. Jarman intertwines two diegetic strands that are dialectically related but different in tone. Queen Elizabeth I (Jenny Runacre) bids her astrologer/confidant John Dee (Richard O'Brien) to deliver her 'knowledge of the future'. Dee summons the spirit Ariel (David Haughton), who transports Elizabeth, Dee and a dwarf lady-in-waiting (punk Helen Wellington-Lloyd, who also appears in *The Swindle*) to 'the shadow of this time': a dystopian near future that happens to look like 1970s London, specifically the derelict hinterland beyond Jarman's studio at Shad Thames. Here law and order have been abolished, sounds of demolition and machine-gunfire can be heard and girl punks use a female captive as a human maypole, dispassionately wrapping her in barbed wire.

The Virgin Queen's double in this future England is the coldly regal, androgynous Bod (Runacre again). She is first glimpsed only distantly as she mugs Queen Elizabeth II on some waste ground, later making her grand entrance into the group's warehouse squat wearing the crown. We have already met most of the other inhabitants – crop-headed pyromaniac Mad (Toyah Willcox), the brothers, Viv and a tightrope-walking French au pair named Chaos (Hermine Demoriane) – via a voiceover introduction from Amyl Nitrate (Jordan), the group's intellectual, who delivers a provocative alternative history lesson ('What separates Hitler from Napoleon? Was Churchill a hero? Did he change history for the better?'). However, as Amyl's own speech and the film's later events uneasily highlight, her professed motto – the Situationist slogan '*Faites vos desirs realité*: make your desires reality' – could be a recipe for fascism or murder as easily as liberation.

Jubilee's future England seems at once lawless and totalitarian (whether of the Left or the Right is unclear and scarcely matters). Power is privatised in the hands of the monopolistic media – embodied by the film's most outrageous creation, the all-powerful proto-Murdoch magnate Borgia Ginz (Orlando, aka the blind actor Jack Birkett), source of the quotation in this chapter's title. Across several superbly aphoristic speeches, he sets out his business philosophy ('As long as the music is loud enough, we won't hear the world falling apart') and sketches a world in which commodified mediation has not only replaced the real but has swallowed political and religious institutions of East and West, Left and Right alike.

Despite their apparent anti-Establishment posturing, Bod, Amyl and Mad – as much as the sexually susceptible Crabs – all prove to be eager acolytes of Ginz's media empire. As Ginz himself predicts, 'They all sign up in the end.' In one of *Jubilee*'s defining set pieces, Amyl, signed by Ginz as 'Britain's entry to the Eurovision Song Contest', mimes to 'Rule Britannia',[34] gyrating in a faded plastic Union Jack apron – Britannia dwarfed by mirrors and dry ice, looking increasingly peeved as the sounds of a Luftwaffe air-raid and Hitler's speeches intrude. The film closes with the foursome holed up in Ginz's stately home in Dorset – now a passport-controlled mini-state with its borders policed by armed guards. Their fellow house guest is Adolf Hitler, 'the

greatest artist of the 20th century', not dead after all. A troubled Elizabeth and Dee end the film in a more elegiac Dorset, but even here 'the sky seem[s] somewhat dark'.

In closing, three particular points should be noted regarding *Jubilee*'s character as a 'punk' film. First, as observed by Julian Upton, it often 'seems less like Jarman's vision than one of a punk cinema collective'.[35] Second is the success of Jarman, his performers and his production designers (John Maybury, plus Kenny Morris of Siouxsie and the Banshees) in translating the visual, verbal and performative aspects of punk aesthetics to film. This is achieved through *mise en scène*, dialogue, styles of performance and *Jubilee*'s structure as a sequence of set pieces. The achievement of a punk *mise en scène* is especially striking in the styling of the warehouse inhabited by Bod, Mad, *et al.* A densely graffiti'd wall serves as backdrop to Amyl Nitrate's history lesson; her customised globe obliterates both superpowers to 'Negative World Status'; her desk is surrounded by books and ornaments (including an ironic Winston Churchill mug); defaced Xeroxed images decorate the walls alongside real late-1970s newspaper headline posters: 'Sex Pistol no. 2 knifed'. Notwithstanding its imaginative design, *Jubilee*'s pleasures are, centrally, verbal and performative, the latter ranging from the over-the-top relish with which Orlando delivers Borgia Ginz's speeches, to Jordan's set pieces. In a different acting mode, Adam Ant's gauche, giggling performance as punk hopeful Kid exposes the absurdity of a po-faced speech from Sphinx ('My generation's the blank generation').

Third, in contrast with most of the other British punk and post-punk films, punk *music* in *Jubilee* is rarely presented directly, but more usually mediated or interrupted. As Tracy Biga notes, Jarman's films tend to disrupt narrative and frustrate its patriarchal logic through strategies including 'the eruption of varied modes, such as the music video . . . [and] use of tableaux'.[36] In *Jubilee*, these interruptions extend to the presentation of the music itself, which thus itself becomes a comment on punk's predicted commodification and neutralisation. In a characteristic scene, three of the film's featured bands appear in succession on the TV in the warehouse squat (ostensibly on *Top of the Pops*) but are largely ignored by the assembled protagonists. *Jubilee*'s only 'live' performance by a real band – Adam and the Ants' audition for Ginz – is truncated, while an audition by Mad (with invented band 'The Maneaters') takes place behind a glass screen, ignored by Ginz while he conducts (more amusing) business with a minion.

In Conclusion

In a dissenting analysis of the films of Jarman and Peter Greenaway, A. L. Rees argues that neither is genuinely avant-garde due to their attraction 'towards the theatrical, the literary and the symbolic', resulting in 'highly text-driven' films.[37] My analysis above has suggested that British punk rock was likewise defined in part by 'text-driven' qualities – and also that, paradoxically, some of the qualities that might disqualify *Jubilee* as an 'avant-garde' film also make it one of the most effective cinematic responses to punk. Notwithstanding their diverse aesthetics, and variable quality and success with audiences, a key achievement of the wider corpus of British punk and post-punk films was precisely that they contributed to the opening up of a hybrid space for alternative possibilities in British cinema unconstrained by either the woefulness of its 1970s 'commercial' sector or the purist notion of 'independent' film favoured by Rees.

(Opposite page) Amyl Nitrate (Jordan) reinvents Britannia for Derek Jarman's *Jubilee* (1978)

In its aesthetics, sensibility and vision of contemporary Britain, *Jubilee* – alongside Petit's *Radio On* and Jarman's wider 1970s work – helped to open up the aesthetics and subjects available to contemporary British cinema, paving the way for the 'new' British art cinema that would emerge more fully in the 1980s. *The Swindle* and *Breaking Glass* can be contextualised as products of a transitional phase in the renewal of a popular genre-based British cinema that would likewise evolve more adventurously during the 1980s. But despite this vanguard role, the one-off iconoclasm of *Jubilee* and *Radio On* – and equally the one-off nature of the other punk films – also set them apart from later developments, while presenting difficulties for their critical interpretation. While in the DVD age (the initially unprofitable) *Jubilee* continues to find new admirers, such factors may explain the relative critical neglect of the British punk and post-punk films, which are barely mentioned in most of the recent work on British cinema.

Notes

1 Kevin J. Donnelly, 'British Punk Films: Rebellion into Money, Nihilism into Innovation', *Journal of Popular British Cinema*, no. 1, 1998, pp. 101–14.
2 For an account of these films, see Donnelly, 'British Punk Films', pp. 103–4 and 107.
3 Stacy Thompson, 'Punk Cinema', *Cinema Journal*, vol. 43, no. 2, 2004, pp. 47–66.
4 Ibid., pp. 47–8.
5 Donnelly, 'British Punk Films', p. 101.
6 Thompson, 'Punk Cinema', p. 47.
7 Donnelly, 'British Punk Films', p. 101.
8 Ibid.
9 I therefore exclude the US documentary *D.O.A.: A Right of Passage* (Lech Kowalski, 1981), which focused on British punk from a US perspective but relied heavily on footage of the Sex Pistols' US tour that had already been released on video, 1986's *Sid and Nancy*, and 2000's *The Filth and the Fury*.
10 Donnelly, 'British Punk Film', p. 105.
11 Stiff (founded 1976) was the blueprint for most of the British independent record labels that followed.
12 Jarman reported that *Jubilee* was funded with a £50,000 cheque from an unexplained source in Tehran by his producer James Whaley 'one week before . . . shooting'. Derek Jarman, *Dancing Ledge* (London: Quartet, 1984), p. 168.
13 Jarman reputedly wanted the Buzzcocks for *Jubilee* but could not afford their fare from Manchester, so instead cast London bands/performers he had already encountered. Toyah Willcox (cast as Mad) was at that time an actress but became a post-punk pop star in the 1980s.
14 McLaren had first attempted a Sex Pistols film in 1977 titled *Who Killed Bambi?* (with Russ Meyer hired as director), but production ceased when the crew walked out due to non-payment. The title survives as a song/segment (performed by Edward Tudor-Pole of the band Tenpole Tudor) towards the close of *The Swindle*.
15 Rotten (John Lydon) walked away from the Pistols on 14 January 1978 and formally left the group three days later.
16 Donnelly, 'British Punk Films', p. 108.
17 Ibid.
18 Ibid.
19 Ibid., p. 107.

20 Thompson, 'Punk Cinema', p. 52.
21 Donnelly, 'British Punk Cinema', p. 108.
22 Ibid., p. 110.
23 Michael O'Pray, *Derek Jarman: Dreams of England* (London: BFI, 1996), p. 96.
24 Simon Frith and Howard Horne, *Art into Pop* (London: Methuen, 1987), p. 155.
25 Donnelly, 'British Punk Films', p. 101.
26 Ibid., p. 105.
27 Jarman, interviewed by Claire Monk, *Psychotic Snark* fanzine, no. 3, 1986.
28 Jarman, *Dancing Ledge*, p. 170 [his spelling].
29 The term 'pornification' was coined by Leon Hunt in his study *British Low Culture: From Safari Suits to Sexploitation* (London: Routledge, 1998). Hunt suggests that 1970s British culture became 'pornified' in the sense that pornographic values permeated mainstream media forms such as TV comedy.
30 See O'Pray, *Derek Jarman*, pp. 73 and 99–104.
31 Jarman, *Dancing Ledge*, p. 168 [his capitalisation].
32 Jordan (real name Pamela Rooke) became prominent in the punk scene as an assistant at Vivienne Westwood's boutique Sex. At the time of *Jubilee*'s production, she was briefly manager of Adam and the Ants, hence the casting of Adam as Kid.
33 Jarman, *Dancing Ledge*, p. 176.
34 'Rule Britannia' is sung not by Jordan but by Suzi Pinns.
35 Julian Upton, 'Anarchy in the UK: Derek Jarman's *Jubilee* Revisited', *Bright Lights Film Journal*, no. 30, October 2000, <www.brightlightsfilm. com/30/jubilee> (accessed 3 March 2007).
36 Tracy Biga, 'The Principle of Non-Narration in the Films of Derek Jarman', in Chris Lippard (ed.), *By Angels Driven: The Films of Derek Jarman* (Trowbridge, Wiltshire: Flicks Books, 1996), p. 13.
37 A. L. Rees, *A History of Experimental Film and Video* (London: BFI, 1999), p. 100.

9 Nothing to do around Here: British Realist Cinema in the 1970s

James Leggott

Many accounts of British cinema suggest, or at least imply, that the 1970s was a fallow period for the production of realist feature films. The development of an indigenous strain of social realist cinema has been traced from its origins in the 1930s documentary movement, via the 'kitchen sink' cycle of the late 1950s and early 1960s, to contemporary manifestations such as *The Full Monty* (1997) and *Nil by Mouth* (1997).[1] While the cultural significance of the New Wave films has been called into question, there is broad agreement that industry and audience alike soon lost patience with the socially committed films produced during this time by Anderson, Richardson, Schlesinger, Reisz, *et al.* According to Geoff Brown, 'by the mid-60s, images of direct social observation were far more likely to be found on television than in the cinema'.[2] Samantha Lay goes further, claiming that the director Ken Loach was 'almost singly responsible for sustaining social realist texts' during the late 1960s and 1970s.[3] That Loach was only able to produce two rather untypical cinema features during the 1970s gives credence to the commonly held view of the decade as a bleak time indeed for the film industry. This was also an era of frustration for another director who has maintained a reputation for a commitment to realist practice (albeit of a very different sort to that of Loach). Mike Leigh began his film career with *Bleak Moments* (1971), but it would be seventeen years before he produced his second theatrically distributed film, during which time, like Loach, he worked mostly for television.

The realist impulse of British cinema, apparently near-dormant since the decline of the 'kitchen-sink' cycle, is generally reckoned to have re-emerged in the 1980s, invigorated partly by a widespread distaste for Thatcherite economic policies, but also, ironically enough, by the opportunities opened up by their application to the industry – most significantly, the arrival of Channel 4 with its patronage of low-budget, socially committed drama.[4] Films such as *My Beautiful Laundrette* (1985), *High Hopes* (1988) and *Letter to Brezhnev* (1985) tend to be bracketed together, alongside the more stylised work of Peter Greenaway, Terence Davies and Derek Jarman, as proof of the arrival of a truly oppositional cinema. For Peter Wollen, these works constitute a wave of 'delayed modernism', a far more challenging cycle of texts than that of the original so-called New Wave.[5] Christopher Williams identifies the evolution of a 'social art cinema', fusing together 'issues of social concern' with aspects more familiar in the tradition of European art cinema.[6]

The generous critical attention given both to the New Wave and the films of the Thatcher era further reinforces the notion of the 1970s as a period of insignificance for realist cinema.[7] Yet there has been some effort to locate a number of the realist-oriented films of the period within discourses of representation: for example, *Pressure* (1977) has been hailed as a landmark work in the development of a vigorous black British cinema.[8] The roots of later developments, such as the emergence of social art cinema and the vogue for regional comedy, have been found in work by Bill Douglas and Bill Forsyth respectively, while the early films of other auteurs (for example, Terence Davis, Loach and Leigh) have been situated within the context of their continuing oeuvre.[9]

It is possible that the relative disinterest in some important films in the realist vein, such as *Bronco Bullfrog* (1969), *Akenfield* (1974) and *Nighthawks* (1978), stems chiefly from their resistance to straightforward categorisation. Despite depicting a range of different experiences, there are sufficient commonalities across these, and other 1970s films, to strengthen the case

Pressure (1977), a landmark in the development of black British cinema

for a thematically coherent, if sporadic, tradition of socially committed British cinema. In particular, these films are characterised by a shared ambivalence towards the idea of home and they frequently invoke a tension between stasis and processes of transformation or escape. This may not be surprising, given that they are produced during an era of social and political upheaval, a decade characterised by industrial disputes, economic hardships and increasingly prominent debates around issues of gender and race. In keeping with the realist texts of the years that preceded and followed, however, there is an emphasis upon individual escape or resistance, rather than collective action.[10]

Taken together, the films under scrutiny here support a definition of the social realist film as a demonstration of the interrelationship between character and place. At the same time, they are often innovatory in their depiction of hitherto under-represented environments and experiences. This commitment to 'social extension', as defined by Raymond Williams, tends to be accompanied by strategies aimed at ensuring authenticity, such as the use of location shooting and the involvement of non-actors as performers or advisers.[11] A concern for naturalism often sits together with a degree of visual stylisation or structural complexity; a conflict between tradition and innovation is thus played out at both a thematic and formal level.

It is not difficult to identify films produced in the 1970s that draw upon, albeit to different ends, the iconography, preoccupations and 'look' of the kitchen-sink films. A fair number are shot in black and white, and texts as diverse as *Get Carter* (1971), *The Likely Lads* (1976) and even, to a much lesser degree, *Spring and Port Wine* (1970) rely on familiar signifiers of the industrial north of Britain: sloping terraces, grimy canals and cramped houses. A notable development, however, is the geographical extension of the realist film from the working-class north to other parts of the UK such as Scotland, the rural south and London (which arguably offers greater scope for the representation of non-dominant communities). More significantly, there is a continued fascination with the struggles of young men to escape the stifling domesticity of urban or suburban environments. Echoes are frequently found of New Wave works such as *Saturday Night and Sunday Morning* (1960), *A Kind of Loving* (1962) and *Room at the Top* (1959) that had led towards (and lamented) the containment of the subversive energies of the 'angry young man' through marriage.

Two consciously backward-looking films of the 1970s, *That'll Be the Day* (1973) and *The Likely Lads*, weigh up the prospect of resistance; that is, they sketch out the paths not taken by the stone-throwing Arthur Seaton and his ilk. Set during the late 1950s, *That'll Be the Day* is the story of Jim MacLean (David Essex), who throws away the chance of a place at university, thereby rejecting the road to middle-class conformity taken by his peers. He chooses instead an itinerant lifestyle of jobs in the leisure industry and at the type of locations traditionally posited in the British social realist text as sites of either transitory escape or sexual experimentation: a seaside resort, a funfair and a Butlins-style holiday camp. Initially unpolished in the skills of sexual conquest, he is mentored in the art of the one-night-stand by Mike (Ringo Starr), a fellow worker, to the point that his increasing boldness – which comes to a peak with his bedding a much younger girl – shocks even his teacher.[12] As in the New Wave films, however, this form of recklessness cannot go unpunished, although here it is Mike who receives a beating for his promiscuity, in a fairground-set sequence that echoes a similar turn of events in *Saturday Night and Sunday Morning*. Seemingly weary of his nomadic adventure, Jim returns home, succumbing at last to a conventional suburban existence when his chaste courtship of a local girl leads to marriage and the birth of a son. But this is not to be. *That'll Be the Day* begins with a sequence showing Jim's disaffected father walking out on his wife and young child and concludes with the repetition of family history. Having become increasingly drawn to the world of rock 'n' roll, Jim abandons his own wife and child, and sets off for new adventures. Liberatory, yet predetermined (by way of his gender and upbringing), this is a gesture both transgressive and habitual.

We find out exactly where Jim goes next in *Stardust* (1974), which outlines the course of his career from overnight pop stardom to his overdose on live television towards the end of the 1960s. A kind of suburban death may well have been narrowly avoided, but the enervation, even emasculation, that results from Jim's newly found life of hedonism and exploitation becomes a belated punishment for his wanderlust. Ensconced in a sterile, Xanadu-like mansion, his creative career reaches its nadir with a pompous rock opera extolling the virtues of womanhood; an insufficient atonement for the wrongs done unto his mother, wife and lovers.

A more light-hearted take on this theme of the restless young male and his bumpy ride to maturity is found in *The Likely Lads*, written by Dick Clement and Ian La Frenais. Typifying the decade's trend for cinematic spin-offs from popular television sitcoms, *The Likely Lads* continues the saga of northerners Bob and Terry, first encountered in the 1960s comedy of the same name (1964–6), then rediscovered almost a decade later in *Whatever Happened to the Likely Lads?* (1973–4). Although the film's episodic plot uses the standard generic device of removing characters from their familiar environment, the relocation of Bob and Terry from the city to the countryside, and then the seaside, neatly illustrates the impossibility of escape. Their trip to a caravan site carries a promise of the kind of rural respite enjoyed by the characters in *The Loneliness of the Long Distant Runner* (1962), *A Taste of Honey* (1961) and *Kes* (1969). However, the rows of identical vehicles at the site offer only a grotesque parody of suburban uniformity. There follows an attempt to recapture the (sexual) freedom of their youth at an appropriately out-of-season seaside resort, but events take a farcical turn and they return home trouserless and penitent.

Of the two men, it is the conformist Bob – safely settled into a life of domestic orderliness – rather than the promiscuous, ever-mobile Terry, who suffers pangs of nostalgia at the demolition of their derelict childhood haunts. In response to his lament at seeing his past being 'bulldozed away', his pragmatic friend retorts that such nostalgia is merely a middle-class indulgence. Such mockery of the sentimentality of the 'outsider' for the decline of working-class tradition is particularly stinging, as it is a charge that has been levelled at British social realist cinema made before and since. Critiques of the New Wave films have examined how the privileged perspective of the (largely) middle-class film-makers is made manifest in the reoccurrence of certain visual tropes, such as, in Andrew Higson's words, 'That Long Shot of Our Town from That Hill'.[13] In contrast, a case could be made for the heightened self-awareness of 1970s realist texts. Both *That'll Be the Day* and *The Likely Lads* acknowledge their ambivalence towards their subjects through the incorporation of characters that embody differing perspectives. In *That'll Be the Day*, Jim's revolt against his future destiny is compared with the university career, and implied embourgeoisement, of a schoolfriend.[14]

A prominent aspect of realist-inflected film-making of the era is its increasing interest in the issue of teenage delinquency; again, the theme of individual escape predominates. A handful of

Bob (Rodney Bewes) and Terry (James Bolam) in the film version of *The Likely Lads* (1976)

films produced towards the end of the decade, such as *Quadrophenia* (1979) and *Scum* (1979), have subsequently achieved near-iconic status for their portrayal of charismatic rebels and introduction of fresh acting talent, and been placed alongside equivalent 'cult' texts such as *If. . . .* (1968) and *Trainspotting* (1996). Based on a 1973 rock opera by The Who, *Quadrophenia* tells the story of a young man who gets drawn into a clash between Mods and Rockers, rival youth tribes that infamously came to blows in seaside resorts in the mid-1960s. As another example of a kind of 'youth heritage' picture, it is a more straightforward work than *That'll Be the Day* in that it ultimately posits adolescent nonconformity as merely a passing phase. The film concludes with the lead character alighting (or so it would seem) from his motorcycle prior to sending it over a cliff; the eradication of this totem of his teenage past signifies his reluctant entry into adulthood.

The austerity in style and setting of the borstal drama *Scum* gives an allegorical resonance to its eventful narrative. While Roy Minton's screenplay makes a case for the dehumanising processes of the reform system (and, indeed, of the hierarchical British class system itself), it also offers a succinct summary of the empowering strategies employed by the youthful rebels of British realist cinema. The articulate, anti-Establishment Archer (Mick Ford), with his claims of vegetarianism and atheism, continues a tradition of bumptious troublemakers vowing not (in

Arthur Seaton's words) to 'let the bastards grind you down'. A more apt reference point, perhaps, is the ambiguously political subversion of Colin Smith in that earlier account of borstal life, *The Loneliness of the Long Distance Runner*. As a contrast, the necessarily bloody rise of Carlin (Ray Winstone) to the coveted position of 'daddy' places him within a line of brawny characters – Joe Lampton, Frank Machin in *This Sporting Life* (1963), Ray in *Nil by Mouth* – that exploit their physical charisma as a means to an end. By way of the fate of two new inmates, Alan Clarke's film also acknowledges the relative invisibility in this mode of film-making of the experiences of those who are 'othered' in some fashion. A sensitive new arrival, singled out for being 'queer', is gang-raped when on gardening duty; the occurrence of this violation in the apparent safety of the potting shed is a grim rebuttal of the trope of the 'rural' as escapist refuge – as found, not least, in *The Loneliness of the Long Distance Runner*. His suicide, following the incident, triggers a futile riot at the end of the film. Another 'trainee' (Angel) suffers violence and racist taunts from warders and other boys for the colour of his skin.

The connection between youth and trauma is even more pronounced in the autobiographical films made during the 1970s by Terence Davies and Bill Douglas. Their highly stylised take on the privations of working-class life and its impact on adult development have stimulated debates as to their place within the realist canon.[15] Nevertheless, their subject matter is in keeping with the predominant concerns of the realist texts discussed here. The main character of the *Bill Douglas Trilogy*, a child in *My Childhood* (1972) and *My Ain Folk* (1973), then finally a young adult in *My Way Home* (1978), is shuttled back and forth, almost arbitrarily, between family residences, authority homes and hostels of equivalent bleakness. The viewer shares Jamie's bewilderment at the complex topography of neglectful, unfaithful or ailing relatives that constitutes his oppressive little universe. Finally, in the last film, his friendship with an Englishman while on National Service in Egypt appears to stimulate a creative impulse; his 'way home' is, more accurately, a way out. No such liberation is available to Tucker, the solitary, troubled protagonist of *Children* (1976), the first part of Davies's own trilogy (completed in 1983). Shifting between the character's childhood and young adulthood, the film diagnoses the lasting damage of sexual and religious oppression, and introduces, too, the methods and themes of the director's subsequent work.

Among the youth-centred films produced during the period, *Bronco Bullfrog* stands out as a rarity for not telling its story of disaffected teenagers from either a satiric, nostalgic or autobiographical perspective. It is a loosely plotted work, with functional black-and-white cinematography and undemonstrative performances that border on the monosyllabic. For his first film feature, the director Barney Platts-Mills drew inspiration from the Italian neo-realist principle of not only reflecting the real experiences of those from a particular neighbourbood, but 'getting the people themselves to act them in their natural locations'.[16] The script was developed out of the suggestions of a group of potentially delinquent Stratford teenagers who had been brought together by Joan Littlewood's Playbarn project to devise work based on their everyday experiences.

The main character, Del, is on friendly terms with both his boss and his father (who he lives with), and takes pride in his work as a welder's apprentice, but he is bored by his environment and social life: '[there's] nothing to do around here', he tells his father. Gang scuffles and petty robbery provide the only means for 'kicks' and, far from being a deterrent, prison provides a valuable education in how to pull off 'jobs' (robberies); Del is chastised by Bronco Bullfrog, a more worldly acquaintance fresh out of borstal, for an unsophisticated burglary that only nets the gang a handful of cake. Del's limited options become apparent when his courtship of a fifteen-year-old girl incurs the wrath of his father and the girl's mother. Hopes of a refuge in the countryside with his uncle are dashed when the scarcity of local work is made clear, and a brief stay in Bronco's flat – where boxes of stolen goods are the only furnishings – gives a taster of the rootless life of those existing beyond the mainstream economy. From this point, the narrative takes a Loachian turn towards escalating crisis: Del's motorbike, his means of mobility, is crushed, he stoically takes a beating – something of a rite of passage in British realist films – and the police are alerted to his 'abduction' of the girl. As in *My Name Is Joe* (1998) and *Ae Fond Kiss* (2004), the protagonist is faced with an impossible choice: he can return home to complete his apprenticeship and settle into conformist adulthood or accept a life of peripatetic labouring. Conjuring up recollections of Truffaut's *Les Quatre cents coups* (1959), the film's freeze-frame ending leaves the young lovers on a quayside, on the run to an uncertain future.

With its representation of characters that could be said to form part of a growing 'underclass', *Bronco Bullfrog* anticipates one of the significant concerns of the British realist cinema of the 1980s and 1990s. As a work of social extension that evolved out of the actual experiences of its participants, it can be ranked alongside *Akenfield* and *Nighthawks*, two similarly pioneering films of the decade.

Akenfield's depiction of a Suffolk farming community takes its inspiration from Ronald Blythe's poetically tinged book of oral history (published in 1969) by incorporating documentary elements within a more artful framework. Filmed at weekends over the course of a year, so as not to disrupt the working lives of the locals (mostly playing themselves), *Akenfield* is notable for its painterly cinematography, reliance upon natural light sources and evocative score by Michael Tippett. At the heart of the film lies the dilemma faced by Tom, a young villager, on the day of his grandfather's funeral: whether to settle into marriage, and into the house vacated by his grandparents, or to leave the town alone and break a generational cycle of farm work. This expectation of continuity is emphasised by the flashback sequences (often introduced by way of seamless graphic matches or trick panning shots) where Tom 'plays' his own father and grandfather. These scenes indicate how Tom is traumatised not so much by the past but by intimations of his own future should he remain in Akenfield.

Throughout the film there is a commentary from Tom's grandfather, musing, without sentiment, on various aspects of rural life – work, religion, education, music and courtship rituals – but revealing his regret for staying and his sympathy for youngsters who no longer wish to be 'beholden to the farmer'. Aside from his service in the First World War, the only time he made a 'decision', rather than letting 'things just lead to another', is when he walked forty miles to Newmarket in a fruitless search for employment. *Akenfield* concludes with young Tom quietly leaving the village, apparently planning to migrate to Australia. Driving out, he 'sees' his grandfather walking back from Newmarket. Tom's break from the past may well prove to be definite but this moment of contact is also a warning, from family history, of the inevitability of return.

Nighthawks, which communicates the social and work life of Jim, a young homosexual teacher in London, has the distinction of being one of the first British feature films to describe everyday gay life. Ron Peck and Paul Hallam used non-actors to play Jim's colleagues, fellow

New approaches to realism: Barney Platts-Mills' *Bronco Bullfrog* (1969)

clubbers and partners, and also incorporated their experiences into the script. If *Nighthawks* has obvious interest as a bona-fide document of the London gay scene of the late 1970s, it was also a belated response to the negative stereotyping of mainstream cinema, which had commonly perceived of homosexuality in terms of either 'camp' or victimhood.

The film is loosely plotted, but establishes a tight rhythm that circumscribes the rituals of Jim's sex life, beginning, as it ends, with his hopeful cruising of a crowded disco; the remaining narrative describes a cycle of one-night stands, reunions with former conquests, more cruising and tentative relationships that fizzle out after a couple of weeks. From the events of the film, and the anecdotes Jim tells his new friend Judy, a supply teacher at his school, it becomes evident that when relationships do get established, these are undone when one party is compelled to move away or return to the cruising circuit. One potential partnership flounders through disagreement on whether to 'stay in' or 'go out', a denotation of the problems of reconciling a long-term relationship with the characteristically transient gay lifestyle (as well as a reminder of the anxieties around 'coming out' as homosexual to work colleagues and family, which Jim has not fully done). This tension is not exclusive to homosexual relationships, however. Judy describes how the stability she has gained through marriage and child-bearing has been at the expense of a varied social life; furthermore, her husband is disapproving of her trips to the pub. While Jim's increasing desperation is symptomatic of the metropolitan gay experience, the film permits a reading of his simultaneous desire for companionship but also for being 'without any ties' as an unresolved stance on commitment that happens to coincide with his sexuality. He tells Judy how the initial pleasure of coming home to a partner in his (cramped) flat soon mutated into claustrophobia at the disruption to his 'work'.

As if to work through his anxieties about permanency, Jim spends some of his spare time taking photographs and collecting slides of derelict and demolished houses. Elsewhere in British social realist cinema, such imagery tends to be bound up with a nostalgia for working-class traditions; here, Jim's fascination with transitional sites evokes his alienation from the mainstream. The act of photography gives permanence to processes of change, offering a resolution of a sort to the film's central opposition between stability and flux. Despite his financial security, Jim's empathy with those who struggle to maintain their societal place is underlined by his interest in a school colleague's plan to screen *Cathy Come Home* (1966), Ken Loach's drama about homelessness: 'I'd like to see that', he says.

It is this concern with place – or, more specifically, the problems of locating home – as much as its naturalistic performances, long takes and commitment to the project of social extension, that secures *Nighthawks* its place within the realist canon, making it an unexpected bedfellow to *Akenfield* and *Bronco Bullfrog*. Furthermore, through its consideration of the potential disjunction between private and public identities, *Nighthawks* recapitulates their narrative concern with the clash between job security and individual freedom. *Nighthawks* is, of course, an unusual realist film in that it concerns the experiences of a professional, and thus middle-class, character, even if Jim's sexual encounters are somewhat egalitarian (they include a working-class northerner, an American stockbroker and a representative of the cultural Establishment). It is fitting, however, that Jim is a teacher of geography, the academic study of human beings and their environment: in one lesson he asks his class to consider the benefits of life beyond the restrictions of the city. A colleague who has failed to live up to his promise of leaving is mocked as a 'permanent fixture' of the school, so as to ward off any suggestion of his own entrenchment. There is a climactic sequence towards the end of the film where Jim reveals his sexual orientation to a class of taunting children, but the final scene returns us yet again to one of Jim's disco haunts and the cyclical search for a partner: the camera pans and zooms listlessly through the crowd to the familiar strains of the forceful, repetitious dance music that dominates the film's soundtrack.

British realist cinema has traditionally been characterised by a prioritisation of male experience; with the odd exception, it is not until the 1980s that a significant number of female-centred films go some way to redress the imbalance. Two of the rare films of the 1970s to challenge this masculinist bias happen to be directed by Ken Loach and Mike Leigh. The repressions suffered by the central characters of *Family Life* (1971) and *Bleak Moments* are as much psychological as political, however. Loach's *Family Life* places the blame for a troubled young woman's deteriorating mental health on misguidedly disciplinary parents and the brutal psychiatric treatment meant to curtail her delinquency. The family home is equally a prison for the lonely, borderline alcoholic Sylvia (and the mentally disabled sister in her care) in Leigh's provocatively slow-paced *Bleak Moments*. Despite the character's apparent inertia, she is actually able to exert a degree of control – and alleviate the tedium of a courtship that is proceeding at a comically glacial rate – through some playful stage-management. Guests, including her potential partner, are slyly mocked, or left to make awkward small talk while their host lingers on thresholds; in other words, for the similar purpose of social satire, Sylvia is demonstrating the director's own improvisatory methods.[17]

A comparison between Loach's didactic, ultimately tragic vision and Leigh's satiric comedy illustrates in miniature the divergent possibilities opening up for the realist film in the 1970s. At the same time, the incorporation of 'realist' elements within other types of film-making played no small role in the success, and even reanimation, of popular genres such as horror, comedy, musicals and the gangster film. Across films as disparate as *Frightmare* (1974), *Steptoe and Son* (1972), *Tommy* (1975) and *Get Carter* there is, to varying degrees, a commitment to social commentary and an attention to locale. While this dispersal of realism further problematises its definition, the theme of escape – or, put another way, the problem of finding one's place in the world – remains a constant. It would seem that the films of the 1970s not only constitute a transitional phase of British realist cinema but are themselves characterised by a concern with processes of change.

Notes

1 See, for example, Samantha Lay, *British Social Realist Cinema* (London: Wallflower Press, 2003).
2 Geoff Brown, 'Paradise Found and Lost: The Course of British Realism', in Robert Murphy (ed.), *The British Cinema Book, 2nd Edition* (London: BFI, 2001), p. 253.
3 Lay, *British Social Realist Cinema*, p. 77.
4 See John Hill, *British Cinema in the 1980s* (Oxford: Oxford University Press, 1999).
5 Peter Wollen, 'The Last New Wave: Modernism in the British Films of the Thatcher Era', in Lester D. Friedman (ed.), *Fires Were Started: British Cinema and Thatcherism, 2nd Edition* (London: Wallflower Press, 2006), pp. 30–44.
6 Christopher Williams, 'The Social Art Cinema: A Movement in the History of British Film and Television Culture', in Christopher Williams (ed.), *Cinema: The Beginnings and the Future* (London: University of Westminster Press, 1996), p. 194.
7 It is perhaps no coincidence that this was also the moment when the notion of realism – hitherto conceived of critically as a straightforward, laudable project – came under theoretical scrutiny in a series of *Screen* debates. For a summary of these, see Lay, *British Social Realist Cinema*, pp. 29–31.
8 See Sarita Malik, *Representing Black Britain: Black and Asian Images on Television* (London: Sage, 2002), pp. 159–60. Also Jim Pines's essay in the same anthology.
9 For an analysis of the film and television work of Leigh in the 1970s, see Ray Carney and Leonard Quart, *The Films of Mike Leigh: Embracing the World* (Cambridge: Cambridge University Press, 2000), and Garry Watson, *The Cinema of Mike Leigh: A Sense of the Real* (London: Wallflower Press, 2006). For scrutiny of Loach's work, see Jacob Leigh, *Ken Loach: Art in the Service of the People*

(London: Wallflower Press, 2002), and George McKnight (ed.), *Agent of Challenge and Defiance: The Films of Ken Loach* (Trowbridge, Wiltshire: Flicks Books, 1997).

10 One of the few exceptions to place an emphasis on collaborative activity is Kevin Brownlow and Andrew Mollo's historical film *Winstanley* (1975), about the suppression of a self-sufficient farming community led by the writer and social reformer in the seventeenth century.

11 Raymond Williams, 'A Lecture on Realism', *Screen*, vol. 18, no. 1, Spring 1977.

12 A variant on this theme of the mentor initiating a naïve subject into sexual experience is found in the comedy *Black Joy* (1977), about a young man who arrives in London from Africa. The film parallels his sexual education with his gradual ability to resist economic exploitation and ends with him coming to the rescue of his streetwise teacher.

13 Andrew Higson, 'Space, Place, Spectacle: Landscape and Townscape in the "Kitchen Sink" Film', in Andrew Higson (ed.), *Dissolving Views: Key Writings on British Cinema* (London: Cassell, 1996), pp. 133–56.

14 It would seem that this figure is a surrogate for the author, Ray Connelly, and the film itself a speculation on the alternative life of one who chose not to follow the 'straight' path. See Alexander Walker, *National Heroes: British Cinema in the Seventies and Eighties* (London: Harrap, 1985), p. 69.

15 For an account of the debates around the 'realist' credentials of Davies, see Wendy Everett, *Terence Davies* (Manchester: Manchester University Press, 2004), pp. 28–30.

16 Quotation taken from the director's 'Biography' on the website <www.platts-mills.com> (accessed January 2007).

17 For a summary of Leigh's working methods, see Watson, *Cinema of Mike Leigh*, pp. 27–31.

10 Heritage Crime: The Case of Agatha Christie

Sarah Street

The Mirror Crack'd (1980), a film adaptation of the novel by Agatha Christie, opens with an establishing shot of an old dark house, filmed in black and white. Thunder crashes in the background and the camera zooms in closer. The next shot is inside the house, the camera tracking past a large grandfather clock that chimes ominously in the hall as, through an archway, we see a group of people who resemble stock characters from a murder mystery, gathered in the grand reception room. The butler admits the Inspector, who breaks the silence by promising to reveal the identity of Lord Fenley's murderer. The denouement is about to take place when we hear the jarring sound of film caught in a projector as the image dissolves into a blur. We have not been watching *The Mirror Crack'd* but a film-within-a-film, projected in the village hall of St Mary Mead, now filmed in colour. The spectators, aghast at not learning the identity of the murderer, begin to speculate. Miss Marple, also there to see the film, demolishes each of their wild theories on the grounds of faulty logic and lack of observation. She finally puts them out of their misery by telling them whodunit with an elaborate, brilliant explanation that is marked by its convincing and penetrating analysis. The main titles for *The Mirror Crack'd* then feature, as the film proper begins with pictorially composed shots of St Mary Mead as a rural idyll that are similar to the sumptuous, languid openings of 1980s heritage films.

This opening, which does not feature in the novel, demonstrates a playful awareness of the conventions of Agatha Christie's detective fiction, the film-within-the-film establishing *The Mirror Crack'd* as being replete with parody, and preparing us for what by then had become an established formula for adapting Christie for the screen. The film features a star-studded cast including Elizabeth Taylor and Rock Hudson, who play respectively an actor and director who have come to Britain to make a heritage film, *Mary, Queen of Scots*. There are numerous stunning settings and a touch of comedy to accompany the unravelling of a mystery that turns on the revelation of information that readers and audiences would have been hard-pressed to second-guess ahead of the indomitable Miss Marple. The production companies, EMI Films and G. W. Films, had used this formula on several previous occasions, hoping to rescue the struggling British film industry with a touch of 'heritage crime'. In addition, as EMI executive Nat Cohen told Alexander Walker: 'I just had the feeling that, considering all the doom and gloom in the country, Agatha Christie would go down well.'[1]

Before *The Mirror Crack'd*, there had been sixteen film adaptations of Christie that were either wholly or part-British produced.[2] The prolific producer Julius Hagen was responsible for *The Passing of Mr Quinn* (based on a short story, 1929) and *Alibi* (based on *The Murder of Roger*

Ackroyd, 1931), but during the subsequent period when Christie's novels were extremely popular there were very few screen adaptations, the most notable being *Witness for the Prosecution* (1957), a Hollywood film directed by Billy Wilder. This pattern continued until the 1960s when MGM, operating in Britain, produced a series of popular Miss Marple films starring Margaret Rutherford and directed by George Pollack: *Murder, She Said* (1961), *Murder at the Gallop* (1963), *Murder Most Foul* and *Murder Ahoy!* (1964). Despite the common assumption that Christie did not like any screen representations of Miss Marple, she nevertheless dedicated the novel *The Mirror Crack'd from Side to Side* (1962) to Rutherford 'in admiration'.[3] The 1970s and early 1980s were the most fertile years, before the explosion of popular television adaptations featuring Miss Marple and Poirot, which then became the major incidence of screen adaptations and appropriations of Christie. The films therefore were important in establishing screen conventions that television drew upon when devising its own formulas for the production of new stories, not penned by Christie, but that highlighted iconic elements of what has become indicative of an imitative 'Christie style'. Alison Light argues that this approach perpetuates a misleading view of Christie, labelling her firmly as a backward-looking conservative, rather than retaining the elements of modernist irony that are evident in her novels, particularly those written in the interwar period when she, and others, were modernising the crime novel.[4]

The formula developed by EMI and G. W. Films involved four films: *Murder on the Orient Express* (1974), *Death on the Nile* (1978), *The Mirror Crack'd* and *Evil under the Sun* (1982). Each was based on a successful Christie novel and, with the exception of the Marple mystery *The Mirror Crack'd*, featured detective Hercule Poirot. The films featured international star casts and showcased remarkable locations that were photographed by highly regarded British cinematographers: Geoffrey Unsworth (*Murder on the Orient Express*), Jack Cardiff (*Death on the Nile*) and Christopher Challis (*The Mirror Crack'd* and *Evil under the Sun*). The British films produced before *Murder on the Orient Express* can, however, be seen to be experimenting with various approaches, some of which were utilised by the EMI team while others were not.

Endless Night (1972), produced by veteran British film-makers Frank Launder and Sidney Gilliat in association with British Lion and EMI Films, demonstrates a very different direction based on one of the few Christie novels that can be associated with thriller/horror, as opposed to the more typical concern to present an intricate mystery whose primary pleasure for the reader is its convoluted and compelling 'narrative games'. As Robert Merrill has observed, Christie possessed 'an uncanny grasp of the plot variations available within the conventional detective format'.[5] While the plot of *Endless Night* is indeed complex, in addition the novel (published in 1967 and not as highly regarded as her earlier works) and film employ the device in which the narrator turns out to be the murderer, a technique Christie had famously employed in *The Murder of Roger Ackroyd* (1926), which was remarkable at that time for signalling 'the collapse of the reliable narrator' in detective fiction.[6]

Hywel Bennett plays Mike, a chauffeur with a passion for fine art, who becomes fixated with buying a plot of land called 'Gypsy's Acre' that appears to hold a mysterious secret, or even be cursed. While surveying it, he meets and becomes attracted to Ellie (Hayley Mills), a woman he subsequently distances himself from when he discovers she is rich. Still in love with Mike and knowing his passion for Gypsy's Acre, Ellie buys the land; they are reconciled, marry and commission an architect to design a new house. Ellie's family disapprove of the marriage and conflict develops when Ellie's friend, Greta (Britt Ekland), comes to visit and ends up staying with the couple in their new house. Ellie dies after a riding accident and in a shocking twist we learn that this was planned by Greta and Mike, who knew each other before Mike met Ellie. Greta and Mike quarrel and he kills her. The film ends at the beginning with Mike recalling his story to a doctor and being asked to start again; in keeping with the novel's ambiguities, the narrator has turned out to be the killer and we are unsure if the story we have witnessed is the 'correct' version.

Endless Night was not well received by critics, who could only find interest in the modernist house, realised by distinguished production designer Wilfrid Shingleton, with novel features such as one-way windows that allow the couple to see who is outside but not to be seen themselves. Bernard Herrmann wrote the music, which experimented with the innovative Moog synthesiser, an electronic instrument invented in 1970. David Robinson considered Bennett and Mills to be 'too modern' for the roles, while Dilys Powell thought that Gilliat had done 'a good job with the script'.[7] Both Alexander Walker and Derek Malcolm considered that the book was not a good example of Christie's writing.[8] A sex scene between Bennett and Ekland that was not present in the novel was considered a mistake, a misguided attempt to give the film a contemporary gloss.[9] Despite these negative perceptions, the film attempts to institute a sense of atmosphere and place with beautiful locations (the Isle of Wight and the Home Counties), the intriguing modernist house and a real feeling of suspense in parts. In many ways it suffers from being a hybrid of several styles that were symptomatic of British cinema during this period. The quasi-modernist feel, together with allusions to Hitchcock's *Vertigo* (1958) and *Marnie* (1964), are combined with a dreamy, European sensibility that gives the film a rather sluggish pace despite brief moments of suspense/horror. Apart from the use of established stars such as George Sanders, the film did not really offer an acceptable model of Christie adaptation, especially since it was based on one of her more unusual novels. But it did register an interest in her work that EMI later exploited by opting for the more populist approach of adapting older classics featuring Poirot and Miss Marple, and employing more well-known stars.

A second model that jettisoned the thriller/horror dimension in favour of a lighter touch was attempted in adaptations of Christie's novel *Ten Little Indians* (originally titled *Ten Little Niggers*, 1939). René Clair directed a highly regarded version in 1945, and a British adaptation was produced in 1965. The novel is notable because it exonerates the most likely suspect (Justice Wargrave) by making him appear to have been murdered; we later discover this is not the case and that he has been responsible for all of the murders. Ten people receive invitations to go to a remote island off the coast of Devon. They do not know their host, Mr Owen, but each has particular reasons for accepting the invitation. Once they arrive, they wait for Owen but he does not appear. A gramophone record plays a message that accuses each character of committing, or contributing, to murder. They cannot leave the island because of bad weather conditions and one by one the characters are murdered. The twist comes when Wargrave persuades the doctor he is innocent and that in order to expose the murderer he should go along with a plan to feign the Judge's death. The reader only discovers this at the end of the novel when all ten characters are dead. Wargrave has written a confession that he places in a bottle and throws out to sea. It is found by a fisherman and from reading it we learn of the Judge's motives to administer justice outside the law and, after years of sentencing murderers, of his desire to experience how it feels to be a killer. As Merrill points out, this plot exemplifies Christie's consummate skill as a

Britt Ekland, Hywel Bennett and Hayley Mills in *Endless Night* (1972)

puzzle-maker by 'forcing us to entertain unlikely solutions we cannot dismiss even though we cannot believe in them'.[10]

The films follow the plot quite closely, but they reject the ending wherein no characters survive. Instead, they allow the young couple to live, thwarting the Judge's plan and lessening the novel's profoundly dark, social resonances. As Light points out, *Ten Little Niggers* is a key text as expressive 'of the fears and desires of respectable England', with its off-coast setting serving as 'a metaphor for the corruptions of insularity . . . as an image of the mental universe of the British middle classes in the late 1930s, shut in and clannish, and increasingly marooned'.[11] The 1965 and 1974 adaptations instead opt for assembling a relatively well-known cast and changing the setting to, respectively, an Alpine retreat and the Shah Abbas hotel, Isfahan, in the Middle East.

Another major difference is the lack of emphasis on the characters' memories of the past, which in the novel creates a sense of psychological motivation and plausibility, particularly concerning the guilt of a governess who was implicated in the drowning of a child.

The 1965 film adaptation can be related to mid-1960s British cinema, particularly in its casting of Shirley Eaton as Mr Owen's secretary, who re-creates her role as love interest in *Goldfinger* (1964). Wilfred Hyde-White plays the Judge, a well-known character actor whose wry charm rather militates against him being as sinister as Wargrave is in the novel. Shot in black and white, the film uses the snowbound, mountainous Alpine location to good effect by emphasising the characters' isolation with use of long shots that show how they are trapped. In scenes when the characters search for Mr Owen, there is an attempt at creating a suspenseful atmosphere by use of low-key lighting and cavernous cellars; by contrast, the setting of the novel is a modern hotel. Rather than focus on the characters' guilt about the past, the film concentrates more on their mutual suspicions and, as has previously been mentioned, on the survival of the young couple who have become attracted to each other. The ending is therefore far more conventional than in the novel, leaving the viewer with a sense of relief.

And Then There Were None (a co-production between France, Germany, Italy, Spain and Britain, 1974) used more or less the same script as the 1965 film, including the survival of the couple at the end. With a remote, desert location and shot in colour, the film features a star cast including Charles Aznavour, Herbert Lom, Oliver Reed and Richard Attenborough. It was not well received by critics, as exemplified by the following comments in the *Monthly Film Bulletin*:

> This multi-national adaptation . . . dilutes the original by transplanting the action to an unspecified locale, substituting an unrelated cast of jet-set characters, adding a happy end and, worst of all, neglecting the victims' relationships in favour of lingering shots of Iranian ruins, while the somnolent cast wanders about the Shah Abbas hotel.[12]

While these comments are certainly valid, it could be argued that the 'lingering shots' are in fact one of the film's most interesting features, and that its cinematographic strategy attempted to replicate an equivalent style to the 1965 adaptation. The emphasis on interiors and exteriors therefore assumes a relevance that to some extent makes up for the film's obvious shortcomings. The Shah Abbas hotel, for example, is in many ways a spectacular location and this is emphasised by frequent use of an unsettling, mobile camera that identifies the Judge's power over the other characters. Thus, while both the 1965 and 1974 adaptations can rightly be criticised on different grounds, they suggested an approach to Christie on screen that emphasised location and the casting of stars. On the other hand, the liberties both films took with the plot and their negation of psychological suspense rendered them less convincing or compulsive than the novel. Although the 'trick' device of killing the most likely suspect before the resolution of the mystery was retained, the happy, romantic endings of both films substituted a lighter touch that was contrary to the spirit of the novel.

These shortcomings highlighted the difficulties of adapting Agatha Christie novels to the screen, difficulties with which every subsequent attempt was forced to grapple. Analysts of her fiction have commented on the sparseness of her prose, of the 'strict formalism of technique' and employment of 'a language of reticence which was able to articulate a conservative Englishness but in a modern form'.[13] She relied on her readers' knowledge of 'stock' characters, but then proceeded to devastate these expectations by exposing their capacity for evil and duplicity. As Mary Anne Ackershoek has commented, this ambiguous landscape provided the dynamism of her fiction as well as its capacity for social comment:

> What these depictions indicate is not a securely powerful leisured class, but a class that is purposeless and doomed. Murder disrupts this world because it calls attention to its falseness; in the course of the investigation, the hidden failures of its inhabitants will be revealed. Once the disruptive force is removed, the society returns to its normal course; but this closure is less a confirmation of society's essential validity than a confirmation of its static nature, its inability to change in response to changing times.[14]

The tightly constructed plots therefore provide scope for adaptations that could aim both to entertain and infer comment. Christie's novels contain large chunks of dialogue that would apparently make the screenwriter's job easy. Yet the films highlight the challenges of presenting whodunit characters and plot in a context of what was to become the EMI formula of exotic locations, established stars in period costumes and all manner of sumptuous detail that, in classic 'heritage' style, could be said to dominate the films. These adaptations also display a degree of parody and excessive stylisation of Christie that encourages performances very much based on a camp sensibility that could be construed as militating against an extensive exploration of the period in which the novels are set.

The most successful of the four EMI/G. W. Films adaptations was the first, *Murder on the Orient Express*, produced by John Brabourne and Richard Goodwin. This was an ambitious production that was able to attract top international stars, partly because of tax laws that were lenient on foreign actors working in the UK.[15] Although the film was registered as British, the director, Sidney Lumet, was American, as were cast members Lauren Bacall and Anthony Perkins; it was co-funded by Paramount and distributed by the company in the USA, Canada and Japan. Other stars included Albert Finney as Poirot, Sean Connery, Wendy Hiller, John Gielgud, Michael York, Jacqueline Bisset, Rachel Roberts, Ingrid Bergman and Vanessa Redgrave. This incredible team signalled an approach that wallowed in the appearance of its stars in often brief scenes that were designed to cover the sparseness of the novel's characterisation. Ingrid Bergman, for example, was awarded an Academy Award as Best Actress in a Supporting Role for her performance as Miss Ohlsson, a Swedish missionary. Comparing the novel and the film, it is clear that the part was embellished for Bergman so that she could invest it with distinctive, memorable qualities while introducing a comic element that is not exploited in the novel. Anthony Perkins's performance as Hector MacQueen plays on his edgy, neurotic persona established in *Psycho* (1960). In contrast to the adaptations of *Ten Little Indians*, the changes introduced by screenwriter Paul Dehn were judicious, and frequently made the plot flow smoothly. In addition, Lumet's visual style works, as Ina Rae Hark has noted, to enhance characterisation by raising the

> emotional temperature of everyone involved. Overall, the film's affective atmosphere is steeped in guilt and hostility, two emotions one might expect in a tale of revenge and murder, and that one certainly anticipates in a Lumet film, but which are virtually absent from Christie's novel.[16]

(Opposite page) Albert Finney as Poirot in *Murder on the Orient Express* (1974)

The opening montage that informs the viewer about the kidnapping and murder of the Armstrong baby creates a suspenseful narrative frame; we eventually learn that it is this event that connects all twelve characters on the Orient Express. Christie's reputation for narrative surprise was again admirably demonstrated in the novel. The stunning revelation delivered by Poirot at the end of the film is that everyone conspired to execute their own form of justice by participating in the killing of a passenger who is the murderer of the Armstrong baby. The train is temporarily halted by snow on the track, creating a moment of stasis as the murder investigation proceeds. This provides a classic Christie situation whereby characters are trapped in a place removed from their usual environment; their temporary displacement is the most significant factor. This was an important Christie trademark whereby

> it is the journey, the voyage, the pleasure of moving from one place to another and the disruptions it may bring with it, as a way of passing time, which engrosses the reader rather than the engagement of actually being abroad.[17]

The success of *Murder on the Orient Express* encouraged Brabourne and Goodwin to adapt another Christie novel, *Death on the Nile*. Christie had agreed to the filming of her novel before she died in 1976. The tax advantages that were a contributing factor to the all-star cast for *Murder on the Orient Express* were no longer operating, which is reflected in the perhaps less overtly 'starry' cast for *Death on the Nile*. There were, however, some distinguished names including Bette Davis, David Niven, Mia Farrow, Maggie Smith and Peter Ustinov as Poirot. Once again, the story presents a puzzle whereby the murderer appears to be the least likely suspect, in this case because of a cast-iron alibi that is later revealed to be part of a crime planned and committed in collaboration with another character. The location cinematography by Jack Cardiff provided a suitably spectacular background for the drama, and the screenplay was by well-known writer Anthony Shaffer. Some of the formulaic elements that had been evident in *Murder on the Orient Express* were further extended in *Death on the Nile*. These include enhancing the material's camp potential, which is articulated primarily through the characters played by Maggie Smith, as Mrs Schuyler's (Bette Davis) companion, and Angela Lansbury as Salome Otterbourne, a flamboyant romantic novelist. Although Albert Finney's portrayal of Poirot in *Murder on the Orient Express* was generally praised, not least by Agatha Christie, the casting of Peter Ustinov permitted a more expressive characterisation. This drew on Ustinov's celebrated ability to speak many languages, although the introduction of repeated references to him being mistaken for being French rather than Belgian becomes tedious. *Death on the Nile* was directed by John Guillermin, a British director who had worked in Hollywood on *The Towering Inferno* (1974). According to Alexander Walker, *Death on the Nile* was particularly successful in Japan and was purchased by several American television networks.[18]

The third film in EMI/G. W. Films' Agatha Christie experiment was *The Mirror Crack'd*, which has already been referenced as a film that demonstrates the evolving formula. It was directed by Guy Hamilton, an established British director who also directed the next Christie adaptation, *Evil under the Sun*. Once again, international stars featured prominently in *The Mirror Crack'd*, including Elizabeth Taylor, Rock Hudson, Tony Curtis and Kim

Importing international stars: Elizabeth Taylor in *The Mirror Crack'd* (1980)

Novak. Angela Lansbury played Miss Marple, prefiguring her portrayal on television of another female sleuth in *Murder, She Wrote* (USA, 1984–96). The game Christie plays this time is to mislead the reader into thinking that the victim was not the person the murderer intended to kill. Rather, we are led to believe that Marina, played by Elizabeth Taylor, who turns out to be the murderer, is in danger of being killed by characters with various plausible motives.

A key scene, which bears a close resemblance to its description in the novel, occurs when a fan, Heather Badcock, tells Marina that she met her years ago. Heather recalls how she was feeling ill but nevertheless went to see Marina, got her autograph and kissed her. During this long, boring story, another character observes as Marina suddenly looks over Heather's shoulder with a 'frozen' expression, as if she has seen something disturbing. Marina offers Heather a cocktail; the drink gets spilled and Marina gives Heather her own, which turns out to be poisoned. We therefore deduce that someone wants to kill Marina and that the poison was intended for her rather than the unfortunate Heather, who dies. Miss Marple later discovers that the key to the crime is the significance of Marina's 'frozen' look, which depends on knowledge that the reader could not possibly have: Marina contracted German measles while pregnant, which resulted in her giving birth to a handicapped child. It is while talking to Heather that Marina realises that she must have caught the disease from her; the 'frozen' look is explained by this sudden realisation as she looks at a painting of the Madonna and Child on the landing in the distance.

As with *Murder on the Orient Express*, the film allows the well-known actors to develop their characters in ways that are not signalled in the novel. Take the scene, for example, when Inspector Craddock (Edward Fox) interviews Marina. In the novel he is not particularly a film buff, whereas in the film he is a devoted fan of Marina's work, so much so that he can identify lines she is repeating from one of her films. She intended the impromptu performance to go unrecognised, but when she knows that Craddock can see through her 'act', she bursts into hysterical laughter. This is very much an Elizabeth Taylor performance, executed with panache and allowing for a momentary, disruptive break from the otherwise serious tenor of the moment. In this and other ways, the film conveys considerable wit and showcases St Mary Mead as an idyllic, English village. This heightens the film's 'heritage' qualities, particularly when it completely cuts out any reference to 'The Development', a nearby housing estate where Heather lives and that features prominently at the beginning of the novel.

Evil under the Sun was the last film to be made in the series. It was filmed in Majorca, rather than the north Devon setting of the novel, with hotel interiors filmed in London; it was chosen as the film for the Royal Film Performance in 1982. Ustinov appeared again as Poirot and other notable stars included Diana Rigg, James Mason and Maggie Smith. There were fewer international stars and in general the film did not do as well at the box office as its predecessors.[19] Combined with judicious use of a beautiful location, the film exaggerates the camp elements that had become increasingly prominent in the other films, particularly Maggie Smith's performance as Daphne and Diana Rigg's as Arlena. The screenplay again highlights the rivalries between the characters, relishing the source novel's scope for wit, misunderstanding and irony. Despite the film being a mature example of the formula, Brabourne and Goodwin decided not to produce any further Christie adaptations. Michael Winner later directed *Appointment with Death* (1987), but it was a poor imitation of the style that had been developed at EMI.

An assessment of the significance of the 'heritage crime' formula needs to place the films discussed in this chapter in relation to previous adaptations of Christie, as well as locate them as an important influence on the trend for heritage-themed films in the 1980s. Many of the conventions associated with heritage are evident in films of the 1970s, in this case those set in the past featuring spectacular locations. Also in line with heritage films, the Christie adaptations feature plots about middle- and upper-middle-class people who are frequently not what they seem. The mood of parody and camp detracts from the darker aspects of Christie's novels and the films present instead hyper-stylised representations of the past. As examples of 'international' productions registered as British films that frequently featured foreign locations, actors and personnel from different countries, they have been rather overlooked by critics and scholars. This neglect is undeserved, since they exemplified the pressures towards co-production and demonstrated some of the pleasures and pains of adapting such a popular novelist's work for the screen. *Murder on the Orient Express* represents the high point of this experiment, even though it was only the first film in the series produced by Brabourne and Goodwin. It is tempting to conclude that, unlike Fleming's James Bond, the Christie novels did not result in an infinitely repeatable formula. Yet the legacy of the film adaptations must surely be the extremely successful television series that have produced David Suchet's arguably definitive screen realisation of Poirot, as well as Joan Higson's and Geraldine McEwan's distinctive portrayals of Miss Marple. Screen interest in Christie has increased rather than abated, establishing a mode of appropriation to which without question EMI and G. W. Films made a significant contribution.

Notes

1 Alexander Walker, *National Heroes: British Cinema in the Seventies and Eighties* (London: Harrap, 1985), p. 129.
2 *The Passing of Mr Quinn* (1928), *Alibi* and *Black Coffee* (1931), *Lord Edgware Dies* (1934), *Love from a Stranger* (1937), *The Spider's Web* (1960), *Murder, She Said* (1961), *Murder at the Gallop* (1963), *Murder Most Foul* (1964), *Murder Ahoy!* (1964), *Ten Little Indians* (1965), *The ABC Murders* (1966), *Endless Night* (1972), *Murder on the Orient Express* (1974), *And Then There Were None* (1974), *Death on the Nile* (1978).
3 See, for example, Charles Silet, 'Christie on Screen' <www.agatha christie.com> (the official Agatha Christie website, accessed 24 January 2007).
4 Alison Light, *Forever England: Femininity, Literature and Conservatism between the Wars* (London: Routledge, 1991), pp. 62–5.
5 Robert Merrill, 'Christie's Narrative Games', in Jerome H. Delamater and Ruth Prigozy (eds), *Theory and Practice of Classic Detective Fiction* (Westport, CT: Greenwood Press, 1997), p. 97.
6 Martin Priestman, *Crime Fiction from Poe to the Present* (Plymouth, Devon: Northcote House Publishers, 1998), p. 21.
7 David Robinson, *Financial Times*, 6 October 1972 and Dilys Powell, *Sunday Times*, 8 October 1972.
8 Alexander Walker, London *Evening Standard*, 5 October 1972 and Derek Malcolm, *Guardian*, 5 October 1972.
9 *Monthly Film Bulletin*, October 1972, p. 209.
10 Merrill, 'Christie's Narrative Games', p. 90.
11 Light, *Forever England*, p. 98.
12 *Monthly Film Bulletin*, February 1976, pp. 23–4.
13 Light, *Forever England*, p. 62.
14 Mary Anne Ackershoek, '"The Daughters of His Manhood": Christie and the Golden Age of Detective Fiction', in Delamater and Prigozy (eds), *Theory and Practice of Classic Detective Fiction*, p. 124.

15 Walker, *National Heroes*, p. 132.
16 Ina Rae Hark, 'Twelve Angry People: Conflicting Revelatory Strategies in *Murder on the Orient Express*', *Literature/Film Quarterly*, vol. 15, no. 1, 1987, p. 39.
17 Light, *Forever England*, p. 90.
18 Walker, *National Heroes*, p. 131.
19 Ibid.

Part Three: Films and Film-makers

11 Folksploitation: Charting the Horrors of the British Folk Music Tradition in *The Wicker Man*

Paul Newland

In this essay I want to examine the ways in which the cult British film *The Wicker Man* (Robin Hardy, 1973) employs a hybrid musical soundtrack, composed by the New York-based musician Paul Giovanni, that merges the syntactical codes and conventions of traditional British folk music with both a classically trained level of performance and the counter-cultural and mass-cultural languages of pop and rock. I will try to show how this soundtrack helps to construct the strange territory in which the narrative of the film takes place; a territory that evokes a particular type of British liminality. But in addition to this, I also want to gesture towards the ways in which *The Wicker Man* showcases the affective nature of music in cinema.

Although it only achieved moderate box-office success when it was released in the UK as the lower half of a double bill with *Don't Look Now* (Nicolas Roeg) in December 1973, *The Wicker Man* has since gained a large cult following and received a reasonable amount of critical attention.[1] Much of this criticism has focused on the ways in which the film resists straightforward generic categorisation. *The Wicker Man* has primarily been associated with the British horror tradition but it does not sit easily within the horror genre.[2] Instead, the film can be read as a detective story, a thriller or as a fantasy 'likely to be watched for as long as audiences retain an appetite for the magical and mystical, the fantastic and the bizarre'.[3] According to Leon Hunt, *The Wicker Man* closely resembles a pagan musical.[4] This, then, is not a horror film in the traditional sense. There are no clearly marked monsters or monstrous figures that 'breach the norms of ontological propriety presumed by the positive human characters in the story'.[5] Moreover, there is no obviously positive human presence in the narrative. Instead, a flawed and essentially dislikeable character, Sergeant Neil Howie (Edward Woodward), comes into conflict with a perhaps more likeable but equally flawed character, the patrician Lord Summerisle (Christopher Lee), a strange, titular leader of a remote British pagan community. While the events that occur at the end of the film are certainly horrific and disturbing in nature (and are indeed instigated by Lord Summerisle), the 'monstrous' appears to reside elsewhere – within what amounts to a disturbed vision of British folk culture.

The horrific events in the film develop out of a clash that occurs between diametrically opposed belief systems and ideologies of governance. On the one hand, we have Howie's rigidly held Presbyterian Christian beliefs; on the other, what he sees as the degenerate practices of an island community that apparently melds aspects of traditional, pagan folk culture with the contemporary counter-culture. The real horror of the film thus lies within Howie's experience of this clash; or, indeed, within his generation of this clash. The narrative comes to operate, then, as a strange and ultimately deadly Freudian 'working through' of Howie's psychological and corporeal conflict; a conflict he has apparently resisted on the mainland but now finds exacerbated by the pagan folk traditions and hippy-type 'free love' he comes into contact with on the remote island.

I want to suggest that Howie's internal conflict is effectively marshalled by Paul Giovanni's score. The diegetic and extra-diegetic musical performances in the film employ a wide variety of strategies that, while always residing within a broad conceptual vision of 'folk' culture, encode the conflicting concepts of space and place that frame Howie's experience and allow the spectator/listener access to his point of view/point of aural reception. Giovanni's songs come to operate as a symptom of Howie's intense trauma. But while his internal conflict exemplifies a wider cultural conflict that was occurring in late 1960s and early 1970s Britain (ostensibly a conflict between traditional modes of behaviour and more forward-looking, open-minded ways of life), these songs serve to evoke an 'other' Britain of long-standing but liminal cultural traditions and liberal progressiveness.

Closer to the Edge

At the beginning of the film, a title card thanks Lord Summerisle and his people for their co-operation during filming. But while a real Summerisle does exist, it was not employed as a location by the film-makers.[6] The Summerisle seen in the film is a composite. Robin Hardy and his production team utilised a number of real places in western Scotland in order to create the chimerical island that draws Howie to his doom.[7] *The Wicker Man* deliberately blurs distinctions between real and imagined space. This fictional, oneiric territory, with its distinct echoes of the long-deserted island of St Kilda, is supposedly situated a number of miles off the western coast of the Outer Hebrides.

In an early sequence in the film, Howie flies a seaplane from mainland Scotland to the remote island. As shots from the plane clearly show, Summerisle is set in the Gulf Stream. Its lush vegetation and tropical flora evoke an exotic mysteriousness. Its location in space and time remains ambiguous. The shots of the seaplane flying over this island, offering us Howie's point of view, show it to be (for him, at least) a sexualised space – all phallic, rocky outcrops and vulva-like cavities. Howie descends from the sky; a movement that, according to David Bartholomew, lends him 'a (Christian) god-like status'.[8] But this is not how he appears to the islanders, who see him emerge – innocent – from his womb-like seaplane. Howie's descent effectively marks his entrance into a dream-like space that manages to evoke both a rural 'folk' idyll and a coeval, prurient hippy commune.[9] Summerisle is a territory in which Howie encounters the type of degenerate practices that he believes should have no place in what he sees as a modern, Christian Britain.

The island is located within a dream-like 'folk chronotope' or time/space; a parallel world in which the heavily policed culture of mainland Britain breaks down.[10] The strange 'otherness' of this remote time/space is effectively evoked by the melding of music with memorable visuals. I aim to show how, in order to construct this oneiric chronotope, the film clearly exploits a concept of British folk culture that is effectively marked as 'other' in terms of its preservation of a shared cultural heritage; or, more accurately, its guardianship of narratives that embrace witchcraft, spirituality, murder, illicit sexual activity and other seemingly pre-Enlightenment cultural practices.

Over the shots of Howie's seaplane swooping across the mysterious landscape in this early sequence, the spectator/listener hears two extra-diegetic pieces of music segued together on the soundtrack. The first song is an adaptation of the Robert Burns ballad 'The Highland Widow's Lament', sung by Lesley Mackie (who plays Daisy in the film) over a backing of Northumbrian pipes.[11] This performance demonstrates a degree of authenticity. Mackie sings in a Highland accent and her voice, echoing around what sounds like a village hall, resembles perhaps more an old field recording than a professional 1970s studio recording. But this level of authenticity is certainly not aimed at, or indeed achieved, by Paul Giovanni's performance of the second song, 'Cornrigs and Barleyrigs', a tune that borrows lines from another Robert Burns ballad, 'Rigs O'Barley'.[12] Giovanni accompanies himself on a crisply played and beautifully recorded acoustic guitar, singing (in a strangely out-of-place middle-class English accent) sexually suggestive lines such as 'Beneath the moon's unclouded light I held awhile to Annie'. Interestingly, the composer has admitted that 'I was trying to make a sound to show that the community was contemporary, in the 1970s, apart from their religious practices.'[13] While this *feels* like folk music, the clarity of Giovanni's vocal performance certainly appears to signify the up-to-date nature of both this recording and the events in the film that it introduces. These performances, either borrowing from and exploiting authentic British folk music or drawing on the high-quality production values of modern mass-cultural recording techniques for their contemporary sheen, manage to evoke a rich, hybridised musical syntax. Indeed, the varying levels of technical skill and authenticity that these performances display together suggest the constructed, inauthentic, hybrid nature of both the folk chronotope in which the narrative takes place and the music that facilitates its construction. However, other musical performances in the film, diegetic rather than extra-diegetic, certainly aim to evoke a greater level of 'folk' authenticity. These are usually the songs of the islanders; songs that come to perform an extremely important role in the development of the narrative that frames Howie's experience.

We soon discover that the people of Summerisle are freely operating beyond the reach of a modern culture industry that 'intentionally integrates its consumers from above'.[14] Although Lord Summerisle runs the island, his people appear to enjoy a measure of socio-cultural freedom. That is, in Theodor Adorno's terms, they can still be seen to be producing their own culture 'from below'. Simon Frith has argued that 'the industrialisation of music means a shift from active musical production to passive pop consumption, the decline of folk or community or sub-cultural traditions . . . '.[15] It seems that the remote Summerisle has escaped these developments. Here, then, in this imagined outpost of 1970s Britain, music is still seen to function as an organic mode of expression that brings the community together and articulates its pagan traditions and shared sense of identity. But the music that the outsider Howie comes into contact with on the island profoundly affects him. Indeed, it is this music that stirs Howie's stolid sense of identity.

Sound Affects?

In one early scene, Howie stands in the Green Man pub, obviously disturbed by the song 'The Landlord's Daughter' being sung by the massed regulars for Willow MacGregor (Britt Ekland). Paul Giovanni has admitted that this 'is the most manufactured song in the film'.[16] While it exploits aspects of the British folk music tradition, it has been clearly updated to evoke contemporary discourse surrounding sexual permissiveness. It features the following bawdy lines:

And when her name is mentioned
The parts of every gentleman
Does stand up at attention . . .

For nothing can delight so
As does the path that lies between
Her left toe and her right toe.

To Howie, a contemporary, ascetic listener, the islanders appear to share a debased vision of sex and the female body in particular. But this song is performed in a style that stands in stark contrast to the aesthetic beauty of Giovanni's extra-diegetic performance of 'Cornrigs and Barleyrigs'. While the islanders' diegetic performances serve to evoke a backward rural community, Giovanni's extra-diegetic performances facilitate, for the film spectator/listener, the location of the narrative within a contemporary frame of cultural reference.[17]

Listening to the different musical performances in the film, we can begin to detect varying vocal modes of expression that oscillate between the codes and conventions of what Roland Barthes distinguished as '*pheno-song*' and '*geno-song*'. In his intriguing essay 'The Grain of the

Updating British folk music traditions: Robin Hardy's *The Wicker Man* (1973)

Voice' (1972), Barthes tries to understand his predilection for one singing voice over another.[18] He argues that what he calls the 'grain' of a voice manages to articulate aspects of the workings of the body of the performer: 'The "grain" is the body in the voice as it sings, the hand as it writes, the limb as it performs.'[19] This 'grain' can be perhaps best thought of as a space that develops between the acoustic properties of the voice and the overpowering presence of the body articulated through this voice. It is within this space that the semantic possibilities of a text might be fully exploited. Developing his argument, Barthes makes the distinction between '*pheno-song*' and '*geno-song*', suggesting that a '*pheno-song*' can be thought of as a flawless musical performance of purity and technical perfection that covers 'all the phenomena, all the features which belong to the structure of the language being sung, the rules of the genre . . .'.[20] He then argues that a '*geno-song*' can be seen to function as a performance in which the workings of the body take precedence over the acoustic purity of the voice, bringing to life 'the voluptuousness of its sound-signifiers'.[21] *The Wicker Man* features Giovanni's extra-diegetic '*pheno-song*' 'Cornrigs and Barleyrigs'. But it also features a number of diegetic '*geno-songs*' sung by a variety of singers (or as a chorus), such as 'The Landlord's Daughter', 'Maypole' and 'Sumer Is A-Cumen In'. These vocal performances, not always concerned with the conventional acoustic beauties of singing, are often delivered in a ribald, carnivalesque style. The full potential of the sexual body can often be seen to be articulated through the energetic physicality of these performances. Indeed, Howie effectively becomes bewitched by the 'grain' that develops in this music.

During his night in the pub, a song is performed that articulates the potential power of a Barthesian '*geno-song*' to elicit an erotic response. This is one of the most extraordinary sequences in the film. Although he believes himself to be safely ensconced in his room above the bar, Howie hears Willow's sensual siren song coming from the room next door:

> Please come, say how do
> The things I'll give to you
> A stroke as gentle as a feather
> I'll catch a rainbow from the sky
> And tie the ends together.

This performance is clearly designed to elicit or effect a '*geno-song*'-type emotional charge or to effect an erotic, visceral, bodily response. Indeed, as Willow rhythmically grinds and thumps the walls of her room like a drum, what we might think of as the Barthesian 'folk grain' of the music reverberates into Howie's room and thus through his body, and his composure begins to crack as he moves towards *jouissance*. Willow's performance in this sequence thus creates what Barthes has termed a 'pulsion', a '*certain demand of the body itself*'.[22] For Howie, then, Willow's song provides more than pleasure. It operates as a blissful text. Through this music he hears and *feels* the proximity of Willow's sexual body. Barthes writes: 'What I hear are blows: I hear what beats in the body, what beats the body, or better: I hear this body that beats.'[23] Howie hears (and *feels*) the beat of Willow's pulsational body, 'one which pushes itself back and forth'.[24] This becomes a truly horrific episode for the ascetic Christian, whose own body thus becomes 'a stunned body (intoxicated, distracted, and at the same time ardent)'.[25]

This sequence articulates aspects of a traditionally puritanical British (or indeed western) denial of the physicality involved in the production and reception of music, a view that had been challenged by a number of counter-cultural texts.[26] Howie's platonic view of music as 'sound only' is clearly challenged by Willow's sexual rhythms. He thus comes under attack not only from Willow's fecund sexuality but also, by association, from the pagan British folk traditions articulated in her song.

A Folk Phonotope

With its utilisation of a dense nexus of folk narratives and a variety of musical codes and conventions, the chronotope constructed in *The Wicker Man* more accurately becomes what I want to call a 'phonotope' or sound/space. The prefix 'phono-', derived from the Greek word for sound, also suggests 'speech'. I want to emphasise here that the phonotopes or sound spaces developed in films such as *The Wicker Man* can speak to us. They have a discursive function. Their constituent parts together develop potent meanings that can profoundly affect our readings of the text. The phonotope or aural filmic landscape or territory constructed in *The Wicker Man* encompasses mythologised visions of material space, the imbricated socio-cultural histories of real and imagined communities, and the corporeally affective music that serves to articulate aspects of these dense discourses. This phonotope is built around concepts of paganism, folk culture and both ancient and contemporary views of sexual permissiveness. It utilises the 'grain' evident in '*geno-song*' performances as a kind of mortar or bonding agent. In this film, the phonotope functions as a territory in which the mind and body are encouraged together to behave in ways that would perhaps be deemed unacceptable elsewhere; specifically, on mainland (or, indeed, in mainstream) Britain. By exploiting a mythical vision or concept of British folk music and folk culture, then, and situating it alongside an early 1970s drive towards sexual freedom, this phonotope provides a thematic discursive space or frame in which the full horror of the sexually repressed Howie's experience can be played out.

The construction of the aural/filmic phonotope in *The Wicker Man* draws on a wide variety of traditional British 'folk' sources. Anthony Shaffer's screenplay initially included fragments of traditional poems and folk rhymes, and clearly indicated which songs were to be used in the film. The director Robin Hardy also tracked down fitting authentic rural ditties in Cecil Sharp's famous collection of English folk songs.[27] Meanwhile, the associate music director on *The Wicker Man*, Gary Carpenter, working together with Paul Giovanni, put together a group of musicians from the Royal College of Music that became known as Magnet.[28] Giovanni later discarded most of Shaffer's lyrics and a number of the musicians, deciding instead to include a selection of material that he himself had composed that combined traditional songs with original contemporary material, brass pieces and nursery rhymes.

Instrumental passages in the score were based on traditional English, Scottish and Irish folk tunes such as 'Miri It Is' and the 'Drowsy Maggie' reel. The tune 'Chop Chop' was written by Gary Carpenter, based on the nursery rhyme 'Oranges and Lemons', while 'The Procession' is a 'wholly original' instrumental tune for brass, based on the fourteenth-century Scottish ballad 'Willie of Winsbury'.[29] Other songs featured on the soundtrack include 'The Tinker of Rye' (sung by Christopher Lee and Diane Cilento), 'The Ram of Derby' (the only song retained from Shaffer's screenplay, also sung by Lee and Cilento), 'The Flame Dance' (with vocals by Rachel Verney and Sally

Presant) and the aforementioned 'Willow's Song' (also sung by Rachel Verney, but re-recorded by Lesley Mackie for LP release).[30] Other sequences in the film utilise traditional Scottish folk music including the Strathspey 'Robertson's Rant' and an Irish variant of the reel 'Drowsy Maggie'.[31]

Many of these tunes evoke aspects of the British folk revival of the 1950s and 1960s, but other musical interludes in the film are also clearly influenced by the folk rock of late 1960s and early 1970s British bands such as Fairport Convention and Pentangle, as they too mix traditional folk music with mass-cultural and counter-cultural musical forms. Indeed, the music that accompanies Howie's search for Rowan, featuring fiddles, electric guitars and Hammond organ, recalls not only folk music but also contemporary early 1970s free jazz, jazz rock and progressive rock. This hybrid music is clearly reflected by the appearance of Lord Summerisle and his followers, who, as seen in the May Day procession sequence, appear to combine Woodstock-era counter-cultural fashions with traditional pagan ceremonial costume in order to create their 'look'. Moreover, this sequence, and others in the film, also serves to remind us that the folk tradition, rock music and the aesthetics of British horror films helped to produce something of a musical subgenre during the late 1960s and early 1970s: 'folk-rock horror'. Perhaps noticing the thematic links between British folk tales, nursery rhymes, horror and exploitation films and contemporary youth rebellion, bands such as Genesis fused grotesque imagery with a rural sensibility, counter-cultural concerns and a progressive musical style in much of the folk-tinged material that they produced during this period. Giovanni's *The Wicker Man* score can certainly be considered within the parameters of this hybrid musical subgenre.[32]

The memorable final 'Wicker Man' ceremony in the film, featuring an adapted version of the Middle English song 'Sumer Is A-Cumen In' ritualistically performed by the massed island folk, takes place high on a cliff top, seemingly at the edge of 1970s Britain. This is highly significant. The remote British countryside has often been marked in British cinema as a space of the past;

Music of the common people: the finale of *The Wicker Man*

as a space in which old, pre-modern folk traditions survive. Theodor Adorno and Hans Eisler advocated that 'even the vestiges of spontaneous folk art have died out in the industrialised countries, at best it subsists in backward agrarian regions'.[33] Songs that have achieved a wide currency among people have traditionally been termed folk songs, and folk music has been understood to encompass narratives that have been passed down through generations by oral transmission.[34] If folk music is subject to the verdict of the community, it is also usually considered to be 'peasant music'.[35] It is thought to have roots in the common experience of a 'people', to articulate an authentic set of cultural practices and beliefs. Folk song is, it seems, 'impersonal, because it is the expression of the community and not merely of the individual'.[36] Furthermore, the folk song collector Cecil Sharp believed that folk song was 'created by the common people . . . an exceedingly small class . . . to be found only in those country districts which, by reason of their remoteness, have escaped the infection of modern ideas'.[37] It is these concepts of folk music and folk ideology that are broadly exploited by *The Wicker Man*.

Steve Redhead and John Street have justly critiqued elements of what they call the 'folk ideology', arguing that

> it is wrong to see music as *emerging* from out of the people (as folk ideology tends to assume), because there is a process of audience *creation* involved and because there is no simple 'people' in which the music can be rooted.[38]

They are rightly concerned about how far folk ideology 'runs the risk of misconceiving the politics of music and encourages an overly deterministic – and hence unsuccessful – merging of music and ideas'.[39] This is what can essentially be seen occurring in Paul Giovanni's score for *The Wicker Man*. His music, facilitating as it does the development of the 'folk phonotope' in which Howie's conflict rages, effectively exploits a concept of 'folk ideology' by suggesting a shared, communal ownership of songs that celebrate free love, paganism and aspects of the occult.

But it should be pointed out that *The Wicker Man* was not the only film of the period to do this. *Witchfinder General* (Michael Reeves, 1968), *The Plague of the Zombies* (John Gilling, 1968) and the Amicus portmanteau *And Now the Screaming Starts!* (Roy Ward Baker, 1973), for example, all depict backward, rural, folk-type British communities in which evil stirs. And other films set in contemporary times such as *Doomwatch* (Peter Sasdy, 1972) and Sam Peckinpah's notorious *Straw Dogs* (1971) (both shot on location in Cornwall) also clearly mark rural folk and folk song as remote, degenerate and horrific. It seems, then, that in the Britain of the late 1960s and early 1970s, a mythic pagan past, rural folk cultures and aspects of the counter-culture were imaginatively elided to form a powerful, 'othered' vision of British culture.

Notes

1 *The Wicker Man* screenplay was written by Anthony Shaffer, based on the 1967 book *Ritual* by David Pinner. For details of the intriguing story of the film's production and exhibition, see Allan Brown, *Inside the Wicker Man: The Morbid Ingenuities* (London: Sidgwick & Jackson, 2000).

2 Brown, *Inside the Wicker Man*, pp. 65–6.

3 Ibid., p. 179.

4 Leon Hunt, 'Necromancy in the UK: Witchcraft and the Occult in British Horror', in Steve Chibnall and Julian Petley (eds), *British Horror Cinema* (London and New York: Routledge, 2002), p. 95.
5 Noël Carroll, *The Philosophy of Horror; or Paradoxes of the Heart* (New York and London: Routledge, 1990), p. 16.
6 David Bartholomew, 'The Wicker Man', *Cinefantastique*, vol. 6, no. 3, Winter 1977, p. 10.
7 Ibid., p. 18. See also Ali Catterall and Simon Wells, *Your Face Here: British Cult Movies since the Sixties* (London: Fourth Estate, 2002), p. 144.
8 Bartholomew, 'The Wicker Man', p. 6.
9 The details of the beliefs and practices of this remote community were drawn by the writer Anthony Shaffer from Sir James George Frazer's twelve-volume *The Golden Bough*. See Brown, *Inside the Wicker Man*, p. 24.
10 According to Mikhail Bakhtin, a chronotope is a 'time-space' – see Mikhail Bakhtin, *The Dialogic Imagination* (Austin and London: University of Texas Press, 1981), p. 84.
11 Gary Carpenter, 'The Wicker Man – Settling the Score' <www.garycarpenter.net/archive/wicker> (accessed 18 December 2006).
12 Bartholomew, 'The Wicker Man', p. 36.
13 Ibid.
14 Theodor Adorno, *The Culture Industry: Selected Essays on Mass Culture*, ed. J. M. Bernstein (London and New York: Routledge, 1991), p. 98.
15 Simon Frith, 'The Industrialisation of Music', in Andy Bennett, Barry Shank and Jason Toynbee (eds), *The Popular Music Reader* (London and New York: Routledge, 2006), p. 231.
16 Bartholomew, 'The Wicker Man', p. 36.
17 'Gently Johnny', performed by Giovanni, was cut from the eighty-four-minute original theatrical version. It was reinstated to the ninety-nine-minute Director's Cut of the film.
18 Barthes's 'The Grain of the Voice' ('Le Grain de la voix') was originally published in *Musique en jeu*, no. 9, 1972.
19 Roland Barthes, *Image-Music-Text* (London: Collins, 1977), p. 188.
20 Ibid., p. 182.
21 Ibid.
22 Roland Barthes, *The Responsibility of Forms: Critical Essays on Music, Art, and Representation*, trans. Richard Howard (Oxford: Blackwell, 1986), p. 175.
23 Ibid., p. 299.
24 Ibid., p. 300.
25 Ibid.
26 Susan McClary, 'This is Not a Story My People Tell: Musical Time and Space According to Laurie Anderson', in Bennett, Shank and Toynbee (eds), *The Popular Music Reader*, p. 23.
27 Bartholomew, 'The Wicker Man', p. 34.
28 The band (which was originally known as Lodestone before becoming Magnet) included the recently graduated students of the Royal Academy of Music Peter Brewis (recorders, Jew's harp, harmonica, bass guitar), Michael Cole (concertina, harmonica, bassoon) and Gary Carpenter himself (piano, recorder, fife, organ, lyre). They were joined by Andrew Tompkins (guitars), Ian Cutler (fiddle) and Bernard Murray (percussion), who had played in a folk rock band with Carpenter called Hocket. See Carpenter, 'The Wicker Man – Settling the Score'.

29 Carpenter, 'The Wicker Man – Settling the Score'.

30 Bartholomew, 'The Wicker Man', p. 36.

31 Carpenter, 'The Wicker Man – Settling the Score'.

32 I am thinking especially here of tracks such as Fairport Convention's version of 'Matty Groves' on *Liege and Lief* (1969) and Genesis's 'The Musical Box' on *Nursery Cryme* (1971) and 'Supper's Ready' on *Foxtrot* (1972).

33 Theodor Adorno and Hans Eisler, 'Prejudices and Bad Habits', in Kay Dickinson (ed.), *Movie Music: The Film Reader* (London and New York: Routledge, 2003), p. 25.

34 Maud Karpeles, *An Introduction to English Folk Song* (Oxford and New York: Oxford University Press, 1987), p. 2. See also Roy Palmer (ed.), *Everyman's Book of British Ballads* (London: J. M. Dent, 1980), p. 14.

35 Ibid., p. 12.

36 Ibid., p. 19.

37 A. L. Lloyd, *Folk Song in England* (London: Panther Books, 1975), pp. 13–14.

38 Steve Redhead and John Street, 'Have I the Right?', *Popular Music*, vol. 8, no. 2, 1989, p. 183.

39 Ibid.

12 Under Siege: The Double Rape of *Straw Dogs*

Sheldon Hall

Though it may well be, as Stephen Farber has suggested, 'a major work, a seminal film of the seventies',[1] *Straw Dogs* still stands as a forbidding title in the imaginations of many film viewers and critics. While it has figured in critical and biographical studies of its American director, Sam Peckinpah, and has been the subject of occasional articles since its scandalous first appearance in late 1971, its subsequent British re-release in 1995 and its long-delayed certification for UK home video in 2002, it has rarely been seen as anything other than a provocation. In the course of its history, the film has often fallen victim to the different yet parallel ideologies of, on the one hand, the conservative forces represented by the British Board of Film Classification, formerly Censors (BBFC), and the moralism of certain sectors of the mainstream press; and on the other, the intentionally progressive movement of academic film and cultural studies, especially feminist film criticism. *Straw Dogs* has become, in fact, as much of a sacrificial object as the ritual tokens to which its title refers.[2] Like the fog that surrounds the protagonists' farmhouse at its climax, much of the critical discussion has tended not to illuminate, but to obscure the film and render it inaccessible to unprejudiced judgment.

Straw Dogs was one of the last, and among the more successful, of thirty-six cinema films commissioned by the theatrical production arm of the American television network ABC.[3] It was produced and released at a time when 'Hollywood' – or more precisely the interlocking system of studio-based production and distribution set-up, relatively stable genre conventions and regular audience attendance, which had previously characterised the American film industry – was in a state of collapse. Box-office admissions, which had been in continuous and precipitous decline since the late 1940s, bottomed out in 1971. The familiar, traditional genres were undergoing a process of transformation and, in some cases, terminal breakdown – a process in which Peckinpah's work played a decisive part. The near-disappearance of the family audience produced, as a further consequence, a relaxation of the permissible limits of narrative subject matter and the manner of its representation, facilitated by the MPAA's introduction of the ratings system in 1968. *Straw Dogs*' assault on 'the sacrosanct values of hearth and home'[4] was also contiguous with a more general crisis of confidence in American – or western – capitalist democracy in the wake of the Vietnam War, a crisis registered in the film by the passing suggestion that the film's protagonist, David Sumner (Dustin Hoffman), has moved to the English village of Wakeley partly to escape involvement in the activist demonstrations and campus protests in his own country.

Along with *The Devils* and *A Clockwork Orange* (both 1971), *Straw Dogs* was at the centre of what came to be regarded as a British censorship crisis, which resulted in an atmosphere of confusion and uncertainty over what the censor would or would not pass for exhibition.[5] One manifestation of this was a collective letter to *The Times* – signed by thirteen British newspaper reviewers – denouncing Peckinpah's film and the censor for seeming to pass it uncut (this was not quite the case, as I shall describe later) while withholding a certificate from a film they claimed to be relatively harmless, Andy Warhol and Paul Morrissey's *Trash* (1970).[6] Challenged by journalists and pressure groups to clarify the situation, the BBFC's secretary, Stephen Murphy, responded to these and other doubts cast on his competence and authority by reluctantly withdrawing from the libertarian position that the Board, under his leadership, had attempted to maintain. Although it may be argued that films such as those mentioned above marked 'a certain watershed . . . and viewers may well have become accustomed to levels of sex, violence and language that were once thought unacceptable',[7] the BBFC under Murphy and his successor in 1975, James Ferman, generally maintained a policy of paternalist conservatism, massively increased after 1986 with the extension of its powers to cover home video. As a consequence of this, and despite a theatrical re-release in 1995, *Straw Dogs* was refused a certificate for release on video until 2002, following Ferman's retirement.[8]

Dustin Hoffman in Sam Peckinpah's *Straw Dogs* (1971)

The hysterical press response that greeted the initial release in Britain of *Straw Dogs* has been described (and deconstructed) at length by Charles Barr, and I would not wish to dispute any of the conclusions he draws.[9] Barr points out the central irony in British newspaper coverage of the film attacking it for its alleged hysteria and overstatement, the critics' own work can be found guilty of the same offences: 'passion swamps reason, and they succumb to that loss of control which they diagnose in Peckinpah, victims of a process which is a leading subject of the film'.[10] The film's alleged offensiveness was often taken to reside not just in the explicitness of its violence (including sexual violence) but also in Peckinpah's supposed endorsement and celebration of that violence, and his conception of a masculinity based on aggression, brutality and domination. Repeated concern was expressed for the film's dubious realistic veracity (mainly in terms of its lack of authenticity in reflecting the presumed real-life conditions in West Country villages similar to the one in which the action is set); the contrived schematism of the narrative and its characterisation; the stridency of Peckinpah's visual style; and the likely emotional or behavioural effect of its violence on audiences. The following remarks seem representative:

> The whole might be more acceptable to British audiences if the setting had been in the past or in a still primitive territory, rather than the possibly backwards but not uncivilised West of England.[11]

> I can tolerate a great deal of screen violence if I can believe in the characters or story . . . [the film] will undoubtedly prove popular wherever such excesses are regarded as the height of entertainment.[12]

> [W]hen you've chosen to take as a theme one of the last remaining taboo subjects, the only topic that still marshals the censor's vigilance, i.e. the thrill of violence, it does pay to tread rather warily and there seems little doubt that Peckinpah has overstepped the mark.[13]

The film's British distributor, Cinerama, made judicious use of some of the more salacious reviews in its publicity campaign, and took out a full-page advertisement in the trade paper *CinemaTV Today* to inform the industry of its record-breaking box-office takings; *Straw Dogs* was ultimately placed fourteenth in the same publication's list of 1972's top earners in the UK.[14] Several reviewers offered first-hand observation of favourable audience responses (the contrast with their own, needless to say, being the point), while Andrew Tudor reported on the relation between the newspapers' accounts and the general public's experience of the film:

> one common comment to be heard from the large crowds leaving after a performance was that it was not as 'bad' as was expected. That is, it was not as evilly violent as the histrionic critical establishment claimed. In fact the various spot researches carried out by interested parties at the time suggest that the audience was in some disagreement with the critical evaluation. Nevertheless they clearly had been influenced seriously in that they attended the film with very specific expectations. Thus, although in disagreement over judgement, they are still bound in a perceptual framework set by the initial critical response, and it therefore becomes impossible to see *Straw Dogs* outside the context set by the institutional opinion-leaders.[15]

A recurrent refrain in the reviewers' complaints was the similarity of the film's scenario to a Western, and the seeming inappropriateness of this to its present-day rural English setting. Compare the remarks of Dilys Powell and, from a retrospective position, Alexander Walker:

> Some people found Mr Peckinpah's *The Wild Bunch* painfully violent. It was violent all right, but in the context of a Western and with the director's superb control of composition and movement it never struck me as offensive. *Straw Dogs* is different . . . One might say that Mr Peckinpah was bringing the outside in, translating the Sioux or the Apache massacre from the Western to an English living-room.[16]

> Perhaps if it had been set in some isolated Western homestead in the 1880s, the terrorising of the newlyweds . . . might have fitted into the traditional expectations of the genre: but the contemporary setting in the West of England . . . seemed like putting on indecent display all the nightmares that could affect the British bourgeoisie.[17]

The critics' anger seems partly traceable to a certain disorientation engendered by the film's failure – or refusal – to fulfil 'traditional expectations' or respect such generic boundaries. Nigel Andrews's *Monthly Film Bulletin* review indicates a further generic disturbance:

> *Straw Dogs* assembles familiar horror-in-rural England motifs (arrival of stranger in remote village, mistrustful locals, dark hints about the past), but develops them in such a way as to shock the spectator out of his faith in the immutable conventions of the horror film.[18]

Leaving aside any quibbles one might have about the 'immutability' of horror movie conventions, Andrews's enlistment of *Straw Dogs* under the rubric of English gothic seems pertinent; and it is confirmed by Terence Butler, for whom 'the film manages to clarify the Gothic nature of [Peckinpah's] preoccupations' (Butler devotes a lengthy chapter of his book to a discussion of the director's centrality to Leslie Fiedler's category of *American* gothic).[19] It is arguably the film's combining of these diverse generic elements, along with the intrusion of an unwelcome American presence into the British cinematic landscape, that was a major cause of critical distress.[20]

Peckinpah was extremely vocal in expressing his dislike of Gordon M. Williams's *The Siege of Trencher's Farm*,[21] the novel on which Peckinpah and David Zelag Goodman based their script, and it seems worthwhile delineating some aspects of the novel he and Goodman changed in making their adaptation, as they provide a number of essential clues to its thematic development. The novel's central couple, George and Louise Magruder, are closer to one another in age than the film's David and Amy Sumner, and have a young daughter, Karen (eliminated for the film). Though Louise is English, she has no previous connection with the village, Compton Wakley (*sic*), in which they settle, with Trencher's Farm (which in *Straw Dogs* is Amy's 'Daddy's house') or with the locals who attack it. Louise is not raped and Henry Niles, who accidentally causes the death of young Janice Hedden, is a fugitive from a mental hospital where he has been incarcerated for previous sex crimes (whereas there is no suggestion in the film that Henry's behaviour has any precedent). It is also revealed that a previous outsider to the village community had been killed by a mob and his body left in a field: a further detail suggesting that the violence brought down on the Magruders is already incipient in the community itself, leaving its victims essentially innocent of responsibility. In one respect, however, and despite its author's repudiation of Peckinpah, the novel is guilty of just the sort of masculinist hero-worship of which the director was so often accused (rather more guilty, in fact, than the film). George Magruder responds to the attack on his home by rediscovering his manhood, winning back the love of his unfaithful, frustrated wife as he repels the invaders:

> He left the light on. Louise was at the top of the stairs, her face white. 'We're winning,' he shouted up. 'Three down, two to go.'
>
> She frowned. There was a funny expression on George's face. At the beginning – God, when was that? She looked at her watch. It was only ten to nine. It seemed to have been like this for *hours* – at the beginning he'd seemed helpless, weak and passive, looking at her for strength. Then there was a stage when he's taken over. She'd liked that. To think that George, her bookish husband, was capable of finding ways to keep a gang of ruffians out of their house.
>
> For the first time in years she'd felt the way she'd always wanted to feel, like a woman. Protected. Given a man to lean on. No longer leaning on herself. Even when they'd been firing the gun at the door she hadn't really felt they were in serious danger. George had been so sensible, so quick to act.
>
> But now . . . why was he looking so pleased with himself?

Peckinpah was clearly drawn to the book by its theme of a man discovering his masculinity through his capacity for violence in defence of his 'territorial imperative' (the anthropologist – and Hollywood screenwriter – Robert Ardrey's book of that title was read avidly by the director prior to his making the film). However, his realisation of this theme, especially in the climactic scenes of violence, is far removed from the simplicities of Williams's novel, and indeed from the accounts given of the film by contemporary writers who, it is not unreasonable to argue, had a vested interest in vituperating the work of a man they considered representative of Hollywood's most aggressively patriarchal, sexist and misogynist recent tendencies.

Brief discussions of *Straw Dogs* appeared in three influential books published in the mid-1970s that offer chronological surveys of the representation of gender in Hollywood movies: Molly Haskell's *From Reverence to Rape*; Marjorie Rosen's *Popcorn Venus*; and Joan Mellen's *Big Bad Wolves*. All three conclude that the 1960s and 1970s mark the nadir for the representation of both sexes; all three see Peckinpah's work as entirely, and perniciously, characteristic of its time, with *Straw Dogs* the *locus classicus*, especially in its treatment of Amy Sumner (Susan George); and all three are riddled with glib generalisations, pat misrepresentations and crude oversimplifications. Haskell's sketch of Amy's 'constant libidinous excitation [making] any man less than a sex fiend look like a fairy' is a rhetorical caricature, and the notion that she is 'constantly fantasising rape' is the author's own fantasy.[22] Rosen not only produces fatuous inaccuracies and plain errors of fact (Amy is not gang-banged, as she describes, but raped twice), she also implies a false causality to the climactic siege. It is essential to the film's irony that David is not aware that his wife has been raped, whereas Rosen suggests that he acts from knowledge to which he never has access. It is not Amy's 'sexiness' that brings about the climactic violence but David's sheltering of Henry Niles (David Warner).[23]

For Mellen, *Straw Dogs* is Peckinpah's 'most important statement on the nature of masculinity . . . a primer in how to be a man'.[24] But comments such as 'Sexual identity flows from the assertion of . . . primitive, primal feelings' reduce to a simplistic platitude a proposition that it is the purpose of the film to dramatise, by following through its implications and thereby laying it open to question. The angled shots of David may or may not be 'surreal', as Mellen claims, but they arguably present his actions as disturbing and oppressive rather than 'transcendent'. Amy's participation in the fight with the last intruder, shooting Riddaway to prevent him from breaking David's spine, is preceded by some considerable hesitation: it seems for a time that she may prefer to kill David. Her help is not easily or unambiguously won, and she is afterwards visibly appalled by what has happened and by her own part in it. Mellen's description of her as being 'full of feeling' suggests mute admiration and glowing hero-worship that are nowhere apparent in the scene as presented. The pay-off, that 'a man who has so completely found himself could hardly become lost', fails to register anything of the sense of numbness and desolation with which many viewers, like Amy herself, tend to be left by the film's final images: for a critic so concerned with the woman's point of view, Mellen seems strikingly insensitive to the nuances of Susan George's remarkable performance.

The accounts of *Straw Dogs* offered by Haskell, Rosen and Mellen do not test out a critical hypothesis but merely illustrate the efficacy of an argument that has already been decided in advance. Those textual elements that do not support their readings are effectively suppressed or distorted, and the complex response the film invites is refused in favour of dogmatic assertions. I want, therefore, to offer as counter-argument a brief discussion of a single sequence from the film, the one that seems most problematic for us now: the rape of Amy.

This scene has always been a problem for *Straw Dogs*' censors and it was cut by several minutes for the American release. Although the film was not cut by the BBFC after completion, Stephen Murphy was consulted during the editing stage, and the sequence was considerably modified on the strength of his advice. It was the suggestion of sodomy in the later part of the sequence that proved unacceptable, with the result that in the severely cut American version (the version of the film re-released in the UK by the British Film Institute in 1995), there remains only a single full shot, lasting perhaps less than a second, showing Venner holding Amy down on the sofa as Scutt stands while penetrating her from behind. It was the scene's potential for arousal that led James Ferman continually to refuse the film a video certificate. Pauline Kael commented of its abridged version: 'The rape is one of the few truly erotic encounters on film . . . [the scene] has heat to it – there can be little doubt of that.'[25] Paul D. Zimmerman went so far as to claim that 'the rape sequence is a masterful piece of erotic cinema, a flawless acting out of the female fantasy of absolute violation'.[26] Naturally enough, it is the distasteful and possibly dangerous implications of interpretations such as these – and what male spectators might do as a consequence of seeing the sequence – that have concerned feminist commentators ever since. The film cannot of course *dictate* how actual spectators respond to it: no film can. But it is my contention that Peckinpah enables us to project ourselves into the sequence through the construction of empathy and partial identification with *both* Amy and Charlie, encouraging some responses and discouraging others.

The scene is, first of all, carefully contextualised within the film's continuing narrative development. Amy's emotions in the first part of the sequence are impossible to pin down precisely, as they change by the moment. It is a tribute to Susan George's skill that she is able to communicate the complexity of the character's experience, though it is not to her discredit that so many

Susan George in *Straw Dogs*

critics have failed to acknowledge it. Charlie Venner (Del Henney) is her ex-lover; her marriage with David is clearly undergoing great stress and conflict, and her embrace of Charlie midway through his rape suggests that she still harbours strong feelings for him that interfere with her feeling for David (confirmed when, during the siege, she shouts to Venner rather than David for help). Her initial resistance to Venner is broken down, but her reaction to the appearance of Scutt (Ken Hutchison) and her subsequent second rape registers only pain and distress. Compare the later sequence at the church social, in which every element of the *mise en scène* forces our close identification, in as vivid a manner as possible, with Amy's traumatic memory of the rape: there is no possibility here of suggesting that Amy looks back on the experience with fondness, or that she can have enjoyed or profited from it. No other character in the film is treated with this degree of interiority.

Our relationship with the characters changes in mid-sequence. Up to the moment of Venner's climax and his embrace by Amy, we see the scene almost entirely from Amy's point of view; this is not contradicted by the brief shot, from Venner's viewpoint, of her breasts, which is matched with her p.o.v. of his torso (the gesture of his taking off his sweater is rhymed, by a split-second flashback, with David's similar one in the earlier bedroom scene: this is Amy's subjective memory as well as the film's editorial comment). Identification switches with the appearance of Scutt, introduced from Venner's p.o.v. with a close-up of his shotgun barrel; the second rape is presented alternately from the positions of Amy, whose distressed face is seen in successive close-ups, and of Venner. Del Henney's performance registers, in his reaction shots, the dilemma in which Charlie has placed himself: obliged to choose between tenderness and brutality, compassion for his former lover and loyalty to his male peer, he takes the latter options. Dominating Amy by forcing himself on her – the only way he knows how to deal with emotion – he is in turn himself dominated by Scutt.[27]

The intercutting of the rape with shots of David on the moor with his shotgun, waiting for the game-birds, was partly necessitated by the demands of the censor to reduce the impact of the second rape. But its effect is also to stress David's own 'victimisation', leading later to his dismissal of the men from the repair work to the roof and his decision to prove his mettle by holding out in the final siege. It is crucial also that he remains unaware of Amy's violation: it is not 'his woman' he believes himself to be defending in the siege (her presence is to him largely an irritant) but the empty principle of 'home' and his own self-respect. His failure to see Amy's point of view is essential to his inability to understand the different meaning the siege has for her.[28] The notion that he 'learns' the value of masculine aggression from the shoot is partly true, but this is presented by Peckinpah with heavy irony (as in his action during the siege, paralleled with that of Venner prior to the rape, of slapping Amy and dragging her by the hair).

Finally, we may further place the film's treatment of Amy (and its alleged representation of 'all women' as sex-obsessed coquettes who want to be raped) by comparing her with the film's only other substantial female character, Janice Hedden (Sally Thomsett), whose disappearance sparks off the villagers' assault on the farm. She initially appears to be constructed in parallel with Amy, almost as a younger version of her, and has been similarly dismissed by critics as a variation on the stereotype of a provocative flirt. Yet her behaviour is equally clearly motivated: the men she flirts with, David and Henry, are the only sensitive, vulnerable types among the village's male inhabitants, and her interest in them may be said to derive from her alienation from the menfolk whose brutality the film insists upon at every turn (she seems to have no female friends, and her only companion is her elder brother). If one also takes into account the brief appearance at the farm of the Reverend Hood (Colin Welland) and his wife, and her ignominious treatment by both David and her husband, it could well be argued that the film, though primarily concerned with masculinity and its definition, has more to say about the oppression, marginalisation and domination of women than has usually been supposed. Of course, there is no 'positive image' to set alongside these characters; but nor does the film offer a positively conceived man, let alone a reconstructed 'hero' or role model to emulate.

Notes

1 Stephen Farber, '*Straw Dogs*', *Cinema* (USA), vol. 7, no. 2, Spring 1972, p. 7.

2 The title derives, as so many commentators have found it necessary to explain (no explanation is given within the film itself), from a saying by the Chinese philosopher Lao Tse: 'Heaven and Earth are ruthless and treat the myriad creatures as straw dogs; the sage is ruthless and treats the people as straw dogs.'

Much speculation has attended the question of which characters in the film are meant as symbolic straw dogs: David and Amy, or the villagers whose attack they repel. Thematic logic would suggest to me the latter, with David as the sage.

3 See Lee Beaupré, 'ABC Films Results: 30 of 36 in Red; Total Loss $47 Mil', *Daily Variety*, 31 May 1973, p. 3. According to this source, *Straw Dogs* earned worldwide rentals of $8m, giving ABC its second largest profit (after 1972's *Cabaret*) from the mere six profitable films it produced between 1967 and 1972, against thirty loss-makers, including Peckinpah's *Junior Bonner* (1972).

4 T. J. Ross, '*Straw Dogs*, Chessmen and War Games', *Film Heritage*, vol. 8, no. 1, Autumn 1972, p. 4.

5 An account of the *Straw Dogs* affair is given in Guy Phelps, *Film Censorship* (London: Gollancz, 1973), pp. 77–80. Stephen Murphy explained his decisions regarding the film in *CinemaTV Today*, 4 December 1971.

6 Extracts from the letter are reproduced in Phelps, *Film Censorship*, pp. 78–9.

7 Julian Petley, 'The Lost Continent', in Charles Barr (ed.), *All Our Yesterdays: 90 Years of British Cinema* (London: BFI, 1986), p. 42.

8 For a brief summary of the film's video censorship history in Britain, see Julian Petley, 'Who Let the Dogs Out?', *Sight and Sound*, vol. 12, no. 12 (NS), December 2002, p. 66. In 1995, *Straw Dogs* had been submitted to the BBFC by BFI Distribution for theatrical re-release and passed uncut with an '18' certificate; but this was the pre-censored American release version, not the longer cut that had originally played in British cinemas. With this decision, surviving prints of the 'uncut' version that still circulated in the UK had to be withdrawn or recut to conform to the abridged version. The source material used for the two best DVD editions of the film – Criterion's Region 1 release and Fremantle's Region 0, both now deleted and out of print but worth seeking out – is the longer original British version.

9 Charles Barr, '*Straw Dogs*, *A Clockwork Orange* and the Critics', *Screen*, vol. 13, no. 2, Summer 1972, pp. 17–31. Barr does not mention the film's more positive treatment by the UK trade press and specialised film periodicals, including Tom Milne in *Sight and Sound*, vol. 41, no. 1, Winter 1971–2, p. 50; Nigel Andrews in the *Monthly Film Bulletin*, vol. 38, no. 455, December 1971, p. 249; and Clyde Scott in *Films Illustrated*, vol. 1, no. 6, December 1971, pp. 26–7. The American critical response was summarised in *Filmfacts*, vol. 15, no. 1, 1972, pp. 1–5, as six favourable reviews, two mixed and seven unfavourable. There seems in general to have been a greater willingness on the part of American reviewers to recognise the film's achievements on a stylistic or technical level; British critics were, as always, primarily concerned with its morality and social effects.

10 Barr, '*Straw Dogs*', p. 20.

11 'Jock', *Variety Film Reviews*, 1 December 1971.

12 Anon., *CinemaTV Today*, 4 December 1971.

13 David McGillivray, *Films and Filming*, vol. 18, no. 6, March 1972, p. 54.

14 Anon., 'The 1972 Box Office Winners', *CinemaTV Today*, 13 January 1973, pp. 1 and 3.

15 Andrew Tudor, *Image and Influence: Studies in the Sociology of Film* (London: Allen & Unwin, 1974), p. 90.

16 Dilys Powell's January 1972 review from *The Sunday Times* is reprinted in Christopher Cook (ed.), *The Dilys Powell Film Reader* (London: Grafton, 1991), p. 391. Compare her later review of Peckinpah's *Pat Garrett & Billy the Kid* (1973): 'the chances are that there will be violence. Why not? This is a Western, and the West was violent: even those of us most addicted to the romantic view would agree to that' (p. 283).

17 Alexander Walker, *National Heroes: British Cinema in the Seventies* (London: Harrap, 1985), pp. 42–3.
18 Andrews, *Monthly Film Bulletin*.
19 Terence Butler, *Crucified Heroes: The Films of Sam Peckinpah* (London and Bedford, Bedfordshire: Gordon Fraser, 1979), p. 69.
20 One should note here the appearance in 1974 of another controversial film with a contemporary setting (this time made by a British director working in America) and a hero who responds to the violation of his home and the assault of his wife by picking up a gun: Michael Winner's *Death Wish*. Like Peckinpah's film, it also draws on Western conventions and ethics, though in a much cruder fashion.
21 Gordon M. Williams, *The Siege of Trencher's Farm* (London: Secker and Warburg, 1969); reprinted as *Straw Dogs* (London: Mayflower, 1971). The edition to which I have had access is the paperback reprint, published as a tie-in with the film's release; my thanks to Michael Walker for the loan of his copy.
22 Molly Haskell, *From Reverence to Rape: The Treatment of Women in the Movies* (second edition, Chicago and London: University of Chicago Press, 1987; first published 1974), pp. 200 and 363.
23 Marjorie Rosen, *Popcorn Venus: Women, Movies and the American Dream* (London: Peter Owen, 1973), p. 340.
24 Joan Mellen, *Big Bad Wolves: Masculinity in the American Film* (London: Elm Tree, 1977), pp. 302–5.
25 Pauline Kael, *The New Yorker*, 29 January 1972, reprinted in *Deeper into Movies* (London: Calder and Boyars, 1975), pp. 393–9. This collection of her reviews shows that Kael saw, in almost unbroken succession in late 1971 and early 1972, *A Clockwork Orange*, *Dirty Harry* (1971), *The Cowboys* (1972), *Straw Dogs* and Polanski's *Macbeth* (1971), all involving violent extremes of one sort or another. This in itself provides a vivid picture of the context in which Peckinpah's film appeared.
26 Paul D. Zimmerman, *Newsweek*, 20 December 1971, reprinted in *Filmfacts*, vol. 15, no. 1, 1972, p. 3. In this review, Zimmerman recasts in wholly positive terms the primitivism and machismo that most other critics deplore, actively celebrating their neo-fascist ethos. For him the film expresses the 'belief that manhood requires rites of violence, that home and hearth are inviolate and must be defended by blood . . . stripped of its contemporary context, the film reads like a Norse epic'. Compare this with Nigel Andrews's similarly laudatory but more temperate account in 'Peckinpah: The Survivor and the Individual', *Sight and Sound*, vol. 42, no. 4, Spring 1973, pp. 69–74.
27 Farber, '*Straw Dogs*', p. 6, suggests that '[t]he two men raping the same woman as a kind of ritual masculine initiation is a classic latent homosexual gesture – they get closer to each other by sharing Amy'.
28 William Johnson's unsupported suggestion that 'David knows what is going on and is conniving in it' (*Film Quarterly*, vol. 26, no. 1, 1972, p. 61) seems to me merely perverse.

13 Don Boyd: The Accidental Producer

Dan North

> I became a producer by accident. . . . I was a writer and a director who produced films but never saw myself as that in professional terms – I still don't, and never will.[1]
>
> Don Boyd, 2003

The principal account of Don Boyd's early career (outside the trade press) came from Alexander Walker's chapter 'The Boyd Wonder' in his *National Heroes* (1985),[2] in which Walker portrays the young producer-director as an ebullient naïf stumbling from one ill-timed near-miss to another.[3] The descriptor 'enthusiastic' that Walker repeatedly applies to his subject (twice in the first sentence alone) sounds, by the end of the chapter, like a compensatory euphemism. Walker uses Boyd to demonstrate the factors that smothered attempts to vivify independent film-making in Britain: disgruntled critics, diffident audiences and a dearth of industrial sponsorship. In the mid-1970s, Boyd had been something of a trade-press talking point, and his company, Boyd's Co., teased critics with the prospect of an imitable model for commercial entrepreneurship that also sought a high level of artistic credibility. Momentarily, the publicity surrounding Boyd's Co. augured a production company that didn't need to adapt a bad sitcom into a worse film, or imitate Hollywood gigantism, in order to bankroll its next project. This chapter aims to re-examine Boyd's early years through the publicity material generated by his work and the critical reception with which it was met, showing how his experiences as an aspiring director informed the films he produced.

Boyd has always been keen to stress that he never saw himself as a producer, and certainly had not intended to manoeuvre himself into such a role. He had wanted to be a writer-director, a creative artist for whom the business side of things was a means to carve out a space in which his own films, along with those of other directors, could be crafted. He told Walker mischievously that he was 'a director-orientated audience-conscious film-marketing editor',[4] showing a knowing facility with business jargon in assessing the rather unnaturally poly-utile position in which he had found himself.

Attending the London School of Film Technique (renamed the London International Film School in 1974), he studied under Ealing director Charles Crichton on a scholarship from the Inner London Educational Authority. He matched the practical schooling with an auto-didactic viewing frenzy, taking in a diverse, if tastefully orthodox, roster of world cinema staples – Pasolini, Mizoguchi, Antonioni, Godard, Truffaut, Rosselini, Fellini and Resnais. His student films were eclectic, often self-consciously strange; defiantly non-narrative or anti-naturalistic, they show Boyd trying to find his own voice through the noise of his new cinematic influences. *Billiard Balls* (1970), for instance, is a critique of middle-class acquisitiveness and domestic automatism. With Pinteresque dialogue and stagy set-ups (it seems to have been shot, apart from a few intertitles and cutaways to suburban locales, in a small theatre), it appears that Boyd was aiming to construct abstract space on set instead of building it through the optical artifices that cinema is so well equipped to provide. This may display vestiges of his initial interest in directing theatre, but it also exhibits the stiffness typical of experimental film that is not sufficiently resourced to actually *be* experimental; the freedom to try out a range of techniques costs time and money.

Boyd knew that he would need to attract funding if his output was to match his aspirations, and a series of fortuitous openings afforded him that opportunity.[5] Most significantly, he joined with Ken Davis of Arrow Productions to direct commercials for companies including Coca-Cola, Schweppes and Shell, for whose film unit he made *The Realm*, a twenty-minute parable of good business practice starring Robert Hardy. The film is ostensibly a celebration of corporate wisdom and benevolence, but Boyd's penchant for distorted close-ups and portentous pacing gave it a sinister air that was probably neither intended nor commissioned. The 'huge amount of money'[6] he made from these commercials would eventually permit him an advantageous level of autonomy as head of Boyd's Co., the company he would establish following his first outings as a director. In a memo to Davis in April 1974, he revealed the scope of his ambitions, his self-belief and the discomfort he felt in making other people's films to sell other people's products:

> As you know, I am very ambitious. Not ambitious in that I want to make millions of pounds, but ambitious because I want to make feature films that are distributed and acclaimed internationally. I have never disguised my aspirations. Anybody that knows me will have heard me discuss my hopes vehemently . . . My only concern is that opportunity will pass me by. I see friends of mine (less qualified and less talented) getting opportunities I would have liked. I am prepared to work hard and make money for the Company, but I must go in the direction I know I am destined for.[7]

Note how, in this and other statements reproduced here, Boyd's artistic objectives are articulated in commercial terms (and vice versa). His work, I will argue, is characterised by this faith in the profitability of artistically creditable cinema.

In his first feature, *Intimate Reflections* (1975), a young couple, mourning the death of their baby, reflect upon their relationship and role-play some trial-run suicides (without ever giving a sense that they actually plan to go through with it). Their scenes of increasingly buoyant fantasising are intercut with monologues delivered direct to camera by two middle-aged characters (Anton Rodgers and Lillias Walker), looking back on their lives and the choices they regret. Both Guy Phelps, in his unpublished biography, and Alexander Walker contend that Michael Deeley and Barry Spikings of British Lion offered Boyd a distribution deal for *Intimate Reflections* because they had overestimated its erotic focus. At the time of *Emmanuelle* (1974), the film whose distribution contract British Lion had recently failed to secure, soft-porn dressed up as existential essaying must have seemed like a safe bet at the box office; the film's promotional poster picked out an image from the film of the young couple naked in bed. The potentially erotic title was added when Deeley and Spikings objected to the more portentous working titles of *Tick Tock* and *Laughing and Crying* – but the sex in the film is playfully chaste, with hands and feet popping out at the edges of the duvet. According to a letter he wrote to publicist Dennis Davidson, Deeley was anxious about how the film might be perceived: '"Art Film" is a term of contempt . . . please talk to Don Boyd and see if we can describe this film in a form which suggests the entertainment it is intended to be.'[8] Even before the film was completed, Deeley and Spikings withdrew their support, disappointed by the rough cut's distance from their own intentions for it as entertainment, but their distribution guarantee had already enabled Boyd to borrow the £35,000 needed for its completion.

Intimate Reflections' changeable tone and pace mark it out as a debut, but one with ambitions to explore character relationships through a range of examinational modes. There is extensive use of Michael Gibbs's original non-diegetic music to comment upon (often very literally) the image track. Boyd scatters autobiographical motes across all the characters; the depiction of cold boardrooms and sociopathic marketing men put his own advertising career in a new intertextual perspective and compounds the ominous sensibility of *The Realm* (he and cinematographer Keith Goddard revisit a fondness they'd shown on that film for the fishbowl distortions provided by wide-angle lenses for some probing close-ups and lengthy tracking shots). The story had been written during Boyd's student days, driven by the collapse of his first marriage, but by the time

Don Boyd's debut feature film, *Intimate Reflections* (1974)

the screenplay was being finalised (and co-written with Richard Meyrick), he had remarried, a fact that might explain the film's oscillations between retrospective despondency and prospective optimism. The only meeting between the two couples is a wilfully weird final montage that further ambiguates the connections between them – are they future/past versions of one another? – but also abstracts the thematic structures of the film into a single expressive sequence with the audacity to which his film school work had only aspired.

Regardless of what critics thought of *Intimate Reflections*, many were keen to trumpet Boyd as a tantalising prospect for the revitalisation of the British film industry. Dilys Powell thought the film looked 'more than promising, it looks accomplished',[9] while the *Daily Mail* thought that *Intimate Reflections* gave viewers 'a glimpse of the British cinema that could be, if only the industry and the public would support it'.[10] Boyd was keen to propagandise his work personally; he was young, articulate and espoused a staunch commitment to nationally specific film-making. In the programme notes for the screening of *Intimate Reflections* at the 19th London Film Festival, he made his position clear:

> British movies have traditionally been parochial. Very few British directors have made films that appeal in content and style to universal audiences (obviously there are exceptions). I think the time has come in Britain for a serious reassessment of the attitude of film-makers or critics (often ridiculous misplaced reverence) to the naturalistic and realistic style of film-making – a style set by directors like Anderson, Richardson, Reisz, etc. over ten years ago (directors who in their time have made valuable and worthy films).[11]

There are no signs here of the anxiety of influence in this hubristic introduction to his first film.

In February 1976, *Screen International* reported that Boyd was to follow up his debut feature with the thriller *Twist* ('a serious attempt to make a good film that will make money'). It was to star Donald Pleasence under Boyd's direction, and James Mason, Helen Mirren and Frank Finlay were to be approached for supporting roles, with a proposed budget of £431,031.[12] In addition, he announced a biopic about the death of the Spanish poet and playwright Federico García Lorca, and script development for an unspecified Kevin Brownlow project. He announced that he was 'ready to spend around £750,000', spreading the cash across five films instead of investing in one prestige production, with the expectation that one international success would pay for any losses on the others. Boyd was sure that he was only enlisting artists who would turn out 'a very commercial product'.[13] Does it matter that none of these films ever came to fruition? They must surely have contributed to the impression of Boyd as abundantly productive, someone to watch.

The premises he'd taken over at 8 Berwick Street offered a multimedia production facility, housing his company offices alongside an editing suite and a basement recording studio. He wanted to pioneer the production of films for the video market, hoping to pre-empt what turned out to be the rather sluggish home-viewing revolution by adapting poetry, classical music and opera for the new medium (as opposed to treating videotape as the cut-rate repository for cinema's second-hand goods); he had tested the water for this with *The Four Seasons* (1979), a short film setting Vivaldi's music to pictures.[14] Around the same time, he completed *The Princess and the Pea*, a short film version of the fairy tale starring Roy Kinnear, Charles Hawtrey and Judi Bowker. It was expected to be the first in a series of such adaptations, at one point under the title

Storybook International in collaboration with Barry Levinson's Hemisphere Productions and HTV.[15] It's hardly surprising that such conspicuous productivity moved John Williams to reach for the tabloid-friendly tagline 'Boyd Wonder'.[16] *Variety* stretched themselves even further with their amply assonant declaration 'Don Boyd new whiz kid in Brit pix biz'.[17]

East of Elephant Rock (1976), Boyd's second film as director, starred John Hurt as a secretary of the British Embassy in an unspecified South-east Asian colonial outpost who is murdered by his lover. It was distributed by Scotia-Barber, who managed to get it shown slightly more widely than *Intimate Reflections* but who nevertheless handled it roughly – after a fleeting first run, they edited it down from ninety to seventy-five minutes so that it could be shunted onto double bills. Some reviews were aggressively unfavourable. David Badder called it 'punishingly inept in every department. Acres of trite dialogue effectively undermine the half-hearted attempt to lift the narrative to a higher plane by introducing a critique of British Colonialism.'[18] Boyd believes that he had set the critical cat among his promotional pigeons with his 'dreadful error' of addressing the assembled press at a press screening in January 1978. He still recalls this incident with bitterness, and cites it as the beginning of a backlash that started to erode the media patronage that might otherwise have helped to attract audiences to his films.[19] It is impossible to certify exactly what he said, though it may have been similar to the plea for a national cinema he wrote in *Screen International* a year earlier:

> People moan constantly about the state of our film industry. What they are normally complaining about is the lack of finance for British films. What I would campaign about as vigorously is that when we actually make British films they should have a chance of being seen in British cinemas and that the distributors promote them as vigorously as anything else they promote . . . Let us make British films with British artists and technicians which make profits in British cinemas.[20]

If this was the kind of rhetoric with which Boyd prefaced *East of Elephant Rock*, it's not difficult to understand why some critics might have turned against a young film-maker sermonising like an elder statesman – they might even have suspected that he was attempting to garner positive reviews by appealing to national pride – but it's not true that the reviews were all vitriolic cavils engineered to humble an upstart entrepreneur. Alexander Walker even compared Boyd's remarks at the screening to 'a wartime speech by the Prime Minister', but blamed the industry for the film's failings, suggesting that Boyd's ambitions were running ahead of the available resources:

> Unfortunately, what the film then goes on to prove is that patriotism is not (quite) enough. . . . Its fault is inexperience – for which it has substituted opportunism. It shows that without a native film industry, the British independent producer can't find the continuity of support which films like this need.[21]

Other reviews made similar concessions on behalf of the film's patriotic intentions. Angela Mason noted that 'this reviewer, it must be said, is biased. Show her a young, independent, *talented* team of British film-makers and she's likely to promise them anything.'[22] Carol Allen of the *London Evening News* even gave him a chance to answer his critics the following weekend, when he complained:

> At a time when the British film industry desperately needs sympathetic encouragement, it is sad that such a worthy endeavour by a young director should be greeted with such a distorted and, to those who know and have seen the film, such an unfair reception.[23]

Such a plea for the best interests of the national film culture could seem like another cry for clemency, but the championing of British film at a time when it was at its most enfeebled was actually the cornerstone of Boyd's Co.'s pitch; a report of suggestions for promotional ideas, probably compiled by James Atherton around the middle of 1977, argues that 'it would be good to stress the British nature of the film, its producers and its content and the distribution organisation behind it'.[24] The promotional trailer for *East of Elephant Rock* implies a sincere belief that audiences' patriotic goodwill towards a local boy's movie would help them to pledge their support.

In a 1980 publicity leaflet marking the delivery of five features (*Sweet William*, *Scum*, *The Tempest*, the rock 'n' roll documentary *Blue Suede Shoes* and *Hussy*, starring Helen Mirren), Boyd put forward his personal statement of the company's aims:

> I believe that it is possible to combine producing modestly budgeted British films with broad international appeal with the production of larger budget American films. My own personal ambition is to make my company an important base of young film makers at the same time as gearing it towards the realities of the commercial film industry.[25]

Roy Tucker's Rossminster group offered the financial backing for this flurry of activity, but it necessitated some fiscal legerdemain behind the scenes. Tucker had a semi-altruistic interest in the arts, and was able to offer some measures to assist Boyd in his film productions. His acrobatic schemes for tax avoidance combined charity status, offshore companies and discretionary trusts to bypass the Inland Revenue.[26] He became a partner in Boyd's Co. and consolidated all of Boyd's interests into a holding company they called Minbourne Ltd, providing the £30,000 needed to finance *Sweet William*, adapted from Beryl Bainbridge's novel and directed, on her insistence, by Claude Watham.

In 1978, Boyd managed to sell, for a quarter of a million dollars, the script by Ed Clinton that would become *Honky Tonk Freeway*, a project he had developed for himself to direct, but which was eventually helmed by John Schlesinger. While he waited for Schlesinger to finish directing Placido Domingo at the Royal Opera House (shooting on *Honky Tonk Freeway* didn't start until 1980), he was able to devote all of his energies to the package of films that Boyd's Co. was preparing. The ensuing roster of films gave the impression of a wildly adventurous, risk-taking venture that was torrentially productive in spite of the financial aridity of the British film-making scene, but it was also produced with the sub-surface props of promised Hollywood cash and complex tax shelters. What looked like production fertility was also evidence of the requirement that shooting on all the films start before the end of the financial year in order to benefit from Tucker's scheme.

Boyd did not develop an array of films with the intention of producing one or two of them; instead, many films were set up with almost impetuous, autocratic bustle. An agreement to make *The Tempest* was made (with a healthy budget of £150,000) on the strength of a single meeting

Elizabeth Welch in Derek Jarman's version of *The Tempest* (1980)

with Derek Jarman and a preview of a thirty-two-page script, and elsewhere it appears that his word, often based on immediate personal responses, was decisive enough to seal a deal and put something into production. He agreed to put money up for the cinema remake of the banned BBC TV film *Scum* immediately after the original version was screened for him, despite the fact that its prospective producer, Clive Parsons, had not yet acquired the rights to it.

None of the Boyd's Co. films had been pre-sold when they finished shooting in spring 1979, so Boyd invested heavily in promotional advertising, mostly evangelising the company to industry insiders rather than stoking anticipation in potential audiences. This is an area that probably should have been entrusted to distributors rather than handled directly by the company director. *The Tempest*, *Hussy* and *Sweet William* were released on consecutive weeks in London in May 1980, each handled by a different distributor and competing for a share of the small domestic audience. In the lead-up to the films' release, it looked as though Boyd's Co.'s productive contribution to British cinema was energetic enough to erase the memories of *Elephant Rock*'s poor reception and prove him to be a serious prospect for the national film culture, as Derek Malcolm suggested in March 1979: '[Don Boyd] is now overdue for some praise. For energy and determination alone, he surely deserves to lay that "dabbler" tag once and for all.'[27]

The 1980 Boyd's Co. brochure lists eight films in preparation, with preliminary artwork in place, including an animated adaptation of Jekyll and Hyde by Ian Emes, Derek Jarman's post-apocalyptic *Neutron*, the Claude Chabrol vehicle *The House on Avenue Road* and Ron Peck's *Actors*. Only one of these films, *Scrubbers* (Mai Zetterling, 1983), would actually make it to the screen. Even in April 1980, Boyd was on the cover of *The Hollywood Reporter* with the announcement of seven new films to be made in the UK within two years.[28] A notice in the *Evening Standard* exploits the productivity of the company in publicising the consecutive release of *Sweet William*, *Hussy* and *The Tempest*. It mentions that Boyd has 'a dozen movies in preparation', confirming that Chabrol would arrive in Britain in September to begin shooting.[29]

This raft of new films, along with *Honky Tonk Freeway*, was to have been the next phase of Boyd's Co.'s development. By packaging the films, it was hoped that a few successes might cover the costs of the others, while the overall image of productivity would give the company a powerful brand. The second package would cost $25m, more than twice the total budget of the first, and working with some of the same artists (Roy Minton, Derek Jarman, Matthew Chapman, Ron Peck) would help to emphasise a house style.[30] Perhaps it would only have taken a US box-office hit to polish Boyd's brand and consolidate his promise for the foreseeable future. Boyd hoped that his sabbatical in America would give him a grounding in Hollywood business techniques that he could then feed back into the UK business.

Matthew Chapman, director of *Hussy*, told *Screen International* that he was seeking a middle ground between 'commercial films and art films' with his 'serious psychological story',[31] while the *Daily Express* preferred to take the tabloid angle with its headline 'Helen [Mirren] becomes a brazen hussy', focusing its attention on the 'sex bomb of the RSC'.[32] Boyd's interest in a cocktail of sensationalism and seriousness permitted this dual identity in the press coverage of his productions, although this approach to publicity in a variety of markets is by no means a unique attribute. It simply shows that Boyd's Co. could not easily be classified as an art-house workshop or commercial production line.

Unlike Michael Deeley, Boyd didn't see 'art film' as necessarily in conflict with popular cinema, as something to play down in publicity material. Despite the appearance of a dichotomous clash between artistic self-interest and economic prudence, Boyd was hopeful that his films should find an audience. His ambitions to corral an audience into the cinema to see his work (through sensational marketing if necessary), while still tackling important subjects, established the template for his future career, foreshadowing his signature desire to commingle high and low cultural elements in an eclectic brew. This can be seen in his amalgamations of the classical and the vernacular in *The Tempest* ([1979] Derek Jarman's candlelit Shakespearean episode), *Aria* ([1987] a compendium of opera music videos by directors including Jean-Luc Godard, Robert Altman, Franc Roddam and Ken Russell) and *My Kingdom* (2001), which relocates *King Lear* to Liverpool's gangland. This gives his work an eclectic clash of registers, but it may also be what led to his downfall; it is arguable that the gap between the two stools of art and commerce was wider in British film at that time than in most other arenas. His insistence upon contemporary British settings for all of the Boyd's Co. films (with the arguable exception of *The Tempest*, which is rendered timeless in Jarman's hands) backs up his claims to a commitment to a national cinema that was reflective of the nation in question, but it could also ensure that the films would at least speak to (and hopefully therefore profit from) the domestic market.

The Boyd's Co. films jointly covered their costs, helped mainly by *Scum* and *The Tempest*, but when it needed to build on this period of productivity and launch the next phase of production, the company was short of funds, and Boyd was away in Hollywood learning valuable, painful lessons on *Honky Tonk Freeway*, whose budget had spiralled out of control to upwards of $23 million. It would recoup only a sliver of that amount at the box office. A more powerful production company might have been able to absorb the damage of isolated misfires, but before it could mobilise the next phase of production packages, Boyd's project as director, *Gossip*, a comedy about celebrity journalists written by Michael and Stephen Tolkin, collapsed just weeks into shooting in 1982; the promise of funding from a group of private investors had turned out to be a fraudulent con trick. The fallout from *Gossip*'s destruction arrested the momentum of the young Boyd and set his career on a very different trajectory, isolating the early years of Boyd's Co. and the package of films it produced as another casualty of the shaky foundations of the British film industry.

This chapter was researched predominantly from the papers held in the Don Boyd Collection (DBC) at the Bill Douglas Centre for the History of Cinema and Popular Culture, Exeter. Thanks are due to curators Michelle Allen, Jessica Gardner and Charlotte Berry for their kind assistance with access to these files.

Notes

1 Don Boyd, interview with Dan North, 20 February 2003.

2 Alexander Walker, *National Heroes: British Cinema in the Seventies* (London: Harrap, 1985), pp. 144–66.

3 Guy Phelps had been writing a biography of Boyd in the 1980s, based on a series of interviews he had conducted with Boyd and some of his contemporaries. This was never finished, and no portion of it has ever been published, though it would have presented the most extensive history of his career to date. Phelps had also attempted to situate Boyd within a broader contextual framework; a draft of his book even began, grandly, with some sketches of cinema's conceptual and technical origins, name-checking Eadweard Muybridge, the Lumière Brothers and R. W. Paul. In 1995, Boyd was contracted to write a memoir of his experiences as a director and producer. Macmillan, the publishers, must have thought they were getting an audacious exposé of British film-making and its personnel. If so, they shouldn't have been disappointed – the extant manuscript is unreservedly personal in naming and shaming those Boyd deemed responsible for the industry's debility. But his aims were broader; he conducted new interviews with Mamoun Hassan, Romaine Hart, Philip French, Simon Relph, Marc Samuelson and many more, devoting separate chapters to his ideas on 'acting', 'directing' and 'producing', anxious to come to terms with the state of British cinema and his sometimes fractious relationship with it. Drafts of the book are held in the Don Boyd Collection (DBC) at the Bill Douglas Centre for the History of Cinema and Popular Culture, University of Exeter, item no. DBC 1349. Macmillan rejected the book, deeming it an over-emotional diatribe repaying some perceived slights

against the author's standing as an artist (letter from Georgina Morley, editorial director at Macmillan, 29 February 1996. DBC 557).

4 Walker, *National Heroes*, p. 266.

5 While scouting locations for what he hoped would become his first feature film, Boyd was commissioned by Overland Trips Ltd to film a promotional record of one of their coach trips to Kathmandu. After six months working on segments for the BBC's speculative science programme *Tomorrow's World*, he was given funding by the Barbara Speake Stage School to make two promotional films about its pupils, then spent six weeks in California vainly trying to arouse studio interest in his clutch of short works. Returning to the UK defeated, he began to make commercials.

6 Don Boyd, interview with Dan North, 19 June 2003.

7 Don Boyd, memo to Ken Davis, 30 April 1974. DBC 1153.

8 Michael Deeley, letter to Dennis Davidson, 15 October 1974. DBC 708.

9 Dilys Powell, 'Intimate Reflections', *The Sunday Times*, 16 November 1975.

10 *Daily Mail*, 22 November 1975.

11 *Intimate Reflections* programme notes, 19th London Film Festival, 1975. DBC 708.

12 Notes attached to a draft screenplay dated 10 March 1976. DBC 1181.

13 Sue Summers, 'Let's *Twist* Again, Says Independent Film Man Don Boyd', *Screen International*, no. 23, February 1976, p. 16.

14 *The Four Seasons* enjoyed some exposure as a supporting film before releases of *The Boys from Brazil* and *Autumn Sonata* in 1979. Memo from James Atherton, 2 November 1979, DBC 018.

15 Correspondence, August 1978, DBC 031. Boyd even planned to launch a publishing firm to be run by Michael Dempsey, with Anthony Burgess's *Moses* as its first product.

16 John Williams, 'Boyd Wonder', *Films Illustrated*, vol. 5, no. 49, September 1975, p. 15.

17 *Variety*, 17 February 1976.

18 David Badder, '*East of Elephant Rock*', *Monthly Film Bulletin*, May 1977, pp. 96–7.

19 Don Boyd, interview with Dan North, 19 June 2003.

20 Don Boyd, letter to *Screen International*, 13 November 1976.

21 Alexander Walker, '*East of Elephant Rock*', *Evening Standard*, 12 January 1978, p. 22.

22 Angela Mason, '*East of Elephant Rock*', *Over 21*, February 1978, p. 11.

23 Don Boyd quoted in Carol Allen, 'Elephant Rock Man Charges His Critics', *London Evening News*, 20 January 1978, p. 23.

24 Production documents, DBC 031.

25 Boyd's Co. publicity brochure, 1980. DBC 477.

26 For more on the controversy surrounding this matter, see Nigel Tutt's *The Tax Raiders: The Rossminster Affair* (London: Financial Training Publications, 1985). A series of partnerships were set up to raise 25 per cent of the total production costs of five films, with Rossminster funding the remainder of the costs. Before the release of the film, the partnership would sell out most of its interest to one of Tucker's offshore companies and claim the whole cost as a tax loss. Partners had to be involved in two different tax years in order to maximise the amount they could claim as losses, which meant that Boyd's production schedule had to take this timing into account – the sudden arrival of this new source of revenue also meant that he had to expand his company so that it could cope with the simultaneous production of five medium- or low-budget features.

27 Derek Malcolm, 'Phoenix of Our Film Industry: Don Boyd, the "Dabbler" Who Has Raised £3 millions', *Arts Guardian*, 31 March 1979, p. 14.
28 Kenelm Jenour, 'Don Boyd Slates 7 Films to Be Made in UK over Two Years', *The Hollywood Reporter*, 16 April 1980, p. 1.
29 *Evening Standard*, 25 April 1980.
30 Adrian Hodges, 'It's Go, Go, Go for Boyd's Co.', *Screen International*, 12 May 1980, p. 44.
31 'Bridging a Gap in the British Film Industry', *Screen International*, 7 April 1979.
32 Victor Davis, 'Helen Becomes a Brazen Hussy', *Daily Express*, 16 March 1979.

14 'More, Much More . . . Roger Moore': A New Bond for a New Decade

Robert Shail

> And what, I can hear you all asking with bated breath, is Mr Roger Moore like as James Bond? Mr Moore as Bond is exactly like the Mr Moore who played The Saint, who in his turn is the nearest approximation to the Mr Moore who plays anything. There are no surprises whatsoever. Which is just as well, since it is extremely doubtful whether Mr Moore could register them. In *Live and Let Die* he is the perfect cypher through which the glamorous hardware of the later Saltzman and Broccoli Bond movies can express themselves.[1]

By 1972, Sean Connery, who had played Ian Fleming's invincible British secret agent James Bond in six highly lucrative film adventures, had seemingly tired of the role. Connery, keen to branch out into more demanding acting parts, had already handed over the mantle of Bond on one previous occasion (to the ill-fated George Lazenby for *On Her Majesty's Secret Service* in 1969) but had been persuaded back for a final outing with *Diamonds Are Forever* in 1971.[2] Unable to secure Connery for the eighth official Bond movie (1967's *Casino Royale* not being part of the main franchise), its American backers, United Artists, were in the market for a replacement. Despite the fact that both Burt Reynolds and Paul Newman were considered for the role, in the end it was given to the British actor Roger Moore. It might have seemed predestined, as Moore had been in the frame for the first Bond film, *Dr No,* back in 1962, and then was considered again as Connery's replacement for both *On Her Majesty's Secret Service* and *Diamonds Are Forever*.

Moore had obvious credentials for playing Bond. Although his acting career stretched back to 1945 and included a variety of bit-parts in films and a good deal of theatre work, audiences new him best as the star of the popular television series *The Saint* (1962–9), where he played Leslie Charteris's suave troubleshooting hero, Simon Templar. Moore had established a public persona as a debonair playboy figure, built principally on his role as Templar and then confirmed by his appearance as Lord Brett Sinclair in another escapist adventure series for television, *The Persuaders* (1971–2). Both parts had placed Moore against glossy backgrounds, put him behind the wheel of stylish sports cars, and frequently into the company of beautiful women. They also allowed him to develop a nonchalant, minimalist acting style that, as he put it, allowed him to 'cover up holes in acting talent by being charming'.[3]

Press coverage of the announcement that Moore was taking over as Bond confirms the sense that he was seen as the heir apparent. The report in the *Daily Mirror* is headlined 'For Simon Templar Read James Bond' and has a picture of Moore bare-chested but for a long cravat; the caption reads 'Roger Moore: the man who had to be Bond'.[4] Moore is interviewed on the patio of the penthouse at the Dorchester Hotel, sipping Scotch and smoking a cigar. When asked if the public will accept him as Bond, he replies: 'I don't see why they shouldn't. I've been typecast for most of my life.' In public, Moore adopted a typically casual attitude to his new job; responding to the inevitable comparisons with Connery, he told the *Sunday Express*: 'The only thing I bring to the role that Sean didn't is slightly whiter teeth.'[5] This throwaway tone was to become central to his approach to the role.

Moore initially signed a contract for three Bond movies, starting with *Live and Let Die* (1973). It's useful to examine the way in which Eon Productions and United Artists incorporated Moore into their promotional campaign for the first film. The most striking thing about the posters for *Live and Let Die* is the degree to which the visual imagery of the franchise remained unchanged. This includes such basics as the typeface used, the pose struck by Moore (dressed in black suit and tie, arms crossed, gun raised to the side of his face) and the arrangement of the design in which all of the action (girls, cars, explosions) radiates outwards from Bond.[6] Above all else, the prospective audience are reassured that the formula remains unaltered. Similarly, the theatrical trailers, from which this essay's title is taken, promise business as usual, with the arrival of a new Bond comparatively insignificant in relation to the stunts, chases and exotic locales on offer.[7]

The new Bond arrives in *Live and Let Die* (1973)

When *Live and Let Die* was released in the summer of 1973, the press reception was lukewarm. The film itself was generally taken as a rather average addition to the Bond cycle, with some concern voiced over the blaxploitation elements in the story. Moore's performance divided opinion. British reviewers frequently refer to him as 'bland', 'lightweight', 'jokey' or 'plastic'. However, many welcomed the element of self-parody that Moore brought to the role, with positive reviews for his performance in most of the tabloids, as well as in the *Sunday Telegraph* and the *New Statesman*. Ian Christie in the *Daily Express* said, 'The new James Bond will do very nicely, thank you.'[8] Others were less complimentary, particularly when comparing Moore with Connery. Nigel Andrews's review in the *Financial Times* is typical:

> Roger Moore's ease, charm and competence are not enough to raise his Bond to the calibre of Connery's. Though the public school snobbery comes through loud and clear, Moore fails to convince either as a ruthless womaniser or as an athletic hand-to-hand fighter. What is needed is rather less of the suave, charm school badinages and rather more of Connery's aggressively mischievous way with his dialogue, his women and with the story's colourfully preposterous succession of villainous encounters and hair's breadth escapes.[9]

Similarly, Felix Barker in the London *Evening News* suggested that 'for all his easy, boyish charm, he lacks the hard sardonic quality of his predecessor'.[10] The repeated conclusion is that Moore's more comic approach had robbed the character of the authenticity that the tougher Connery had brought to it. However, this judgment requires further consideration, as it can be argued that Moore's characterisation was deliberately designed to undermine any 'real life' credibility the character might have contained.

Whatever reservations the critics might have had about the new Bond, the box-office response was clear enough. *Live and Let Die* was the fourth highest-grossing film in the American market during 1973. Although its takings in America were down on *Diamonds Are Forever*, this was more than compensated for by its international returns that made it the second most profitable Bond movie to date, only bettered by *Thunderball* (1965).[11] Moore's tenure as 007 was secure and he appeared in three further adventures during the decade – *The Man with the Golden Gun* (1974), *The Spy Who Loved Me* (1977) and *Moonraker* (1979) – followed by three more outings during the 1980s. *The Spy Who Loved Me* recorded the third highest number of admissions at the British box office of any of the Bond movies, while *Moonraker* and *Live and Let Die* rank at four and five on this list.[12] Until the arrival of Pierce Brosnan in 1995, *Moonraker* had the highest gross of any of the Bond films. For audiences, if not for critics, Moore's version of the myth was successful enough to ensure the profitable continuation of the series.

The comparison between Connery and Moore remains a useful starting point for considering the direction taken by the Bond films in the 1970s. Connery's success in the 1960s was partially a result of his ability to translate the mythology of Fleming's original creation and make it relevant to the fantasies of a contemporary audience. Fleming's characterisation largely conforms to James Chapman's definition of the traditional British imperialist spy hero (as given in his exemplary study of the Bond films).[13] Fleming's hero was every bit the white colonialist abroad, restoring order and exhibiting reverence for the symbols of British power; the personification of a dominant race whose position in the world, as protectors of all that is civilised, has remained

Roger Moore adopts a familiar pose, with Gloria Hendry and Jane Seymour, for *Live and Let Die*

apparently unscathed by the impositions of the Cold War or the collapse of the Empire. The films toned down these elements, along with the sadomasochistic violence that sometimes characterises the books. Most strikingly, the images of Bond's lifestyle have been altered, taking him away from Fleming's gentlemen's clubs towards a more international style of consumerism. Connery's Bond often resembles an affluent holidaymaker out to enjoy the plush hotels, fine food and drink, exciting nightlife and good times offered by his trips abroad. This is particularly apparent in the depiction of his female conquests. The original Honey of Fleming's *Dr No* is a childlike waif who comes under Bond's fatherly protection. In the film, she has become Ursula Andress, emerging from the surf clad in a white bikini. The Bond of the Connery films is a charming womaniser, but the aristocratic dominance of Fleming's original has given way to a kind of international playboy whose aim is the pursuit of hedonistic pleasures that might seemingly be open (at least as fantasy) to all 1960s men.

Connery's Bond plays out an exaggerated projection of the archetypal 1960s 'Swinging' male lifestyle. Connery said of Bond: 'He enjoys the freedom that the normal person doesn't get. He likes to eat. He likes to drink. He likes girls.'[14] Tony Bennett and Janet Woollacott are surely correct in observing that Fleming's innate conservatism had been replaced by a rampantly capitalist dream world,[15] but it is a world rooted in the context of 1960s Britain. The pleasures afforded by the Bond films are those of an increasingly affluent male audience, experiencing their first foreign holidays, purchasing domestic 'gadgets' and feeling the beneficial effects of a gradual erosion of traditional moral straitjackets. The transition from imperialist gentleman-hero to 1960s hedonist was recognised in contemporary reviews of Connery's Bond. David Robinson in *The Times* suggested that over the first three films, the series had 'crossed the borderline from the baroque into the fantastic'.[16] The key factor in this success was clearly Connery himself. As an archetypal working-class hero of the period in his own right, he reflected one of the era's central myths. Both United Artists and the media were fond of reminding audiences of the actor's authentic streetwise toughness and his rise from the working-class neighbourhoods of Edinburgh. His Scottishness helped to distance Bond from the class connotations with which Fleming had defined him. Fleming's Bond is a class snob who carries his knowledge of wines, clothes and food with him as an indicator of his superior social status. In Connery's version, this connoisseurship is an indication of Bond's modern, and potentially classless, sophistication.

The figure of the hedonistic playboy became one of the central media myths of 1960s culture, and working-class male stars like Connery, Michael Caine and Terence Stamp were essential to its creation. Its main features were a dedication to conspicuous consumption and a freer attitude towards sexual morality, combined with a new form of democratic accessibility. The most public embodiment of this new lifestyle was offered by the American entrepreneur Hugh Heffner, both in his own personal life and in his creation of the Playboy clubs, with their promise of entry to a world of easy sex, gambling and self-indulgence. Such an apparent paradise was now to be available not just to those of a certain class but to anyone who could afford it (and who was also male). For a British heterosexual male emerging from the dreariness of the postwar period, the attractions of such a mythology, however shallow, are obvious enough. As James Chapman argues, for all of their fantastical absurdities, the Bond films of the 1960s were rooted in a form of aspirational imagining for their audience.[17]

It is in relation to this aspirational dimension of the character, as well as through their relationship to the wider context, that Moore's Bond films of the 1970s differ most strikingly to Connery's of the 1960s. The Britain of the 1960s out of which the series grew was a comparatively affluent, stable and optimistic place. Although eschewing generalisations, the historian Arthur Marwick describes the 1960s as a time when 'life was good and all seemed far from lost. Still there was a joy in the present, and hope for the future.'[18] By contrast, Marwick designates the 1970s as 'The Time of Troubles', among them accelerating economic decline, the collapse of traditional manufacturing industries, increasing numbers of industrial disputes marked by outbreaks of violence, rising racial tensions and the reawakening of sectarian conflict in Northern Ireland. For Marwick, the era saw the 'break-up of the optimistic consensus which had, according to one point of view, successfully carried Britain through the difficult post-war years into the affluence of the sixties'.[19] The response of the Bond films, which had always shown a remarkable ability to acknowledge the changing mood of their audience, was to shift decisively from the aspirational to the escapist.

One way in which this was expressed was in the increasingly self-deprecatory and humorous tone adopted by the films, a strategy designed to dispossess them of the rougher-edged authenticity of the Connery period. Connery had always employed self-consciously arch one-liners delivered with a deadpan wink to the audience, but Moore was to carry this much further. The new attitude is established in *Live and Let Die* when Bond is invited to return to bed by one of his sexual conquests and replies: 'Well, there's no sense in going off half-cocked.' At the conclusion of *Moonraker*, Bond is inevitably caught in flagrante with his female co-star (Lois Chiles), this time while in outer space; Q's explanation is that he is simply 'attempting re-entry'. In an interview, Tom Mankiewicz, screenwriter on *Live and Let Die* and *The Man with the Golden Gun*, explained that he deliberately shaped the style of the scripts to take advantage of Moore's established skills as a light comedian.[20] In the Connery vehicles, the effect of the one-liners is to draw attention to the harshly amoral outlook of Bond, whereas Moore's elaborately risqué remarks tend simply to draw attention to themselves.

This approach is extended to other typical features of the Bond formula such as the chases and stunts, the gadgets and the villains. *Live and Let Die* features a chase with Bond at the wheel of a red double-decker bus (whose top half is removed by a low bridge), while *The Spy Who Loved Me* includes a fight in an ambulance that concludes with the 'heavy' zooming downhill on a hospital trolley and crashing into an advertising hoarding. In the same film, Bond's glamorous sports car turns into a submersible (providing one of the film's highlights as he drives it from the sea straight onto a crowded holiday beach). *Moonraker* provides Bond with a motorised Venetian gondola that then turns conveniently into a hovercraft that he drives nonchalantly through St Mark's Square. In both *The Spy Who Loved Me* and *Moonraker*, the villain is the gigantic 'Jaws'

Moore's James Bond gets to grips with 'Jaws' (Richard Kiel) in *The Spy Who Loved Me* (1977)

(Richard Kiel), nicknamed for his metal teeth, a character who proved so popular with audiences that he is effectively turned into a hero at the end of the latter film and given his own love interest. Even the much-anticipated pre-credit sequences are handled in humorous mode; the opening of *The Spy Who Loved Me* finds Bond in bed with yet another conquest and then follows him, after a barrage of one-liners, through a superbly executed snow chase on skis to a finale where he plummets over a cliff-edge only to be saved by his Union Jack parachute. Again, these sequences invite the audience to applaud their ingenuity and wit, rather than thrill to their tense excitement.

One consequence of the humour in these films is to push the audience out from identification and involvement in the narrative. Although it may have been far from the minds of the films' creators, it gives the finished products a superficial air of postmodernism. By borrowing two terms, 'prefabrication' and 'intertextuality', from Susan Hayward's useful description of postmodernism, we can examine further the effect achieved by Moore's Bond movies.[21] Prefabrication describes the tendency to reuse motifs or plot elements from earlier films with the intention of playing on the audience's pre-knowledge of cinematic conventions. This is used quite blatantly in Moore's Bond films, although the references tend to invoke only those films featuring Moore, rather than the whole series. For example, the red-neck sheriff who is used for comic effect in *Live and Let Die* returns as a tourist in *The Man with the Golden Gun*. Moore's exit by car from the sea onto a beach in *The Spy Who Loved Me* is witnessed by a holidaymaker who thinks he is hallucinating from too much drink. This gag is then replicated in the St Mark's sequence in *Moonraker* with the same actor (his double-take is outrageously mirrored with a shot of the similarly amazed reaction of a pigeon). These running gags invite the audience to be complicit in the self-conscious artificiality of the films.

Similarly, intertextuality is used to reference contemporary films and genres in an overtly knowing manner. The most obvious point of filmic reference in *Live and Let Die* is blaxploitation, which features prominently in the Harlem sequences, with the 'Fillet of Soul' nightclub and extras kitted out in Afros. Yaphet Kotto's Mr Big is a caricature black drug baron, but racist overtones tend to be countered by the ironic handling of the stereotypes. *The Man with the Golden Gun* selects another contemporary genre that was then popular with audiences, the martial arts film. Here Bond infiltrates a kung-fu training school and is rescued by two high-kicking schoolgirls during a fight sequence that is again played largely for laughs. *The Spy Who Loved Me* manages a filmic quote from *Lawrence of Arabia* (1962), but it is *Moonraker* that goes overboard on cinematic references. The current audience vogue for science fiction is structured throughout the film's narrative but appears specifically in the concluding laser-gun fight that is heavily reminiscent of *Star Wars* (1977) and in a joke where the entry-pad code for a secret laboratory plays the theme tune from *Close Encounters of the Third Kind* (1977).

These postmodern devices tend to draw the audience's attention to the film as text rather than as social practice. Susan Hayward suggests that postmodern strategies usually operate within two possible modes: parody or pastiche.[22] Parody implies an aspect of ideological critique that would necessitate a direct relation between text and context, whereas pastiche suggests a deliberate attempt to sever this connection and to offer text as playful distraction from context. The latter definition echoes Frederic Jameson's analysis of postmodernism as a symptom of the alienated subject in late capitalism.[23] It is difficult to discern much that might be described as parody in these terms in the Roger Moore Bond films; a sympathetic reading might be made of elements in *The Spy Who Loved Me* where the narrative development offers a mild condemnation of Cold War politics and makes the case for détente between East and West – a reading made persuasively by James Chapman.[24] The films do, however, conform closely to the concept of pastiche. The pleasures they offer rely heavily on self-referentiality and intertextual knowledge on the part of the audience. Their form and tone repeatedly draw attention to their constructedness and status as cinematic objects, abstracting them from wider social discourse or historical placement. Playfulness is (almost) everything here; the audience are invited into an experience that is, in cinematic terms, hermetically sealed. Of course, as Jameson points out, such an exercise is always ultimately futile; by their very evasiveness, these films acknowledge that there is something that needs to be evaded.

Admittedly, there are aspects of the films which don't fit quite so neatly with this analysis of their ideological function. Moore's Bond occasionally exhibits signs of his innate chauvinism in an overt way. The narrative provides him with justification for physically abusing Maud Adams's character in *The Man with the Golden Gun* (albeit that Moore looks particularly unconvincing in this sequence), while his sexual dominance is reaffirmed by Solitaire (Jane Seymour) in *Live and Let Die* when, after she has lost her virginity to him, she confesses, 'You make me feel like a whole woman.' Elements of racial and class snobbery remain; Bond's treatment of the black agent Rosie Carver (Gloria Hendry) in *Live and Let Die* is bordering on the patronising. Topical references sometimes occur, such as the mention of the energy crisis as a plot point in *The Man with the Golden Gun*. Such features might be read as evidence of the inherently conservative nature of the franchise. Jeremy Black certainly interprets them as a means of hanging on to increasingly outdated attitudes and prejudices.[25] This in itself could be seen as a means of denying their interrelation to a contemporary context in which such attitudes were being challenged. However, these aspects are relatively secondary in relation to the overall strategy of pastiche. In some cases they are directly countered by other sections of the same film, so that Rosie is also treated with real affection by Bond, and Lois Chiles in *Moonraker* is given the chance to match Moore in one-liners and repartee. The scene of Bond hitting Andrea Anders (Maud Adams) was apparently considered a serious error of judgment by the film-makers themselves.[26]

In a promotional interview for *The Spy Who Loved Me*, Roger Moore, in a characteristically mock-grandiose manner, explained that the Bond films have a surprising affinity with classical Greek theatre in that they share the same aspiration to give the audience a glimpse of the Gods, to take them out of themselves and into another realm.[27] In the violently pessimistic political landscape of Britain in the 1970s, perhaps it was inevitable that the always fantastical world of the Bond movies should turn in on themselves in such an exaggerated fashion. It was a profitable response to the zeitgeist, but what the series had gained in sustainability it may have lost in cultural resonance. If Connery's Bond is a product of the aspirations of the 1960s, then Moore's 007 may be a symptom of their loss.

Notes

1 Derek Malcolm, *Guardian*, 5 July 1973.

2 There are many accounts of the Bond series but for a highly detailed production overview, see John Cork and Bruce Scivally, *James Bond: The Legacy* (London: Boxtree, 1972).

3 Roger Moore quoted by Deborah Murdoch, 'Why the Saint Is Pleased to Be Scared', *Daily Mail*, 30 August 1969.
4 Don Short, 'For Simon Templar Read James Bond', *Daily Mirror*, 2 August 1972.
5 Roderick Mann, 'The New Bond with the Whiter Teeth', *Sunday Express*, 22 April 1973.
6 Tony Nourmand, *James Bond Movie Posters* (London: Boxtree, 2001) provides handsome reproductions of promotional posters from a variety of territories.
7 The United Artists two-disc special edition DVD releases of the Bond movies contain a plethora of interviews, documentaries, artwork and trailers, which provide fascinating material for those interested in the marketing and promotion of the Bond franchise.
8 Reviews/previews of *Live and Let Die*: Margaret Hinxman, *Sunday Telegraph*, 8 July 1973; John Coleman, *New Statesman*, 6 March 1973; Ian Christie, *Daily Express*, 4 July 1973.
9 Nigel Andrews, *Financial Times*, 13 July 1973.
10 Felix Barker, *London Evening News*, 5 July 1973.
11 For box-office figures on the Bond films, see Cork and Scivally, *James Bond: The Legacy*, pp. 300–3.
12 Information on British box-office admissions can be found in The Ultimate Film Chart at <bfi.org.uk/features/ultmatefilm/facts> (accessed 7 August 2007).
13 James Chapman, *Licence to Thrill: A Cultural History of the James Bond Films* (London: I. B. Tauris, 1999), p. 20.
14 Sean Connery quoted in Sheldon Lane (ed.), *For Bond Lovers Only* (London: Panther, 1965), p. 75.
15 Tony Bennett and Janet Woollacott, *Bond and Beyond: The Political Career of a Popular Hero* (London: Macmillan, 1987).
16 David Robinson, *The Times*, 17 September 1964.
17 Chapman, *Licence to Thrill*, pp. 68–9.
18 Arthur Marwick, *British Society since 1945* (London: Penguin, 1996), p. 181.
19 Ibid., p. 184.
20 Tom Mankiewicz is interviewed in the documentary *Inside Live and Let Die* featured on the two-disc DVD edition of the film released by United Artists.
21 Susan Hayward, *Cinema Studies: The Key Concepts, Second Edition* (London and New York: Routledge, 2000), p. 277.
22 Ibid.
23 See Frederic Jameson, 'Postmodernism and Consumer Society', in Hal Foster (ed.), *Postmodern Culture* (London: Pluto Press, 1983).
24 Chapman, *Licence to Thrill*, p. 189.
25 Jeremy Black, *The Politics of James Bond: From Fleming's Novels to the Big Screen* (Lincoln, NB, and London: University of Nebraska Press, 2005), pp. 146–7.
26 Interviews with director Lewis Gilbert and writer Christopher Wood for the special edition DVD of *The Spy Who Loved Me* indicate that they wished to move away from any violence against women and adopt a much lighter approach.
27 Roger Moore interviewed in *My Word Is My Bond*, a promotional documentary for *The Spy Who Loved Me* featured on the DVD special edition of the film.

15 The BFI and British Independent Cinema in the 1970s

Christophe Dupin

> It is a measure of the importance of such a small and inadequate fund that it arouses so much controversy and debate about the way in which it is dispensed.[1]
>
> Michael Relph, Chairman of the Production Board, 1977

Set up in 1952 as the Experimental Film Fund and revived as the Production Board fourteen years later, the British Film Institute's film production scheme was presented at the turn of the 1970s with an opportunity to transcend its initial role as a minor, and largely unrecognised, research and development unit for the British film industry. This chapter introduces the modest origins of the scheme and examines how it established itself in the 1970s as a key independent production agency in Britain, thanks to an increase in its financial resources, the professionalisation of its practice and a redefinition of its relationships with film-makers. It also looks at the Production Board's sympathetic response to the aesthetic and political radicalisation of independent film-making in Britain through its support of a number of avant-garde and political projects, until the refocus of its resources on the funding of low-budget narrative features at the turn of the 1980s.

In December 1970, in an article defending the Production Board's achievements against recent criticism, the BFI Director, Stanley Reed, observed that 'what is overlooked is that the British Film Institute until recently had no brief to get involved in film production at all'.[2] The reason for the unofficial, pragmatic way in which the BFI's film-making operation developed from the early 1950s onwards is that from its inception in 1933 the Institute was prevented from engaging in any activity that could potentially interfere with the commercial interests of the film trade. Yet its progressive incursion into film sponsorship and production stemmed from the realisation that nothing was done for the training of young film-makers or the encouragement of new ideas in British film-making. The setting-up of the Experimental Film Fund was made possible, rather unexpectedly, by the provision of a token grant by the film trade itself through the allocation of a small percentage of the Eady Levy. From the start, the Fund was allocated to projects selected by a committee of eminent producers led by Michael Balcon, and administered on a daily basis by senior BFI officers.

Despite its extremely limited resources and unofficial status, the scheme managed to provide small but strategically invaluable financial (and very occasionally technical) support mainly to untried film-makers seeking to gain the experience that would allow them to enter the film and television industries. Between 1952 and 1965, it sponsored, wholly or in part, about fifty short films of a great thematic and stylistic variety, its most notable achievement being its support of the majority of films associated with the Free Cinema movement. By 1963, however, the Fund had been exhausted and it became dormant for several years, until Jennie Lee's appointment as Britain's first Arts Minister in 1964 provided new prospects for the scheme. As she significantly increased the BFI's annual grant-in-aid from the Department of Education and Science, she insisted that part of this increase should go to experimental film production. As a result, the scheme – renamed the BFI Production Board – was officially reconstituted in July 1966, under the supervision of the same committee and with a similar brief as its previous incarnation. With the promise of an annual budget, a permanent production unit with offices, cutting rooms, basic equipment and supporting staff, the BFI's production activity entered a new phase of its development marked by the professionalisation of its practice.

These changes made possible an improvement in the technical standards of the films, and allowed for more efficient training of inexperienced film-makers. In the late 1960s, the Board financed and often produced, on shoestring budgets, nearly seventy films (all shorts but two), largely thanks to the dedication of its first production officer, the young Australian film-maker Bruce Beresford (1966–71). Its compact and well-organised production unit, referred to by Stanley Reed as a 'round-the-clock film factory' (it accommodated up to twelve projects at a time), provided a creative environment where film-makers with diverse backgrounds and interests (from young directors seeking to work in the industry like Stephen Frears and Tony Scott, to experimental film-makers such as Jeff Keen, Mark Boyle and Tony Sinden) could meet and exchange ideas. The positive reviews of BFI-funded films in the press and the prizes won in short film festivals attested to the success of the scheme. Yet with a meagre average annual budget of £12,000 between 1966 and 1971, the Board's influence was bound to be limited, both as a training centre for the new generation of feature film-makers and as a sponsor of non-commercial films. Besides, new independent film-making practices associated with the emerging counter-culture started challenging what they saw as the Board's obsolete views on film-making.

In the fast-changing context of British cinema at the turn of the 1970s, the Board faced its first serious crisis. The establishment of the long-awaited National Film School in 1970, as well as the development of practical film courses in art schools, polytechnics and universities, threatened to deprive the Board of its 'training' function. The Arts Council's new funding scheme for artists' films the same year also encroached on the Board's brief.[3] Meanwhile, the low-budget end of British feature-film production had virtually disappeared following the withdrawal of American finance after 1968, which made it almost impossible for first-time directors to find a way into commercial film-making. Hopes that the state-supported National Film Finance Corporation would play a major role in reversing this situation were quickly shattered by the Conservative government's refusal to finance its development sufficiently.

In those circumstances, the shake-up of the Production Board's policy, methods and finances in the early 1970s was inevitable. This had been anticipated by Stanley Reed as early as May 1968 when he had first advocated the Board's move to low-budget feature-film funding in order to 'bridge the gap between the making of a modest film for the Board and [the film-maker's] first commercial feature'.[4] An early beneficiary of this new policy was Tony Scott, who was given the opportunity to direct first a short, *One of the Missing* (1968), then a low-budget featurette, *Loving Memory* (1970). However successful this example was, it was bound to remain an exception until the Production Board had the financial means for its new brief. Several years of campaigning finally paid off in 1972, when the Board obtained substantial financial support from the industry through the allocation of an annual grant from the Eady Levy (but only after Balcon had publicly threatened to resign from the Production Board), and convinced the Arts Minister, Lord Eccles, of the worth of its proposed feature-film policy. After obtaining the usual guarantee that the Production Board would not compete directly with the commercial film industry, Eccles agreed to a significant increase in the government money made available for the BFI's production activity. The Board's operating budget for that year reached £75,000, three times the level of the previous year, but hardly enough to embark on an ambitious feature-film production programme (see Figure 1).

The change in the scale of the Board's financial resources coincided with a double change in personnel, as Bruce Beresford resigned in July 1971 to pursue his film-making career and Michael Balcon retired in January 1972. The latter's successor, Michael Relph, had been one of his close collaborators since the 1930s and shared most of his views on what the role of the Production Board should be. However, Relph lacked Balcon's charisma and authority, and his reign over the Board (1972–8) is remembered by many as a subdued one. The substitution of all Board members between March 1972 and February 1973 completed the overhaul of the scheme.

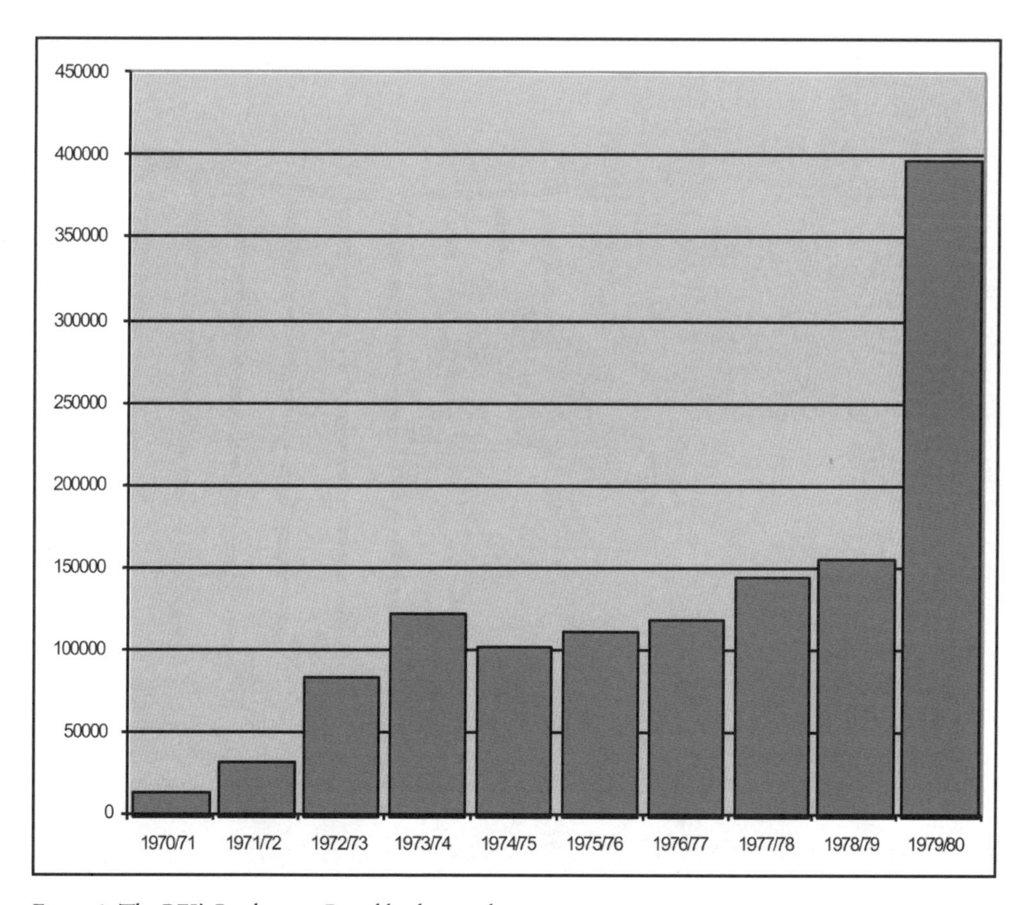

Figure 1: The BFI's Production Board budget in the 1970s

On the whole, the new generation of members were younger and more aware of the latest developments in British cinema than the 'great and the good' whom they replaced, and represented a wider range of qualifications and interests.

When Michael Relph took up his position on the Board, the new Head of Production, Mamoun Hassan, had been in place for a year and had already announced his plan to create a mini-studio where a British cinema based on narrative feature forms could flourish, neither outside nor against the industry but rather at its more 'cultural' end. One of its first decisions in July 1971 was to recommend the allocation of a £3,650 grant to a semi-autobiographical mini-feature film about poverty-stricken childhood in a Scottish mining town, submitted by London Film School graduate Bill Douglas. Shot by a limited crew, with non-professional actors and on 16mm, the forty-eight-minute *My Childhood* proved a turning point in the Production Board's history. A deeply personal and poetic film, it went on to gather high critical praise and was awarded the Silver Lion for Best First Feature at the Venice Film Festival, thus proving the validity of the Board's new policy while earning Douglas the chance to direct two more films for the Board, *My Ain Folk* (1974) and *My Way Home* (1978).

A turning point in the BFI Production Board's history: *My Childhood* (1971)

In Hassan's mind, the Board should not only back first-time directors but also more experienced ones who were unable to find financial support elsewhere. Kevin Brownlow and Andrew Mollo, who, despite the success of *It Happened Here* (1966), had seen their next script rejected by the industry on several occasions, epitomised the latter category.[5] On Hassan's advice, the Board agreed to back their ambitious project – a full-length feature on the Diggers' radical movement during the English Civil Wars in the 1640s. With a budget of £24,000, this was the most expensive project ever funded by the Board. Yet, for a period piece produced to rigorous standards of historical authenticity, it was a shoestring budget. The film took several years to complete and, like *My Childhood*, was made in the semi-amateur conditions (shot in black and white and partly on 16mm, mostly at weekends, with a largely non-professional cast) that characterised all the narrative feature films funded under Hassan, from Peter Smith's *A Private Enterprise* (1974), a sensitive portrayal of the problems surrounding Asian immigrants in Britain, to Chuck Despins's musical *Moon over the Alley* (1975) or David Gladwell's *Requiem for a Village* (1975). One significant breakthrough in the industrialisation of the Board's practice was Hassan's demand that the producer, director, crew and main actors be paid during the making of the films, albeit below the minimum union rates, thanks to special dispensation informally negotiated with them. The Board also introduced the idea of small script-development grants to film-makers about to embark on feature-length projects. As for the commissioning of 'test sequences' (a regular feature of the Fund/Board's work in the past), it became an essential exercise in the context of the selection of increasingly expensive projects.

Despite its emphasis on low-budget, narrative feature films, the Board still funded a great variety of shorts (twenty-eight of the thirty-eight films initiated under Hassan were under sixty minutes). A majority of these were professionally produced narrative shorts and featurettes by first-time directors, such as Michael Alexander's *Home and Away* (from a script by Bill Douglas), Terence Davies's *Children* (1976) and Alan Brown's *Brown Ale with Gertie* (1974). The Board also perpetuated its initial role as a patron of short, non-professional experimental films by giving out a few small grants (generally under £2,000) to projects ranging from animation (Stan Hayward's *The Mathematician* [1976], Chris Majka's *Dialogue* [1974]) to documentary (Giovanni Gnecchi-Ruscone's *L'Année 71* [1975], David Pearce's *A Portrait of David Hockney* [1972]). Finally, the Board's decision to devote a small proportion of its budget to the funding of alternative film-making practices such as the London Film-makers' Co-op stemmed from the pressure exerted on the Board by one of its new members, the avant-garde film-maker Malcolm Le Grice. Although Hassan, like the majority of the Board, had little interest in what he saw as a marginal aesthetic, he nevertheless supported his appointment to the Board when he realised that it had become impossible to ignore this growing trend of independent film-making.

Le Grice systematically supported all avant-garde film-makers who applied for a grant, and vigorously campaigned for better recognition of both the structuralist avant-garde and the emerging politically committed film collectives, and for the replacement of the Board's traditional script-based, project-by-project selection system by one better adapted to the modes of production of these areas of film-making. He obtained significant results over the next three years, with the selection of avant-garde projects by Stuart Pound, Steve Dwoskin, William Raban, Peter Gidal, Gill Etherley and Tony Sinden. The Board also made a gesture towards film-making collectives by setting aside £10,500 towards a Group Support Fund that awarded equipment grants to twelve independent film and video groups (including the Berwick Film Collective, the London Women's Film Group, the LFMC, Cinema Action and Liberation Films) in April 1974. The following year, the Board swapped the Group Support Fund for a scheme whereby technical equipment was made available for free to collectives. Le Grice also convinced the Board to make a one-off £16,000 capital grant to the LFMC before the BFI Regional Department took over responsibility for capital funding in April 1976.

By the time Hassan resigned in early 1974, the Board was a transformed operation and its profile had been considerably raised. His plan to regenerate cultural British cinema through a programme of low-budget features was praised by mainstream film critics, who welcomed the advent of a body of films made not only in Britain with British funds but also 'in the continuing British cinematic tradition'.[6] The Board's achievements enhanced its status within its parent organisation, with the Production unit finally promoted to the status of stand-alone BFI Department (April 1972). It coincided with a shift in the balance of power between the Board and the Head of Production. Although the authority over the selection of projects lay ultimately with the Board, in practice Hassan used his negotiating skills and enthusiasm for particular projects to win the Board's confidence. In his own words, 'I made the selection and they [the Board] were there to moderate my exuberance.'[7] His informal commissioning of certain film-makers, his knowledge of the projects submitted for selection and of those in production, gave him an advantage over the Board at all stages of the production process. But the Board's success remained fragile, as Hassan's more professional approach to production had not been matched by changes in the Department's operational structure. The Lower Marsh premises and equipment were inadequate for the standard of production to which Hassan aspired and the unit was still effectively managed by three people at a time when as many as twenty films were in production simultaneously.

The scheme's major flaw in the early 1970s remained the poor distribution and exhibition of the completed films. Screenings of BFI productions at the National Film Theatre, which were once the only chance for most film-makers to have their film shown to the press and to London audiences, were discontinued under Hassan, who failed to implement a more dynamic scheme. As for the distribution debacle, Hassan blamed it on the nonexistent market for short films in Britain, the difficulty of distributing 16mm films in commercial cinemas, the lack of expertise of the BFI's Distribution Department and the failure to involve film-makers in the process. One of his last decisions before his departure was to bring Peter Sainsbury, a film buyer for the BBC, to the Department in order to 'place the films at a roughcut stage'.[8] By having a say in the appointment of his successor, the BBC producer Barrie Gavin, he hoped that the tighter links between the Board and the BBC would benefit BFI productions. What he probably did not expect, however, was the significant change in direction that Gavin and Sainsbury were to bring with them.

The move away from narrative feature films and the new emphasis on social and political documentaries in 1974 was due primarily to Gavin's own background in television arts programmes and documentaries. As he later remembered:

> If the Production Board's job was not only to find new or young filmmakers but also to reflect the country in which we lived, then you could not ignore documentary cinema. I also knew from my own experience that you can make money go a considerable distance further if you're not paying for make-up, costumes or actors.[9]

If he questioned the affordability of Hassan's programme at a time of rampant inflation and the stagnation of the Board's budget (see Figure 1), he was equally sceptical about the coming of a low-budget cultural British cinema promised by Hassan:

> I didn't recognise what Mamoun said was there. I couldn't see it. He was very proud, and rightly so, of *Winstanley* and Douglas' biographical trilogy . . . In my view, these were Mamoun's leading cards, you played the cards but then you didn't have any more in your hand.[10]

Instead, the new two-headed leadership of the Production Department formed by Gavin and Sainsbury was eager to recognise the radical end of independent cinema as one of the Board's key constituencies.[11] Significantly, it was around that time that this sector organised itself into a pressure group, the Independent Filmmakers' Association (IFA), which started formulating its demands on the Board in a more concerted way. At the other end of the independent film spectrum, the supporters of a low-budget commercial cinema soon reacted by forming their own lobby, the Association of Independent Producers.

As an institutional sponsor open in principle to all trends of independent cinema, the Board suddenly became the stage of a heated ideological battle between these radically opposed independent film-making practices. Where Hassan had enjoyed having to convince the Board of the worth of specific projects, Gavin found the confrontational nature of this relationship utterly frustrating and he resigned within fourteen months. As Nicholas Pole put it, 'this was not simply a difference of personality; it was a symptom of a deeper rift between Gavin and the Board over the development of a self-consciously political movement in the independent sector to which Gavin wished to give expression'.[12] Despite the Board's scepticism, his short tenure remains one of the most audacious periods in the Board's history in terms of the number of aesthetically and politically challenging projects he supported. Of the thirty-two films selected for production during his term, twelve were (mainly feature-length) documentaries 'concerned with social issues, with the structure of society and the necessity to change it'.[13] The majority of these were the work of far-left and feminist film collectives (from the Berwick Street Collective to the London Women's Film Group or the Newsreel Collective) who rejected conventional documentary modes and instead sought to produce political meaning at all stages of their film-making practice.

They showed a strong engagement with political debates of the 1970s, such as workers' struggles (*Miners' Film* [1974], *Occupy!* [1976], *'36 to '77* [1978], *So That You Can Live* [1981]), abortion and women's liberation (*Abortion – An Egg is Not a Chicken* [1975], *Whose Choice?* [1976]) or Northern Ireland (*Ireland – Behind the Wire* [1974]). Other selected documentaries were more conventional in their mode of production but were critical enough of the deficiencies of the state's bureaucratic apparatus to expose the Board to public controversy (Nick Broomfield and Joan Churchill's *Juvenile Liaison* [1975], Ben Lewin's *Welcome to Britain* [1976]). Another novelty was that most of these documentaries received relatively large grants (up to £20,000) previously reserved for low-budget feature films. As for the aesthetic avant-garde, it also received more attention from the Board than ever before, with relatively large grants awarded to Peter Gidal, Chris Welsby and Mike Dunford, and to Peter Donnebauer for his exploratory work on video. Among the few fiction films selected under Gavin, the two most significant projects

(Horace Ové's *Pressure* [1975] – the first black feature film in Britain – and Bill Douglas's *My Way Home* [1978]) had actually been recommended by Hassan, while other narrative fictions (Ken McMullen's *Resistance* [1976] and Stewart MacKinnon's *Justine* [1976], for instance) were close to the avant-garde for the way they disrupted the narrative codes of conventional cinema.

When Peter Sainsbury succeeded Barrie Gavin as Head of Production in late 1975, his first task was to clear the backlog of forty films initiated by his predecessors and still in production. New government regulation about cash flow in public organisations, which required that all film-making grants awarded by the Board should be spent by the end of the financial year, helped him to rationalise the BFI's production activity. He set up a better planned and more focused selection procedure whereby all applications were received, shortlisted and selected between January and April each year, rather than on an ad-hoc basis. He believed that the new system would be fairer for applicants, increase the effectiveness the Board's work throughout the year and rationalise the deployment of the Production Department's resources. It was also meant to ensure that all productions would be completed within one of two financial years. Despite this positive development, 1976 proved one of the most difficult years in the history of the Board, which went through three major crises exposing deep-rooted problems of identity, policy and effectiveness left unresolved since its establishment ten years earlier, as well as the Board's difficult adaptation to a fast-changing context of independent cinema.

The first of these crises revealed the ideological differences between the majority of the Board and the Head of Production. It was triggered by Sainsbury's call for a rationally accountable policy for the Board, through the definition of a set of explicit criteria for the selection of projects, in order to avoid having to rely on implicit choices dictated by the Board members' personal prejudices. Although he justified the need for such a transparent policy by citing the widening gap between the number of grant applications received and the scarcity of resources at the Board's disposal, the vast majority of the Board challenged this materialistic approach to decision-making, which they regarded as an evident manifestation of the politicisation of certain BFI departments (in particular Film Availability Services, the Educational Advisory Service and the Production Department).[14] They also suspected that the Head of Production's real motives were to dictate to the Board the terms of this 'stated policy' according to his own interests. The controversy escalated in October 1976 when Sainsbury and the BFI's FAS programmed a Production Board retrospective at the NFT in which they opted for an openly critical assessment of its recent work rather than a celebration of 'the best of the Production Board', while simultaneously publishing a booklet reiterating their controversial ideas about an explicitly formulated policy for the Board.[15] Several independent film-makers, past Board members and grantees rallied behind an enraged Mamoun Hassan to attack what they considered 'an attempt at manipulation of the filmmakers' works in pursuit of petty political purposes within the British Film Institute' in a manifesto sent to the BFI Governors, the Arts Minister and the national press.[16] After months of impassioned discussions, the Board and the Head of Production eventually reached a compromise by publishing new *Guidelines to Applicants* that clarified to some extent the Board's policy by setting out a number of practical selection criteria, but fell short of the explicit policy advocated by Sainsbury.

The second crisis publicly exposed the Board's ill-defined relationship with its parent body, as well as the ambiguous status of both the Head of Production (a BFI employee at the service of the Board) and the Board Chairman (who was also a BFI Governor). Its origin was the objection by the Lancashire police to the screening of the recently completed *Juvenile Liaison* (a documentary on the workings of the Juvenile Liaison scheme of the Lancashire police). After the BFI (as the film's copyright holder) gave in to the police's pressure and refused to screen the film publicly, seven of the nine Board members threatened to resign should the Governors refuse to reconsider and to guarantee the Board's independence. This mutiny was followed by six months of dispute, which only died down after the bulk of the mutinous Board members retired at the end of the year – without settling the case (the film was not shown to the public for decades) or solving the Board's constitutional crisis. An implication of this crisis was the level of public interest it generated for the Board. One of its new members, Tony Rayns, remembers that

> the fact that *Juvenile Liaison* got so much press attention was instrumental in a way in refocusing the Production Board. . . . It made us conscious for the first time of the potential level of interest that there could be in the Production Board films.

But it also exposed the Board's poor distribution of its films, which triggered the third crisis of 1976.

The controversial documentary *Juvenile Liaison* (1975), which the BFI withdrew

By the time Sainsbury took over as Head of Production, none of the recently completed features had found a commercial distributor, the main reason being the cost of transferring films made on 16mm to 35mm. He quickly made the improvement of the distribution system one of his top priorities, his plan being to incorporate a distribution set-up within the Production Department and to appoint a 'specialist film officer who knows and is interested in the Board's work in progress and points them in the right distribution direction'.[17] He also aimed to build up a new distribution and exhibition network better suited to the specificity of Production Board films by pursuing an active collaboration with non-commercial outlets such as film studies departments, film societies, film-makers' workshops, Regional Film Theatres and independent cinemas, while the sale to commercial distributors should still be sought for the more marketable films. He was helped in his quest for prompt action by another press campaign (from Philip Oakes in *The Sunday Times* to Chris Petit in *Time Out*) that condemned the BFI's incompetence over the distribution of films like *Pressure*, *Brown Ale with Gertie* and *Welcome to Britain*. The new Films Promotion Officer was appointed in September 1976 by a panel including independent film-makers. The opening of several important new exhibition outlets for independent films in London between July and October 1976 (Derek Hill's Essential Cinema, the ICA's new cinema club and The Other Cinema's own theatre) eventually made possible the commercial release of six BFI features in the space of six months.[18] Over the next few years, the strengthening of the Films Promotion unit (with the addition of a second member of staff in 1977 and an increase in its budget) had tangible results on the circulation of the Production Board films.

Between 1977 and 1979, a dozen new BFI films had a London theatrical release followed by screenings in RFTs, six of these being bought by the BBC for television transmission. For the first time, every new BFI film was also automatically added to the Institute's distribution catalogue and advertised to a wide range of non-theatrical venues. Beyond its practical implications, Sainsbury regarded this strategy as a new holistic approach to the public funding of independent film and video, whereby distribution was, beyond its sole commercial purpose, an integral part of the film-making process.[19]

As well as the modernisation of distribution, Sainsbury was committed to pursuing the professionalisation of the production activity initiated by his predecessors, with the intention to establish a stronger, more legitimised state-funded independent sector in which the Board would be a key agency able not only to respond to the changing needs of independent film-makers but also to play an active role in shaping independent film culture. In order to improve the BFI's standards of film production, the Production Department augmented its staff numbers from three to seven between July 1976 and April 1977, which led to higher job specialisation between the administration, production and distribution sides of the operation. Although the Department remained structurally under-equipped, every spare penny was spent on the acquisition of film-making equipment, in particular to avoid the escalating costs of equipment hire. Sainsbury campaigned for, and to some extent obtained, an increase in the discretionary powers of the Head of Production made necessary by the increasingly complex nature of film production. As for the practice of commissioning projects, although the Board still officially proscribed it, in practice the Department started encouraging film-makers to contact it for assistance in writing their applications. As many as seven film-makers were funded more than once between 1976 and 1979.

Commissioning was further formalised by the setting-up in 1979 of a Project Development Fund, which allowed the Head of Production to approach film-makers informally. The normalisation of the remuneration of technicians and actors working on BFI productions was another indication of the industrialisation of the Board's practice in that period. In 1978, Sainsbury took the initiative to formalise dealings with the ACTT and Equity. After months of negotiations with union leaders, both parties finalised a Code of Practice towards the end of 1979. The agreement stipulated that BFI-funded films produced by the Board would be allowed special dispensation to pay their crews at the short and documentaries rate, the full feature rate being paid in residuals should the film go into profit. It also allowed the employment of a number of non-union technicians and actors on certain non-commercial projects.

Sainsbury was also committed to improving the working conditions of independent film-makers as well as their relationship with the Board. On Le Grice's proposal – and despite the reservations of certain Board members – he invited two IFA members onto the Board.[20] Towards the end of the decade, he pursued the overhaul of the Board's membership by ensuring representation of other areas and organisations associated with independent film, such as the ACTT (Roy Lockett), regional workshop production (Alan Fountain) and intellectuals sympathetic to the latest theoretical and practical developments of independent film culture (John Ellis, Sylvia Harvey, Tony Rayns, Geoffrey Nowell-Smith).[21] Sainsbury initiated a close working relationship with the IFA by meeting its representatives on a regular basis. One result of this collaboration was the negotiation of a standardised contract between film-makers and the Board, which increased the film-makers' rights over the distribution of their films and their royalties.[22]

The consolidation of the Production Department and the improvement of film-makers' conditions, combined with rampant inflation and the increase in the number and sophistication of the applications received, proved costly. When Sainsbury launched a campaign for more funds in early 1978, he naturally appealed to the Department of Education and Science and the film industry. Efforts paid off in early 1979 when the new BFI chairman, Sir Basil Engholm, used his connections within government to obtain a significant increase in the BFI's grant-in-aid and made the Board the main beneficiary of this increase. The film industry followed suit and doubled its contribution via the Eady Levy, making the Board's budget for 1979 the highest in its history (over £480,000 against £213,000 the previous year). The Head of Production also sought more modern types of financial arrangements for the films, such as pre-production sale agreements with television companies and co-productions with other production companies or organisations in Britain and abroad. The first example of this new strategy was Chris Petit's *Radio On*, co-produced not only with the National Film Finance Corporation but also with Wim Wenders's production company. In 1978 and 1979, four other projects were selected on the basis of such co-production arrangements.

An examination of the BFI's production programme between 1976 and 1979 shows the sharp reduction in the number of projects funded each year and the simultaneous increase in the average film-making grant (see Figure 2). Despite the increased sophistication of the projects selected, they were still strongly situated within the debates on film theory and far-left politics that characterised British independent cinema of that period. Most of them openly deconstructed the conventional narrative and representational rules of classical fictional and documentary cinema, without totally rejecting narrative and representation. Several films resorted to

Year of selection	Projects selected	Projects abandoned or postponed	Grants for full production	Completion grants	Average grant for full production	Co-productions
1971–2	11	0	9	2	£4,386	0
1972–3	19	6	9	3	£6,210	0
1973–4	13	1	10	2	£9,290	0
1974–5	17	0	13	4	£6,752	0
1975–6	15	1	11	2	£6,492	1
1976–7	7	1	4	2	£15,237	0
1977–8	8	1	6	1	£13,750	0
1978–9	8	1	5	0	£16,200	2
1979–80	8	1	4	1	£41,504	2

Figure 2: Statistics on projects funded by the Production Board in the 1970s

Brechtian techniques of *mise en scène*, from Phil Mulloy's *In the Forest* and Susan Shapiro, Esther Roney and Francine Winham's *Rapunzel Let Down Your Hair*, to Ed Bennett's *Life Story of Baal* (all 1978). Others combined documentary and fiction, for instance by mixing archival footage with dramatisation in order to question historical truth, examples ranging from Jonathan Lewis and Elizabeth Taylor-Mead's *Before Hindsight* (1977), Conny Templeman's *Home* (1977), Thaddeus O'Sullivan's *On a Paving Stone Mounted* (1978) to Anthea Kennedy and Nick Burton's *At the Fountainhead* (1980). Some combined animation and live action, such as *Rapunzel Let Down Your Hair* or Vera Neubauer's *Animation for Live Action* (1978)and *The Decision* (1981).

The radical aesthetic of these films was matched by their post-1968 politics. The area that received the most support from the Board was that of feminist politics, particularly the struggle to challenge traditional representations of women in film. From 1976 to 1979, ten films selected by the Board for production dealt with such issues, ranging from Laura Mulvey and Peter Wollen's *Riddles of the Sphinx* (1977) or *Rapunzel Let Down Your Hair*, to Jane Jackson's *Angel in the House* (1978), Anna Ambrose's *Phoelix* (1979), Carola Klein's *Mirror Phase* (1978) or Vera Neubauer's animation work. The number of BFI-funded films directed by women dramatically increased in that period, reaching 41 per cent. Sainsbury's controversial production programme again polarised critical debates on British independent cinema. While anti-Establishment magazines such as *Time Out* praised the Board's support of political and theoretical film-making in the late 1970s, mainstream critics – not least the BFI's own *Sight and Sound* – virulently rejected what they saw as a dogmatic and narrow view of British film culture.[23]

Sainsbury's own views on what films should be produced started evolving towards the end of the decade. One of the first indications of this change was his backing of Peter Greenaway's *A Walk through H* (1978). Greenaway, then a film editor and director for the Central Office of

(Opposite page) Opening new horizons for the British avant-garde film: Peter Greenaway's *A Walk through H* (1978)

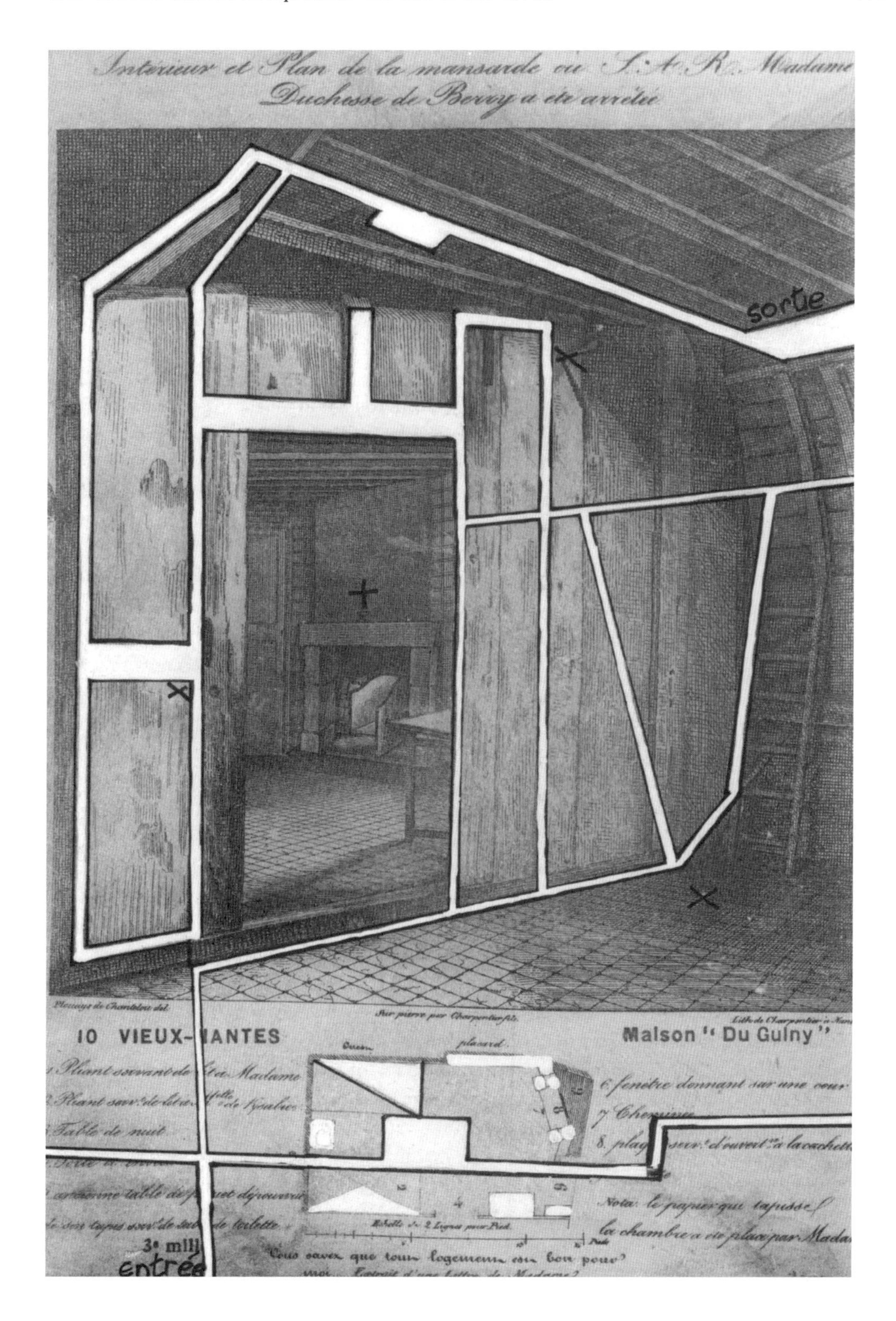
Intérieur et Plan de la mansarde où S. A. R. Madame
Duchesse de Berry a été arrêtée
sortie
10 VIEUX-
ANTES
Maison "Du Guiny"
placard
6. fenêtre donnant sur une cour
entrée

Information (as well as a painter and novelist), was not aligned with any of the groups of independent film-makers and theorists who dominated British film culture in that period. Although his film was experimental in how it challenged conventional narrative, its playfulness and absurd (or even surrealist) approach opened new horizons for the British avant-garde. In an enthusiastic review of the film for the 1977–8 catalogue of BFI productions, Sainsbury welcomed Greenaway's novel attitude:

> What has been rediscovered, readmitted for modernist filmmaking is the pleasure of art and the history of its means and materials – both dangerously exiled since British avant-garde filmmakers shrugged off the dynamic trace of narrative lying in Snow's *Wavelength* and misconceived material as materialism, impleasure as seriousness, and structure as meaning more than ten years ago.[24]

The gap between the kind of cinema that the Head of Production sought to create and the reality of the projects applying to the Board explained his growing frustration with the 'official' avant-garde. So did the lack of audiences for films whose aesthetics and politics were often seen as intimidating and elitist. As Sainsbury admitted: 'Perhaps the pleasure of getting an audience beyond a recognised interest group was part of the motivation of making films that were easier to promote.'[25]

Several other projects soon followed *A Walk through H* in this new trend of innovative yet less 'dogmatic' BFI-funded films, such as Greenaway's *The Falls*, the Quay Brothers' *Nocturna Artificialia*, which borrowed from the tradition of Polish surrealist animation and Chris Petit's debut feature film *Radio On* (all three initiated in 1978–9). The latter was certainly the clearest sign of the Board's change of orientation. Shot on 35mm with a budget of £100,000 (the Board's contribution being £40,000 over two years), it was the most expensive project yet produced by the Board. Although it was a narrative film in many ways, its black-and-white aesthetics and disruption of subjective narration, its creative use of contemporary popular music and landscapes, its cultural references and modes of production and promotion owed more to contemporary European art cinema than to the recent political avant-garde. The film was selected for the Directors' Fortnight at Cannes, an event that epitomised art cinema and auteurism, and was then released in the art-house circuit (first at the Screen on the Hill in London). Geoffrey Nowell-Smith observed that *Radio On* was unique in the history of British cinema in that it was 'a British film inserted into the context of a non-existent British cinema', since it did not correspond to any existing pattern in Britain, either on an economic or cultural level.[26] For Steve Neale, this film reflected a change in the Board's overall strategy, which he defined as the production and promotion of films 'capable of penetrating a sector of the commercial industry at the level of exhibition and, perhaps, of opening a space within that sector for the development of a kind of British Art Cinema'.[27] The IFA's reaction to the funding of such films was unsurprisingly sceptical.

This latest strategy owed as much to new circumstances as to Sainsbury's own vision. The continuing decline of British feature-film production, added to the newly elected Conservative government's intention to dismantle what was left of the institutional support of the British film industry (quotas, NFFC, Eady Levy), reinforced the Board's responsibility as a producer of low-budget features. Another important development was the appointment of new BFI personnel –

especially Anthony Smith as Director and Jeremy Isaacs as Production Board Chair – who immediately embraced the art-cinema project. But the key factor was without a doubt the establishment of the fourth terrestrial television channel. The appointment of Isaacs as its first Chief Executive and of Alan Fountain as its commissioning editor for independent film and video largely accounted for the privileged relationship between Channel 4 and the BFI Production Board throughout the 1980s and beyond. A crucial co-production agreement was negotiated between the two organisations in 1981, whereby the television company took a first option on broadcast rights in BFI films in return for an annual subvention not tied to any specific project. The first of those, amounting to £420,000, almost doubled the Production Board budget and enabled it to engage even further in low-budget feature film-making. Indeed, if *Radio On* had been the first sign of a new orientation for the Board, the critical and box-office success of Greenaway's *The Draughtsman's Contract* (1982) fully established the Board as one of the three pillars of the institutional funding of British art cinema in the 1980s, along with Channel 4 and the NFFC (replaced in 1986 by British Screen). In John Hill's words, 'more than any other film in that period it appeared to demonstrate the economic viability, and cultural cachet, of the newly emerging British art cinema'.[28]

The transition from one policy to the other was not, however, as abrupt as it seemed. Under the combined pressure of the IFA and the ACTT, the Board continued to fund a number of non-feature and non-commercial projects (mainly the work of regional workshops and experimental film-makers) in the 1980s. Perhaps more importantly, many of the feature films backed by the Board in that period, from Mulvey and Wollen's *Crystal Gazing* (1982) to Sally Potter's *The Gold Diggers* (1983), fitted the art-cinema format (length, increased production values, non-rejection of narrative) while retaining a number of aesthetic and political concerns of 1970s avant-garde and political film-making. The level of funding suddenly made available to the independent sector by the Production Board and Channel 4 led to a transformation of its practice and, as Michael O'Pray and others have argued, to a progressive amalgamation of avant-garde, oppositional and art cinema through the 1980s.[29]

Notes

1 Michael Relph in John Ellis (ed.), *1951–1976: British Film Institute Productions* (London: BFI, 1977), p. 9.

2 Stanley Reed, 'Helping Filmmakers', *The Times*, 10 December 1970.

3 In 1972, a Committee of Enquiry set up by the Arts Council and chaired by Richard Attenborough concluded that the Arts Council should retain responsibility for funding film 'as a fine art medium', while the Production Board should focus on the funding of cinema as an 'industrially-produced dramatic art'. The BFI Governors rejected these conclusions and the overlap problem was left unresolved.

4 Stanley Reed, 'Future Policy', paper presented to the Production Board, 29 May 1968, Special Collections of the BFI National Library.

5 See Kevin Brownlow, 'Before the Deluge', *Sight and Sound*, Autumn 1972.

6 See David Wilson, 'Images of Britain', *Sight and Sound*, Spring 1974, pp. 84–7, and David Robinson, 'British and Proud of It: Uncommercial Cinema', *The Times*, 14 May 1976.

7 Interview with the author, 4 February 2003.

8 Ibid.

9 Interview with the author, 18 February 2003.
10 Ibid.
11 The fact that Sainsbury was one of the early promoters and theoreticians of alternative cinema, first at Essex University, then with the distributor of political films The Other Cinema and as co-editor of the magazine *Afterimage*, partly explained the Board's responsiveness to the claims of the independent sector.
12 Nicholas Pole, 'MacCabe & Mrs Matheson: 10 Years of the BFI Production Board', *AIP&Co*, March 1986, p. 22.
13 Barrie Gavin in Ellis (ed.), *British Film Institute Productions*, p. 132.
14 For a personal account of this 'cultural struggle' within the BFI, see Colin McArthur, 'Two Steps Forward, One Step Back: Cultural Struggle in the British Film Institute', *Journal of Popular British Cinema*, no. 4, 2001, pp. 112–27.
15 Alan Lovell, *The Production Board* (London: BFI, 1976).
16 'Broadsheet', *Roughcut*, Special issue on independent British cinema, 1976, p. 20.
17 Sainsbury interviewed in *Time Out*, 6 February 1976, p. 9.
18 The Other Cinema's exhibition project, set up thanks to a capital grant by the BFI, proved a major outlet for BFI-funded films during the fifteen months of its existence. This period marked the apogee of British independent cinema in the 1970s and its closure was symptomatic of the economic fragility of this sector and its non-subsistence without institutional support.
19 The publication between 1977 and 1981 of three catalogues of BFI Productions that provided not only a critical examination of the films and the Board's practice, but also in-depth analyses of various aesthetic, institutional and technological concerns of the independent sector, epitomised this integrated distribution strategy.
20 The Board only agreed to appoint the first two IFA members, Steve Dwoskin and Anna Ambrose, in their individual capacity rather than as official IFA representatives, even though in practice they acted as such.
21 Although the AIP was not officially represented, several of its members sat on the Board in their individual capacity, not least its Chair Michael Relph.
22 The terms of the distribution contract, which had since 1952 been favourable to the Production Board, suddenly made its prospect of making a profit so difficult that Sainsbury had to persuade the IFA to renegotiate them in 1980.
23 See 'The triangle in the tower', *Time Out*, 27 October 1978, pp. 11–12, and Nigel Andrews, 'Production Board Films', *Sight and Sound*, vol. 28, no. 195, Winter 1978/9, pp. 53–5.
24 Peter Sainsbury, '*A Walk Through H*', in Elizabeth Cowie (ed.), *Catalogue: British Film Institute Productions 1977–1978* (London: BFI, 1978), p. 90.
25 Interview with the author, 17 March 2003.
26 Geoffrey Nowell-Smith, '*Radio On*', *Screen*, vol. 20, no. 3/4, 1979, p. 30.
27 Steve Neale, 'Art Cinema as Institution', *Screen*, vol. 22, no. 1, 1981, p. 12.
28 John Hill, 'The British Cinema and Thatcherism', in John Hill (ed.), *British Cinema in the 1980s* (Oxford: Oxford University Press, 1999), p. 20.
29 See Michael O'Pray, 'The British Avant-Garde and Art Cinema from the 1970s to the 1990s', in Andrew Higson (ed.), *Dissolving Views: Key Writings on British Cinema* (London and New York: Cassell, 1996), pp. 178–90.

Select Bibliography

Andrews, Nigel, 'Production Board Films', *Sight and Sound*, vol. 28, no. 195, Winter 1978/9

Armes, Roy, *A Critical History of British Cinema* (London: Secker and Warburg, 1978)

Askwith, Robin, *The Confessions of Robin Askwith* (London: Ebury Press, 1999)

Bartholomew, David, 'The Wicker Man', *Cinefantastique*, vol. 6, no. 3, Winter 1977

Bennett, Andy, *Popular Music and Youth Culture: Music, Identity and Place* (Basingstoke, Hampshire: Macmillan, 2000)

Bennett, Tony and Janet Woollacott, *Bond and Beyond: The Political Career of a Popular Hero* (London: Macmillan, 1987)

Beresford, Bruce, 'One Way In', *Films and Filming*, May 1971

Black, Jeremy, *The Politics of James Bond: From Fleming's Novels to the Big Screen* (Lincoln, NB, and London: University of Nebraska Press, 2005)

Boot, Andy, *Fragments of Fear: An Illustrated History of British Horror Films* (London: Creation, 1996)

Bright, Morris and Robert Ross, *Mr Carry On: The Life and Work of Peter Rogers* (London: BBC, 2000)

Brown, Allan, *Inside the Wicker Man: The Morbid Ingenuities* (London: Sidgwick & Jackson, 2000)

Brown, Geoff, 'Paradise Found and Lost: The Course of British Realism', in Robert Murphy (ed.), *The British Cinema Book: 2nd Edition* (London: BFI, 2001)

Brown, Paul J., *All You Need Is Blood: The Films of Norman J. Warren* (Upton, Cambridgeshire: Midnight Media, 1995)

Brownlow, Kevin, 'Before the Deluge', *Sight and Sound*, vol. 41, no. 4, Autumn 1972

Bryce, Alan, *Amicus: The Studio That Dripped Blood* (Liskeard, Cornwall: Stray Cat Publishing, 2000)

Carney, Ray and Leonard Quart, *The Films of Mike Leigh: Embracing the World* (Cambridge: Cambridge University Press, 2000)

Catterall, Ali and Simon Wells, *Your Face Here: British Cult Movies since the Sixties* (London: Fourth Estate, 2002)

Chapman, James, *Licence to Thrill: A Cultural History of the James Bond Films* (London and New York: I. B. Tauris, 1999)

Chibnall, Steve, *Making Mischief: The Cult Films of Pete Walker* (Guildford, Surrey: FAB Press, 1998)

Chibnall, Steve and Julian Petley (eds), *British Horror Cinema* (London: Routledge, 2002)

Conrich, Ian, '*The Man Who Haunted Himself*', in Tim O'Sullivan, Paul Wells and Alan Burton (eds), *Liberal Directions: Basil Dearden and Post-war British Film Culture* (Trowbridge, Wiltshire: Flicks Books, 1997)

Conrich, Ian, 'Traditions of the British Horror Film', in Robert Murphy (ed.), *The British Cinema Book* (London: BFI, 1997)

Conrich, Ian, 'Forgotten Cinema: The British Style of Sexploitation', *Journal of Popular British Cinema*, no. 1, 1998

Cowie, Elizabeth (ed.), *Catalogue: British Film Institute Productions 1977–1978* (London: BFI, 1978)

Davies, Russell (ed.), *The Kenneth Williams Diaries* (London: HarperCollins, 1994)

Dickinson, Margaret and Sarah Street, *Cinema and State: The Film Industry and the British Government, 1927–84* (London: BFI, 1985)

Dixon, Wheeler Winston, *The Charm of Evil: The Life and Films of Terence Fisher* (Metuchen, NJ, and London: Scarecrow, 1991)

Dixon, Wheeler Winston, *The Films of Freddie Francis* (Metuchen, NJ, and London: Scarecrow, 1991)

Docherty, David, David Morrison and Michael Tracey, *The Last Picture Show? Britain's Changing Film Audience* (London: BFI, 1987)

Donnelly, Kevin J., 'British Punk Films: Rebellion into Money, Nihilism into Innovation', *Journal of Popular British Cinema*, no. 1, 1998

Ellis, John, 'Production Board Policies', *Screen*, Winter 1976–7

Ellis, John (ed.), *1951–1976: British Film Institute Productions* (London: BFI, 1977)

Everett, Wendy, *Terence Davies* (Manchester: Manchester University Press, 2004)

Halligan, Benjamin, *Michael Reeves* (Manchester: Manchester University Press, 2003)

Hamilton, John, *Beasts in the Cellar: The Exploitation Film Career of Tony Tenser* (Godalming, Surrey: FAB Press, 2005)

Hark, Ina Rae, 'Twelve Angry People: Conflicting Revelatory Strategies in *Murder on the Orient Express*', *Literature/Film Quarterly*, vol. 15, no. 1, 1987

Higson, Andrew, 'A Diversity of Film Practices: Renewing British Cinema in the 1970s', in Bart Moore-Gilbert (ed.), *The Arts in the 1970s: Cultural Closure?* (London: Routledge, 1994)

Hill, John, 'The British Cinema and Thatcherism', in John Hill (ed.), *British Cinema in the 1980s* (Oxford: Oxford University Press, 1999)

Hunt, Leon, *British Low Culture: From Safari Suits to Sexploitation* (London: Routledge, 1998)

Hunt, Leon, 'Necromancy in the UK: Witchcraft and the Occult in British Horror', in Steve Chibnall and Julian Petley (eds), *British Horror Cinema* (London and New York: Routledge, 2002)

Hunter, I. Q., 'Deep Inside Queen Kong: Anatomy of an Extremely Bad Film', in Ernest Mathijs and Xavier Mendik (eds), *Alternative Europe: Eurotrash and Exploitation Cinema since 1945* (London and New York: Wallflower Press, 2004)

Hutchings, Peter, *Hammer and Beyond: The British Horror Film* (Manchester: Manchester University Press, 1993)

Hutchings, Peter, 'The Amicus House of Horror', in Steve Chibnall and Julian Petley (eds), *British Horror Cinema* (London: Routledge, 2002)

Hutchings, Peter, *The Horror Film* (Harlow, Essex: Pearson, 2004)

Isaacs, Jeremy, 'Winning the Pools', *Sight and Sound*, vol. 50, no. 1, Winter 1980–1

Jameson, Frederic, 'Postmodernism and Consumer Society', in Hal Foster (ed.), *Postmodern Culture* (London: Pluto Press, 1983)

Jarman, Derek, *Dancing Ledge* (London: Quartet, 1984)

Johnson, Tom and Deborah Del Vecchio, *Hammer Films: An Exhaustive Filmography* (Jefferson, NC: McFarland, 1995)

Kinsey, Wayne, *Hammer Films: The Bray Studio Years* (London: Reynolds & Hearn, 2002)

Lay, Samantha, *British Social Realist Cinema* (London: Wallflower Press, 2003)

Leigh, Jacob, *Ken Loach: Art in the Service of the People* (London: Wallflower Press, 2002)

Lippard, Chris (ed.), *By Angels Driven: The Films of Derek Jarman* (Trowbridge, Wiltshire: Flicks Books, 1996)

Lovell, Alan, *The Production Board* (London: BFI, 1976)

Marwick, Arthur, *British Society since 1945* (London: Penguin, 1996)

McArthur, Colin, 'Two Steps Forward, One Step Back: Cultural Struggle in the British Film Institute', *Journal of Popular British Cinema*, no. 4, 2001

McGillivray, David, *Doing Rude Things: The History of the British Sex Film 1957–1981* (London: Sun Tavern Fields, 1992)

McKnight, George (ed.), *Agent of Challenge and Defiance: The Films of Ken Loach* (Trowbridge, Wiltshire: Flicks Books, 1997)

Medhurst, Andy, 'Carry On Camp', *Sight and Sound*, vol. 2, no. 4, August 1992

Murphy, Robert (ed.), *The British Cinema Book* (London: BFI, 1997)

Neale, Steve, 'Art Cinema as Institution', *Screen*, vol. 22, no. 1, 1981

Nowell-Smith, Geoffrey, '*Radio On*', *Screen*, vol. 20, no. 3/4, 1979

O'Pray, Michael, *Derek Jarman: Dreams of England* (London: BFI, 1996)

O'Pray, Michael, 'The British Avant-Garde and Art Cinema from the 1970s to the 1990s', in Andrew Higson (ed.), *Dissolving Views: Key Writings on British Cinema* (London and New York: Cassell, 1996)

Perry, George, *The Great British Picture Show* (London: Pavilion, 1985)

Petley, Julian, '"There's Something about Mary . . ."', in Bruce Babington (ed.), *British Stars and Stardom: From Alma Taylor to Sean Connery* (Manchester and New York: Manchester University Press, 2001)

Pirie, David, *A Heritage of Horror: The English Gothic Cinema 1946–1972* (London: Gordon Fraser, 1973)

Ross, Robert, *The Carry On Companion* (London: B. T. Batsford, 1996)

Sangster, Jimmy, *Inside Hammer: Behind the Scenes at the Legendary Film Studio* (London: Reynolds & Hearn, 2001)

Sanjek, David, 'Twilight of the Monsters: The English Horror Film 1968–1975', in Wheeler Winston Dixon (ed.), *Re-viewing British Cinema, 1900–1992: Essays and Interviews* (Albany: State University of New York Press, 1994)

Sergeant, Amy, *British Cinema: A Critical History* (London: BFI, 2005)

Sheridan, Simon, *Come Play with Me: The Life and Films of Mary Millington* (Guildford, Surrey: FAB Press, 1999)

Sheridan, Simon, *Keeping the British End Up: Four Decades of Saucy Cinema* (London: Reynolds & Hearn, 2001)

Spittles, Brian, *Britain since 1960: An Introduction* (Basingstoke, Hampshire and London: Macmillan, 1995)

Street, Sarah, *British National Cinema* (London: Routledge, 1997)

Street, Sarah, *Transatlantic Crossings: British Feature Films in the USA* (New York and London: Continuum, 2002)

Sweet, Matthew, *Shepperton Babylon: The Lost Worlds of British Cinema* (London: Faber and Faber, 2005)

Thompson, Hilary and Rod Stoneman (eds), *The New Social Function of Cinema: Catalogue of British Film Institute Productions '79/80*, (London: BFI, 1980)

Thompson, Stacy, 'Punk Cinema', *Cinema Journal*, vol. 43, no. 2, Autumn 2004

Upton, Julian, 'Anarchy in the UK: Derek Jarman's *Jubilee* Revisited', *Bright Lights Film Journal*, no. 30, October 2000, <www.brightlightsfilm. com/30/jubilee>

Upton, Julian, 'Carry on Sitcom: The British Sitcom Spin-off Film 1968–80', *Bright Lights Film Journal*, no. 35, January 2002 <www.brightlightsfilm. com/35/britishsitcoms1>

Walker, Alexander, *National Heroes: British Cinema in the Seventies and Eighties* (London: Orion, 2005)

Walker, John, *The Once and Future Film: British Cinema in the Seventies and Eighties* (London: Methuen, 1985)

Watson, Garry, *The Cinema of Mike Leigh: A Sense of the Real* (London: Wallflower Press, 2006)

Williams, Christopher, 'The Social Art Cinema: A Movement in the History of British Film and Television Culture', in Christopher Williams (ed.), *Cinema: The Beginnings and the Future* (London: University of Westminster Press, 1996)

Wilson, David, 'Images of Britain', *Sight and Sound*, vol. 43, no. 2, Spring 1974

Wollen, Peter, 'The Last New Wave: Modernism in the British Films of the Thatcher Era', in Lester D. Friedman (ed.), *Fires Were Started: British Cinema and Thatcherism: 2nd Edition* (London: Wallflower Press, 2006)

Wood, Linda (ed.), *British Films 1971–1981* (London: BFI, 1983)

Index

Note: Page references in *italics* indicate illustrations.

List of Illustrations

While considerable effort has been made to correctly identify the copyright holders this has not been possible in all cases. We apologise for any apparent negligence and any omissions or corrections brought to our attention will be remedied in any future editions

Life of Brian, Python (Monty) Pictures; *Carry On Emmannuelle*, © National Film Trustee Company Ltd; *Jubilee*, Whaley-Malin Productions/Megalovision; *Eskimo Nell*, Salon Productions; *Confessions of a Window Cleaner*, Swiftdown Productions/Columbia (British) Productions; *Take an Easy Ride*, © Midas Films; *Frankenstein Must be Destroyed*, Hammer Film Productions; *To the Devil, a Daughter*, © Hammer Film Productions/Terra Filmkunst Gmbh Berlin; *Death Line*, © Harbor Ventures, Inc.; *Theatre of Blood*, © Harbor Productions Inc.; *Vampyres*, © Essay Films; *Carry On Abroad*, © Rank Film Distributors; *Carry On at your Convenience*, © Rank Film Distributors; *Carry On Emmannuelle*, © National Film Trustee Company Ltd; *The McKenzie Break*, © Brighton Pictures; *The Eagle has Landed*, Associated General Films/ITC Entertainment; *The Human Factor*, © Sigma Productions; *The Land That Time Forgot*, © Amicus Productions; *Warlords of Atlantis*, EMI Film Productions; *The Duellists*, © Paramount Pictures Corporation; *That'll Be the Day*, Goodtimes Enterprises; *Raise the Titanic*, ITC Productions/Marble Arch Productions; *The Great Rock 'N' Roll Swindle*, Boyd's Company/Virgin Films/Matrixbest; *Rude Boy*, Buzzy Enterprises Ltd; *Pressure*, British Film Institute Production Board; *The Likely Lads*, Anglo-EMI; *Bronco Bullfrog*, Maya Films; *Endless Night*, National Film Trustee Company Ltd; *Murder on the Orient Express*, © EMI Film Distributors; *The Mirror Crack'd*, © EMI Films Ltd; *The Wicker Man*, © British Lion Film Corporation; *Straw Dogs*, © ABC Pictures; *Intimate Reflections*, Kendon Films/Arrow Productions; *The Tempest*, Boyd's Company; *Live and Let Die*, Danjaq LLC/Eon Productions; *The Spy Who Loved Me*, Danjaq LLC/Eon Productions; *My Childhood*, British Film Institute Production Board; *Juvenile Liaison*, British Film Institute Production Board; *A Walk Through H*, British Film Institute Production Board.